W9-APV-708

PLAUTUS: THE COMEDIES

Complete Roman Drama in Translation

David R. Slavitt and Palmer Bovie, Series Editors

PLAUTUS:
THE COMEDIES
Volume IV

EDITED BY

DAVID R. SLAVITT
AND PALMER BOVIE

THE JOHNS HOPKINS UNIVERSITY PRESS
Baltimore and London

© 1995 The Johns Hopkins University Press
All rights reserved. Published 1995
Printed in the United States of America on acid-free paper
04 03 02 01 00 99 98 97 96 95   5 4 3 2 1

The Johns Hopkins University Press
2715 North Charles Street
Baltimore, Maryland 21218-4319
The Johns Hopkins Press Ltd., London

Library of Congress Cataloging-in-Publication Data

Plautus, Titus Maccius.
    [Works. English. 1995]
    Plautus : the comedies / edited by David R. Slavitt and Palmer Bovie.
        p.   cm. — (Complete Roman drama in translation)
    Includes bibliographical references.
    Contents: v. 1. Amphitryon / translated by Constance Carrier — Miles gloriosus
/ translated by Erich Segal — Captivi / translated by Richard Moore — Casina /
translated by Richard Beacham — Curculio / translated by Henry Taylor . . . [etc.]
    ISBN 0-8018-5070-3 (v. 1 : alk. paper). — ISBN 0-8018-5071-1 (v. 1 : pbk. : alk.
paper)
    1. Plautus, Titus Maccius—Translations into English.   2. Latin drama (Comedy)
—Translations into English.   3. Greece—Drama.   I. Slavitt, David R., 1935–   .
II. Bovie, Smith Palmer.   III. Title.   IV. Series.
PA6569.S55   1995
872'.01—dc20   94-45317

ISBN 0-8018-5056-8 (v. 2 : alk. paper). — ISBN 0-8018-5057-6 (v. 2 : pbk. : alk. paper)
ISBN 0-8018-5067-3 (v. 3 : alk. paper). — ISBN 0-8018-5068-1 (v. 3 : pbk. : alk. paper)
ISBN 0-8018-5072-X (v. 4 : alk. paper). — ISBN 0-8018-5073-8 (v. 4 : pbk. : alk. paper)

A catalog record for this book is available from the British Library.

Acknowledgments of prior publication may be found at the end of this book.

CONTENTS

PREFACE

A motley crew of slaves, parasites, courtesans, and procurers assembles in the *Persa* to let Plautus make fun yet again of the Roman pieties. Saturio's daughter, "Virgo," is unwilling to disguise herself as a Persian captive to be sold in a complicated Murphy game in an attempt to defraud Dordalus, the pimp. She is reluctant and tells her father, "I want you to be honest." She is afraid that he'll turn her into a bad girl. But Saturio tells her, "Any girl's bad if she pretends to know / More than her parents want her to."

Finally, she consents to do what he has asked, enters into the game, and plays her part to perfection, handling Dordalus's investigative questions with nimble assurance. She becomes a quick-witted fellow conspirator and all but steals the show. There are similarities between the *Persa* and the *Mercator* and the *Asinaria*, in the rough-edged exchanges of dialogue and underhanded plotting, but the temper of the *Persa* is redeemed by Virgo's charm and by the affable presence of Lemniselenis, Toxilus's true love. As in the *Mostellaria*, the players here seize the occasion to put on a show for one spectator. As they are about to stage their impersonations, Toxilus wants to make sure the actors have been well rehearsed. "Do you have your parts down pat?" he asks. Sagaristio answers, "No comic or tragic actors have ever learned their parts better."

The *Menaechmi* or, *The Brothers Menaechmus*, is Plautus's best-known comedy, the one most often read and reproduced. It is familiar to English and American audiences by way of Shakespeare's brilliant imitation and expansion of Plautus's text in *The Comedy of Errors*. There is also the fast-moving, resonant musical comedy adaptation by Rodgers and Hart, *The Boys from Syracuse*, which has gained popularity on the American stage. It is not hard to see why this comedy should have predominated so among Plautus's plays. It is tightly, almost perfectly constructed; it moves forward briskly through a counterpoint of mistaken identities to a final confrontation presided over by a slave and laid out with Euclidean aplomb. The recognition is inevitable, but, until it comes, we watch with breathless delight as the identical twins range through the same city being mistaken for each other and, as they go, meeting with inexplicable frustrations and unpredictable rewards.

The breakneck action slows down from time to time so that we can catch up with it, and Plautus can give us a series of set-piece speeches about being a parasite, being married to a suspicious spouse, the law, old age, doctors, and being a slave. Then the whirlwind of entrances and exits resumes, and there is another brother—inevitably the wrong one—coming on stage to be beaten or else to be invited to a sumptuous lunch. There is a kind of fourth-dimensional grace in the play's structure where everything that seems discordant and causes conflict falls nearly into place. Confusion is swept away in a final burst of brotherly affection as the Menaechmi twins join hands and prepare to return to Syracuse to live happily in their newfound identity.

The *Cistellaria* also revolves around the search for a missing daughter, and there is the usual complication of frustrated love. Gymnasium, a courtesan, reminds us that "amor et melle et felle est fecundissimus" ["love is abundantly supplied with honey and gall"], adding that "it gives you only a taste of sweetness but piles up bitterness until you can hold no more."

The plot is complicated enough to require the elucidation of a god, Auxilium, to explain to the audience the background of these confused characters. It is only when a little jewel box (*cistella*) is dropped onstage and its contents revealed that Phanostrata recognizes her long lost daughter's birth tokens.

The drama of the dropped jewel box has had something else dropped out of it during the centuries of transmission down to the Renaissance manuscripts. Whole passages and many fragments of the text are missing. The continuity of act 2, from lines 230 to 491, is virtually indecipherable, either missing or in fragments in the manuscripts. Our contemporary translator in this series, R. H. W. Dillard, has dealt decisively with this insoluble problem, reinforcing the potholed text with two additional characters, Lacuna and Hia-

tus. They come in to comment on the action, create a kind of continuity, and bounce off each other in vigorous byplay as they drift in
and out of Plautus's gap-ridden texts. There is also a third man,
Tertius, and a shadowy character named Anonymous to be found in
Dillard's text. It is a daring stroke, but characteristically Plautine, for
if one Auxilium can be summoned onstage to explain things, why not
a whole band of auxilia?

If, in the *Cistellaria,* the lover is rescued by sheer luck, in the
Pseudolus, Calidorus, the forlorn son of Simo, is saved from despair
by the strenuous deviousness of Pseudolus, the family slave. Unless
money can be found to pay off Ballio, the pimp, Calidorus can kiss
his mistress, Phoenicium, good-bye. Pseudolus promises that he
will get the money, and then addresses the audience to notify us that
he is not to be trusted. His name, after all, means "Liar."

His antagonist, Ballio, is a degenerate flesh peddler, altogether
vile—the kind of man we like to see get taken by a trickster like
Pseudolus, who improvises, seems to make up the play as he goes
along, discarding one plan when an obstacle appears, then another
when he is blocked again. He slips and slides and swivels and tap-
dances along, enjoying the challenge of each moment:

> Here you are, Pseudolus, on your own . . . without a shred of a
> plan, cashless and clueless. No idea of where to start to finish
> weaving one's web. Well, after all, that's how a poet works when
> he takes up his pen in hot pursuit of something that doesn't
> exist—yet somehow finds it and fashions fantasy into fact. I fancy
> I'll play the poet now.
>
> (ll. 394–408)

Pseudolus's undaunted tone is that of an experienced dramatist, sure
of his ability to put on a good show.

But the atmosphere of improvisation of this play suggests the
earlier stages of Italian folk comedy, in which the actors in their
different types would play out their complementary and opposing
parts casually, making up the script as they went along. It resembles
the style of the *commedia dell'arte* invoked centuries later in Italian
drama. For Plautus, Pseudolus crowns the hierarchy of inventive
personalities in the line of Tranio and Epidicus, not to mention
Messenio, Chrysalus, and Palaestrio, the self-appointed *architectus*

doli ("framer of the plot") in the *Miles Gloriosus*. He is a slave but he is the master of the moment, exerting control over a nexus of cross-purposes and arranging their ultimate and equitable resolution.

Richard Beacham's stunning translation of this play contributes many songs, in addition, which serve to reflect the lyric aspect of Plautus's work. The lyric settings in Latin, the sensuous solos, the shouting matches, the line-for-line name-calling offer a vitality of rhythms unavailable in prose. Beacham's songs indicate how close Plautus comes to the modern idea of musical comedy.

The *Stichus* was presented at the *Ludi Plebeii* in 200 B.C. According to the official notice that survives in the manuscript, it was "From the Greek play of Menander, 'The Brothers' . . . and produced by Titus Publius Pellio. The music, on Tyrian flutes, was composed by Oppius' Marcipor." Pellio was a famous actor of the day, and Marcipor a talented musician, the slave of Oppius. From a few scant lines of the official announcement we can infer that Plautus, midway in his writing career, took over and adapted an earlier Greek plot but changed the title and drew attention to the musical component. In the middle of the play, Stichus, who makes a late entrance, reassures the audience as to how this drama is supposed to end, as it does, with festive singing and dancing at a party given by the slave. Such behavior, which might disconcert Romans by reversing the usual order of things, is conventionally acceptable in an Athenian setting:

> You, in the audience, don't be astonished
> That slaves can dine out and drink and have mistresses:
> These things were perfectly legal in Athens.
>
> (ll. 446–48)

The unruffled sequence of events in the *Stichus* does indeed proceed toward a final concoction of singing and dancing that expresses a resonant musical climax to the story's varied measures of monody. If the *Pseudolus* could be seen as a musical comedy on a large scale, buoyed up with bold and colorful lyrics, the *Stichus* is an almost Debussy-like conversion of a standard plot into a shimmering enchantment.

The *Vidularia*, or *The Traveling Bag*, survives only in the form of a few passages of dialogue and separate fragments of several lines.

Scholars have assembled these parts in a plausible plot sequence, leaving some unassigned. Modern printed versions of the Latin text indicate the identifiable gaps in the manuscript by asterisks.

When working with *The Little Box* (*Cistellaria*), where lines are also missing in the manuscript, R. H. W. Dillard ably kept a ravaged Latin text afloat by introducing the characters Lacuna and Hiatus and endowing them with speech. But no such expedient is available for the *Vidularia*, whose bare bones reveal only a tenth of the play's original lines.

In his new translation John Wright has addressed the problem of continuity, and in his introduction offers interesting insights into the situation and tone of this pastoral drama and its strong resemblance to the other play of Plautus in this genre, *The Rope* (*Rudens*).

In a lonely setting near the seashore a young castaway named Nicodemus finds unexpected if rough-hewn hospitality among strangers, principally the older man Dinia. Meanwhile, another person, named Gorgines, plans to hide Nicodemus's traveling bag, which is being claimed by quarreling finders. While this is going on the older man Dinia thinks he recognizes the voice of his own long lost son in the voice of Nicodemus, the young castaway he has befriended.

Could it be that, as in the *Rudens*, where the lonely old Daemones discovers his long lost daughter delivered to him, as it were, on his doorstep by the sea, here also in the *Vidularia*, the old man will miraculously recover his child? Will father and son discover their true identities and be reunited? Plautus has often shown how perfectly capable he is of handling ideas like these.

Palmer Bovie

THE PERSIAN

(*PERSA*)

Translated by Palmer Bovie

INTRODUCTION

In the *Persa* Plautus has created a cast of low characters in search of a scenario. The slaves are the prime movers of the plot, and they are assisted by the parasite Saturio, a free man and a freeloader, and his daughter, simply listed as Virgo. One of the slaves, Toxilus, is in love with the courtesan Lemniselenis, owned by the pimp Dordalus. It is to get her out of Dordalus's clutches and into his own that Toxilus and his friends mount their performance.

Persa, in the masculine gender, can mean "the Persian man" in Latin (as in *poeta* or *nauta*). But it can also be taken in the feminine sense and mean "the Persian girl." And a kind of convenient moral ambiguity colors the side-slipping behavior of the insouciant characters in this play. Their action and their revenge on Dordalus are clever and unforgiving. "Virgo" is the only good character in the lot; her virtue and good sense are altogether admirable, and bear comparison with the noble Alcmena in Plautus's *Amphitryon.* She does, however, help with the scheme to deceive Dordalus by impersonating Persians. Dordalus thinks he has made quite a bargain when he buys this lovely girl from the traveling Persian "alibabble Ayatollahso de Monet."

Meanwhile, the slave Sagaristio has acquired the sum needed by his friend Toxilus for the purchase of Lemniselenis. Sagaristio's master (unnamed) has entrusted him with the money to buy some plow-broken oxen at the fair in Eritrea. He will hand the money over to Toxilus and then report that there was no fair and there weren't any oxen anyway.

Saturio rushes on stage to claim the maiden as his daughter; Dordalus feels the waves of disaster falling on him. He had bought the girl thinking her owner, the count de Monet, had acquired her as a captive prisoner of war when the Persians captured the city of

3

Chrysopolis ("Goldburg"). Now he will be forced by law to hand her over to her legitimate father. And that is not all; the players attack Dordalus for his wrongdoing, knock him around the stage, and drive him off, beaten and bowed.

So Plautus has directed his actors to put on a performance, and they willingly comply. They are good actors, but not particularly good people. Saturio is a free man, but woefully in need of a dinner, as all of his ancestors, in the canonical manner of the *mos maiorum*, have always been. His daughter, a model of moral stability and unpretentious beauty, protests against the meanness of the illusion, while she gives in to her father's wishes. She steals the show.

Palmer Bovie

THE PERSIAN

CHARACTERS

M TOXILUS, a slave
M SAGARISTIO, a slave in another family and friend of Toxilus
M SATURIO, a parasite
F SOPHOCLIDISCA, the maid of Lemniselenis
F LEMNISELENIS, a courtesan
M PAEGNIUM, a boy in the family of Toxilus's master
M VIRGO, a maiden and the daughter of Saturio
M DORDALUS, a procurer

SCENE: *A street in Athens, showing the houses of* DORDALUS *and* TOXILUS's *master, with a passageway between.*

ACT I

Scene 1

(TOXILUS *and* SAGARISTIO *enter, from opposite sides*)

TOXILUS: (*To himself*) If a man without money falls in love
    His troubles are going to soar up, above
    The labors of Hercules.
    I'd rather fight with these:

A Nemean lion; or the *excetra*,
That is, the Hydra's constant cluster
Of snakes; a bronze-footed stag;
A boar whose snout could snag
You fatally; Stymphalian birds; *ugh!*
Rather wrestle Antaeus loose from earth   10
Then fight with Love. By now my drastic dearth
Of funds has sent me hunting for friends
To borrow from, but the quest ends
Where it started: money? they haven't got it.

SAGARISTIO: (*Soliloquizing likewise*)
    The slave who wants to serve his master well,
    In the best kind of servitude . . . well . . . his attitude
    Should be to store up lots of notions in his chest
    As to how to please him best! To figure out ways
    To please him, whether he's at home or away.
    But somehow I don't seem to slave in my actions   20
    To his satisfaction. It's as if I were a sty
    In my master's eye and he just can't keep from rubbing
    Or ribbing me; he has to give me orders and cares:
    He has to have me propping up his affairs.

TOXILUS: Who's that standing over there?

SAGARISTIO: Who's that opposite me?

TOXILUS: Looks like Sagaristio.

SAGARISTIO: Of course, it's my friend
    Toxilus, one and the same.

TOXILUS: That's who it is, for sure.

SAGARISTIO: I do think it's him.

TOXILUS: I think I'll go up to him.

SAGARISTIO: I'll go to meet him.   30

TOXILUS: Sagaristio, *ciao!* Gods bless you!

SAGARISTIO: Oh, Toxilus! May the gods grant your every wish.
   How are things?

TOXILUS: I get along, somehow.

SAGARISTIO: What's doing with you?

TOXILUS: Well . . . I still exist.

SAGARISTIO: A good enough existence?

TOXILUS: If what I insist on
   Wishing for works out, I'll be happy.

SAGARISTIO: But that's a sappy way to handle your friends.

TOXILUS: How so?

SAGARISTIO: Here's how: you should order them around.

TOXILUS: But you were as good as dead to me; you see:
   You weren't around to order around.

SAGARISTIO: Was I busy!   40
   Ask Pollux.

TOXILUS: Some iron bands on your hands?

SAGARISTIO: No: down at the mill I've been promoted
   To first sergeant in charge of flogging.

TOXILUS: Oh, you're an old hand at that; you've earned your
   stripes.

SAGARISTIO: But how about you? Are you up to scratch?

TOXILUS: Not really.

SAGARISTIO: So that's why you're pale as Pollux, dead white.

TOXILUS: Fact is: in the battle of Venus I've been wounded;
    Cupid has pierced my heart with his arrow.

SAGARISTIO: Don't tell me slaves fall in love around here?

TOXILUS: What to do? Contend with gods, as if   50
    I were the son of Titan, go to war
    Against forces I cannot compete with?

SAGARISTIO: Well, just make sure that certain catapults,
    Fashioned from elm rods, don't make inroads
    On your ribs.

TOXILUS: At least, I'm king for a day;
    It's like Freedom Day, the festival in honor of the way
    We beat the Persians at Plataea.

SAGARISTIO: How do you mean?

TOXILUS: My master's gone abroad.

SAGARISTIO: So he's off, is he?

TOXILUS: If you can stand having a good time, come along
    And share with me. I'll treat you like a king.   60

SAGARISTIO: Oof! My shoulders itch already, just listening
    To what you're saying.

TOXILUS: But there's one little thing left over;
    And it's ex-cru-ci-a-ting.

SAGARISTIO: And what would that thing be?

TOXILUS: Today is the very last day my mistress can be
   Free; otherwise she'll slave like a slave forever.

SAGARISTIO: So what is it then you want? I want to know.

TOXILUS: Well . . . you can buy an eternal friend for yourself.

SAGARISTIO: And how?

TOXILUS: Give me the six hundred *nummi* I need
   To pay for her freedom. I'll pay you back, of course,
   Three days from now, or four. So come, be good   70
   And come to my rescue.

SAGARISTIO: Some nerve you've got, asking me
   For a sum of money like that; you're really something!
   Why, if I should sell myself, one, whole and entire,
   I wouldn't fetch that high a price. You're asking
   For water from pumice stone, which is so dry itself
   It's dying of thirst.

TOXILUS: So, this is the way
   You're treating me?

SAGARISTIO: How should I be treating you?

TOXILUS: How can you ask? What you ought to ask is:
   Someone to lend you the money.

SAGARISTIO: No: *you* ought to ask
   What you're asking of me.

TOXILUS: I've searched and inquired   80
   And found a source nowhere.

SAGARISTIO: I'll give it a try:
  Somebody might trust me.

TOXILUS: You mean, somewhere,
  Not out of this world, there's a possibility?

SAGARISTIO: If I had the money at home, I promise you'd get it;
  What I can do is try real hard.

TOXILUS: Well, fine . . . whatever . . .
  But come to my house anyway, whatever . . . *but*
  Don't stop looking, whatever you do, and *I'll* . . .
  Do whatever I can.

SAGARISTIO: If there's a chance, any chance
  Whatsoever, be sure I'll take good advantage.   90

TOXILUS: I'm down on my knees, I beseech you . . .

SAGARISTIO: Up off your knees!
  You're making me queasy with your fawning.

TOXILUS: Just do
  Me this one faithful favor.

SAGARISTIO: Ugh! And enough! You're killing me with this kind
  Of kindness.

TOXILUS: It's love's fault, not mine, that I've become,
  Such a monologuing moron.

SAGARISTIO: By your leave, Pollux,
  I'll be leaving.

TOXILUS: You're taking off now, are you?
  Have a good ramble. But do come back as soon
  As you can: don't make me go looking for you. I'll   100

Be hanging around here close to home, and concocting
A good piece of nasty work to give that procurer.

Scene 2

SATURIO: *Ecco mi!* A sight for a pair of sore eyes:
  The perfect parasite, descended from a long line
  Of ancestors, none of whom ever failed
  To fill his stomach with meals at others' expense.
  And I mean long line: father, grandfather, his father;
  And farther back, my great-grandfather's father,
  Or even farther, his father. Like mice, they fed
  On food provided by others, and none could surpass   110
  Them in their taste for good eating. Hard-headed men,
  With arms long enough to cover the whole triclinium.
  (*Sings a snatch of the melody "Volare"*)
      Mangiare, yum . . . yum!
      Circolare . . . sul
      triclinium!
  I take after them; when invited, I leave the forum
  And willingly dine out: it's my *MOS MAIORUM*.
      But about other people's property, it wouldn't be proper to
  Say I'm trying to lay hands on it. I'm not like informers
  Who try to pick up a cool twenty-five percent
  Of the damages by turning others in to the authorities.
  I don't care for those types at all, going for profit
  Without incurring any risk. Those "quadruplers"   120
  Turn me off. Am I making myself quite clear?
      Ah, but suppose an informer turns someone in
  As a matter of public interest, not private profit?
  I would accept him as an upright citizen. But if
  He fails to win the case against the lawbreaker: ah, then—
  He ought to pay half the damages expected
  Into the public purse. And here's another law
  I think ought to be passed. If any informer
  Prosecutes anyone, the defendant in turn should have

The right to sue him for the exact amount,   130
And approach the triumvirs on equal terms.
If this were done I'd make sure that not a one
Of those dirty crooks, with their whitened nets for snaring
Other people's property, was anywhere to be seen.
         But I guess I'm rather foolish to be looking out for
The public interest, when we have our magistrates,
Whose duty this ought to be.
                                    Let me just step over here
Indoors, and see what's been left over from yesterday
And whether these tidbits have had a good night's rest,
And been kept warm; also, kept well under covers   140
So no one could creep up on them. Oh, but wait—
The door's opening; I'd better hold back my steps.

Scene 3

(TOXILUS *enters from his master's house, speaking to himself*)

TOXILUS: I've got the whole thing figured out, how today
    That procurer will procure her liberty, *and*
    (*Looking across the stage*)
    With his own money, . . . but . . . *ecco!* the parasite:
    Just the one whose help I need to work my plan.
    I'll pretend I don't see him and inveigle him into it.
    (*Calls back inside*)
    Hey, you folks in there, look sharp! Step on it!
    I want everything ready by the time I come back here:
    The honey dripped into the wine; the quinces minced;   150
    The trifle trifled with, to feel nice and warm in the dish;
    And don't forget the spiced calamus—toss it in.
    By Pollux, my pal will be along any time now.

SATURIO: (*Aside*) He means me, hot dog!

TOXILUS: Probably coming right here,
  All washed and clean, straight from the baths.

SATURIO: (*Aside*)   He's so right.

TOXILUS: Make sure the cakes and cheese biscuits are good
    and hot;
  Don't put them out for me half-baked.

SATURIO: (*Aside, but a bit louder*)
  That's a very good point he's making: those biscuits,
  If they're left undone, taste terrible; what you want
  Is to swallow them warm and moist. And for the
    gravy-cakes   160
  You need a good thick filling; if it's thin and weak
  They're not worth anything. The sauce needs to be
  Full-bodied and juicy. I want it making its way
  Straight to my stomach, and not slipping off to the side
  And heading for my bladder.

TOXILUS: (*Looking around*) I hear somebody talking near me . . .

SATURIO: (*Aloud*)   Oh, my Jupiter
  On earth! It's your fellow banqueteer: says hello.

TOXILUS: Saturio, what perfect timing!

SATURIO: But to call me Saturio
  Is wrongly stated: I come up hungry, not sated.

TOXILUS: Well, you'll get something to eat. Inside there
  What warms our insides is already simmering: 170
  I've told them to heat up the leftovers.

SATURIO: The rule is
  That next day the ham is served up cold.

TOXILUS: Just as I
   Told them to do.

SATURIO: Do you have some herring and sour cream?

TOXILUS: You're asking me?

SATURIO: Oh, I forgot; you're a genius
   At knowing what tastes just right.

TOXILUS: But do you remember
   That business I was discussing with you yesterday?

SATURIO: About lamprey and eel? Don't warm them up, strip
      them
   Until their skeleton looks like a comb; done cold,
   Their meat tastes better. But why do we delay
   The start of battle? While it's still the morning   180
   All mortal beings should eat.

TOXILUS: Rather too early morning,
   I rather think.

SATURIO: The enterprise you start in on
   First thing in the day lasts you all through the day.

TOXILUS: Now, do listen to this. Yesterday I told you about it
   And begged you to lend me six hundred *nummi*, didn't I?

SATURIO: Of course I remember your asking me, and my not
      having
   Anything to give you. A parasite isn't much
   Of a parasite if he's got money stacked up at home.
   He gets the urge right away to mount a dinner party
   Or he digs right into his own provisions, at his own   190
   Expense. What becomes a parasite is to become, indeed,
   A cynic in need: a leather bottle for his scent,
   A strigil, a small carryout bag, and a cloak

And a pair of slippers, and a purse for small change,
To keep his own household in a good mood.

TOXILUS: I don't want money; I do need to borrow your daughter.

SATURIO: Well, I've never loaned her out to anyone, so far.

TOXILUS: Not for what you think I have in mind.

SATURIO: What do you want her for, then?

TOXILUS: You'll find out:
   She's certainly beautiful and has a lovely figure.   200

SATURIO: That she is and has.

TOXILUS: Now this procurer of mine—
   He doesn't know you, does he, or your daughter?

SATURIO: How could someone know me unless he'd set me
   Up with some food?

TOXILUS: Exactly. And so, this way
   You can find my money for me.

SATURIO: By Hercules,
   I wish I could.

TOXILUS: Then, you want to let me sell her.

SATURIO: *You* sell her?

TOXILUS: No, I'm appointing another
   To do the selling, someone who'll identify himself
   As a foreigner. It hasn't been six months as yet
   Since our procurer moved here from Megara.   210

SATURIO: The leftovers are getting cold. This business
   Can be taken care of later on.

TOXILUS: But don't you see how?
   You won't get a bit to eat here today, and don't
   Fool yourself about that, until you tell me for sure
   That you'll do what I'm asking; and furthermore,
   If you don't bring your daughter with you right now,
   As soon as you can, I'll drum you out of the ranks.
   What's wrong? What's up? Why don't you speak up and say
   What you'll do?

SATURIO: You might as well sell me myself,
   So long as my stomach's full.

TOXILUS: If you'll go through with it,   220
   Then go ahead and do it.

SATURIO: I'll be glad to do
   Just what you want.

TOXILUS: Very good of you. Now hurry home
   And instruct your daughter cleverly and cunningly
   In her part, ahead of time. She is to say:
   Where she was born, who her parents were, and how
   She was kidnapped. And she must state strongly
   That she was born quite far away from Athens,
   And shed a tear or two when she mentions this.

SATURIO: No need to go on and on: she's three times worse
   Than you could want her to be.

TOXILUS: What you're saying   230
   Is perfectly delightful, by Hercules, I admit.
   Now do you know what you have to do? Get a tunic,
   And a sash; and bring a scarf and a broad-rimmed hat
   For the man who's going to sell her to this procurer
   To wear . . .

SATURIO: Good show!

TOXILUS: As if he were a foreigner . . .

SATURIO: Exactly! I approve.

TOXILUS: And bring your daughter dressed
   Smartly in the latest foreign fashion.

SATURIO: *Ma . . . da dove queste cose?*

TOXILUS: Oh, just get them from the stage director:
   He ought to lend them out. The aediles have invested
   Plenty of money in this show.

SATURIO: Well, I'll go and get   240
   These acts together. Meanwhile, I don't know a thing
   About what's going on?

TOXILUS: Not a single thing.
   But when I've got the money, then you want to claim
   Her back from the procurer.

SATURIO: He can have her for himself
   If I don't take her away right away.

TOXILUS: So, off with you,
   And look after things.
   (SATURIO *exits*)
                    Meanwhile I want to send
   A boy to my mistress to tell her to take heart,
   That I'm going to work things out today.
   But I'm talking too much again . . . too much to say.

(*He exits into house*)

ACT II

Scene 1

SOPHOCLIDISCA: (*In a remonstrating tone*)
  It should be enough just to tell any uneducated girl who's thought-
  less and weak in the head the same thing over and over. But I
  suppose you must take me for some kind of stupid country hick. I
  may drink wine, but I'm not in the habit of guzzling down your
  orders along with it.   254

  I thought that I and my habits were familiar to you by now—for
  my part, I've looked after you closely for the past five years. If
  some muttonhead attended school for that length of time, he'd
  know his letters. But it looks like in your childhood or in your
  speaking years you never found out at all what I'm like.

  Can't you hold your tongue? Can't you stop telling me what to
  do? Oh, yes: I remember it; I know it; I grasp it; I have it in
  mind—

  You're in love, poor thing! And that's why your mind is bubbling
  over. I'll see that it quiets down.   264

LEMNISELENIS: (*Reflectively*) Someone who is in love is indeed a
  very poor thing.

SOPHOCLIDISCA: (*To herself*) Well . . . certainly, someone who's in
  love with nothing at all, is reduced to nothing. For someone like
  that, what's the need of life at all? I ought to go now and do what
  my mistress tells me. And with my help she may become a free
  woman. I'll go find Toxilus and load his ears with the things I've
  been told to tell him.

Scene 2

(TOXILUS *and* PAEGNIUM *enter from the house*)

TOXILUS: Is that all clear and firm? You remember, and have it
  All well in mind?

PAEGNIUM: Even better than you, the one who taught
  Me the lesson.

TOXILUS: Oh, you say so do you, you good-for-nothing?

PAEGNIUM: That's just what I do say.

TOXILUS: Then: what did I say, then?

PAEGNIUM: I'll tell it, all of it, to her exactly right.

TOXILUS: I don't think you know what I said.

PAEGNIUM: By Hercules' fist,
  You want to bet whether I know it all, *cold?*—
  And while we're at it, want to bet you know   280
  How many fingers you've got on your hand today?

TOXILUS: Me bet with you?

PAEGNIUM: Right on, if you like losing.

TOXILUS: Better to make peace.

PAEGNIUM: Well, then, let me go.

TOXILUS: So I do,
  And ask it of you. And I also ask this of you:
  Hurry—so that you're back home again, while I
  Still think you're *there.*

PAEGNIUM: Easy to handle.

TOXILUS: Hey! Where
    Do you think you're going?

PAEGNIUM: Back home, so you'll think
    I'm over there when I'm already home.

TOXILUS: You're really something:
    Quite the rascal; and I've got a little something
    Tucked away
    (*Touches his crotch*)
                    to reward you with!

PAEGNIUM: I know   290
    How owners can promise anything and not be compelled
    By the justices at court to appear before them on charges.

TOXILUS: So, take off, now.

PAEGNIUM: I'll see to it that you are glad
    You told me off.

TOXILUS: And take this letter, Paegnium,
    To Lemniselenis herself; and tell her what I
    Told you to.

SOPHOCLIDISCA: (*Aside*) Why am I waiting to go where I was
        sent?

PAEGNIUM: I'm off.

TOXILUS: So, off with you.
                            I'm heading home. Now do be sure
    And give this matter your full concentration. Make tracks.

PAEGNIUM: I'll dash all out, flaps up, like the ostriches we hunt
    In the circus.

(*As* TOXILUS *goes indoors*)
                    But who's the woman coming over?   300

SOPHOCLIDISCA: (*Coming forward*) It must be Paegnium.

PAEGNIUM: (*Seeing her*)   Ah, Sophoclidisca!
    The personal maid
Of the very person I've been sent to see.

SOPHOCLIDISCA: (*Aside*)   They tell me
    That no one is better at getting away with smooth tricks
Anywhere around than this lad.

PAEGNIUM: (*Aside*) I'll go up to her.

SOPHOCLIDISCA: (*Aside*)   I'll wait around a bit.

PAEGNIUM: (*Aside*) I'd better halt at this barrier.

SOPHOCLIDISCA: (*Aloud*) Paegnium, you charming fellow!
    Greetings: How goes it?
And what are you up to these days?

PAEGNIUM: Well, gods bless me, if it isn't Sophoclidisca!

SOPHOCLIDISCA: What about blessing me?

PAEGNIUM: Of course I include you. But it's up to them which
    one   310
Of us they see fit to favor. If they reward you
By your just deserts, they'll hold you high in their hate
And treat you spitefully.

SOPHOCLIDISCA: Oh, please don't speak so undelightfully.

PAEGNIUM: But since it's you I'm addressing, the subject can only
    Agree with the object.

SOPHOCLIDISCA: So what is it you're up to?

PAEGNIUM: I'm up to, that is, leaning against, a treacherous
     female:
Standing right beside you and looking you up and down.

SOPHOCLIDISCA: As for me, I don't know a more good-for-
     nothing lad
Than you.

PAEGNIUM: I'm doing something wrong or insulting someone?

SOPHOCLIDISCA: Someone? Everyone you have the chance to.

PAEGNIUM: Not a single
     Soul has ever thought so.

SOPHOCLIDISCA: But plenty of them know so.   321

PAEGNIUM: Wow!

SOPHOCLIDISCA: And wow again!

PAEGNIUM: You're judging other people
     By your own ways of acting.

SOPHOCLIDISCA: I must admit I'm perfect
     In the role of attendant in the house of a hard-working
     procurer.

PAEGNIUM: Well . . . that's enough of your gabbing.

SOPHOCLIDISCA: But what about you?
     Guilty or not of what I'm charging you with?

PAEGNIUM: If so, I'd admit it.

SOPHOCLIDISCA: Well, off then: You've won the
   game.

PAEGNIUM: Ah yes, and you—you might as well be on your way.

SOPHOCLIDISCA: Just tell me this one thing: where are you going?

PAEGNIUM: And you, where are you?

SOPHOCLIDISCA: But you speak up first.   331

PAEGNIUM: No: you first.

SOPHOCLIDISCA: But I *was* the first, to ask.

PAEGNIUM: So . . . you'll be the last to know.

SOPIIOCLIDISCA: Not far from here.

PAEGNIUM: Me too: not far.

SOPHOCLIDISCA: But *where*, you piece of misery?

PAEGNIUM: You've got to tell me first; otherwise, no way
   You'll get an answer to what you're asking.

SOPHOCLIDISCA: As Castor
   Is my witness, you won't discover where today
   Until I've heard from you.

PAEGNIUM: Is that a fact?

SOPHOCLIDISCA: It's a fact, in fact.

PAEGNIUM: You're such a poor specimen . . .

SOPHOCLIDISCA: You're such a rotten example . . .

PAEGNIUM: As is quite in keeping
    With my character.

SOPHOCLIDISCA: But not in keeping with mine.   341

PAEGNIUM: How about it, you worst of possible women—decide
    To make a secret of where you're going?

SOPHOCLIDISCA: And you,
    You miserable mutt, you've made up your mind to hide
    All knowledge of your destination?

PAEGNIUM: Heard you the first time:
    You're just handing back my words, word for word.
    But I really don't want to know, anyway, so farewell!

(*He starts to move off*)

SOPHOCLIDISCA: Hold it!

PAEGNIUM: I'm in a hurry.

SOPHOCLIDISCA: So am I.

PAEGNIUM: (*Pointing to her hand*)   Got something in there?

SOPHOCLIDISCA: (*Pointing to his hand*)
    And you in the other hand?

PAEGNIUM: Nope, not a thing.

SOPHOCLIDISCA: Well, then, just show me your hand.

PAEGNIUM: (*Showing his right hand*)   This the one
    you mean?   350

SOPHOCLIDISCA: Where's the left, the one you use for stealing?

PAEGNIUM: (*Hiding it behind his back*)
  Oh, I didn't bring it along with me: I *left* it at home.

SOPHOCLIDISCA: (*Grabbing his hand*)
  You've got something in there, but I can't tell what it is.

PAEGNIUM: (*Pushing her away*)
  Stop pawing me, you feeler-upper.

SOPHOCLIDISCA: Ah, just suppose I loved you?

PAEGNIUM: It wouldn't be worth the effort, at all.

SOPHOCLIDISCA: Why not?

PAEGNIUM: Because . . . when you're in love with someone who
    does not
  Love you back, you're in love with nothing at all.

SOPHOCLIDISCA: What best suits a lad with your youth and good
    looks
  Is to look for a good time early along in life,
  So that when your hair changes color, you won't be chained
  To perpetual slavery. So slight! You can't weigh more than
    eighty!   361

PAEGNIUM: But the battle is fought more in terms of energy
  Than of poundage. Well . . . I'm wasting my time.

SOPHOCLIDISCA: How so?

PAEGNIUM: Making points to someone who knows it all.
  And here I am, idling.

SOPHOCLIDISCA: Oh, please do stay around.

PAEGNIUM: You are some pain.

SOPHOCLIDISCA: I'll keep right on being one until
   I find out where you're going.

PAEGNIUM: If you must know:
   I'm going to your house.

SOPHOCLIDISCA: And *I'm* going to *yours.*

PAEGNIUM: Why there?

SOPHOCLIDISCA: What's it to you?

PAEGNIUM: (*Blocking her way*)   You won't go until I find out.

SOPHOCLIDISCA: You are some pain.

PAEGNIUM: Oh, I like to needle people.
   You'll never worm it out of me by being a worse hypoderm
   Than I am.   371

SOPHOCLIDISCA: It's a lot of work to compete with you in being
       clever.

PAEGNIUM: And you're a pretty poor piece of merchandise
       yourself.
   What's got you so worried?

SOPHOCLIDISCA: The same thing as you.

PAEGNIUM: Which is . . . ?

SOPHOCLIDISCA: Ah, but I've been told not to tell
   A single soul; strictly enjoined that all the dumb
   In the world would speak up about it before I did.

PAEGNIUM: Me too: instructed that all the dumb in the world
   Would sound off on this before I would.

SOPHOCLIDISCA: Still . . . let's sound off.
   If we give our word to each other, then we can trust   380
   One another.

PAEGNIUM: But here's something I know for sure:
   A procuress's word is about as weighty as a water-skeeter.
   They are, all of them, too light to trust.

SOPHOCLIDISCA: Come on, out with it!

PAEGNIUM: Come on, out with it! I'll love you for it.

SOPHOCLIDISCA: I'm not
   After your loving me.

PAEGNIUM: Point readily taken and granted.

SOPHOCLIDISCA: Keep the wish to yourself.

PAEGNIUM: (*Shows her a letter*)   And keep this to
   yourself.

SOPHOCLIDISCA: It'll be a secret.

PAEGNIUM: No one will know about it.

SOPHOCLIDISCA: (*Shows him a letter*)
   I'm taking this letter to Toxilus, your master.

PAEGNIUM: Well, go right ahead: he's at home in there.
   Meanwhile:
   I for my part am taking this pinewood tablet,   390
   Seal intact, to Lemniselenis, your mistress.

SOPHOCLIDISCA: What's written on it?

PAEGNIUM: If you don't know, I too
　Am in the same predicament; gentle words, I suppose,
　Of love and affection.

SOPHOCLIDISCA: Well, here I go: I'm off.

PAEGNIUM: And I'll be on my way.

SOPHOCLIDISCA: *Andiamo, allora.*

Scene 3

(*Enter* SAGARISTIO, *soliloquizing*)

SAGARISTIO: By Jove, I'm the lucky one! I got this windfall
　From the jovial power source, the opulent son
　Of Ops, the goddess of wealth: a father who lavishes largess
　On lesser luminaries: riches, high hopes, *plenty*—
　Plenty of what you need.   400
　So I'll raise my voice
　To rejoice in thanksgiving
　For the friendly way
　Jove gives me the means to pay
　My friend the money he had to have today.

　I never would have dreamed
　Or imagined, or even thought
　I'd have a chance like this.
　It just dropped down from heaven.   409
　You see, my master sent me off to Eritrea with money to buy some
　oxen trained to the plow, and told me the cattle auction would be
　held at the fair a week from now. Well . . . you can see he's rather
　absent-minded, trusting a lump sum like that to a fellow like me
　with my tendency to let the money run out on me. What I'll do
　with it is invest it elsewhere. I couldn't find any oxen to buy!

This way I'll be helping my friend in his dependency
And giving full rein to my characteristic tendency
Of not being able to hang on to money.
Don't trust me with cash!
I'll plunge it in pleasure, in one bash,   420
For once and for all, instead of doling it out
Bit by bit. I'll suffer for that. It'll be my back
That gets thrashed. But I don't care—
I like life with a little dash—
In it! I've got those oxen in my bourse,
Well broken to the yoke, to present to my friend.
It's a delightful sensation
To take a good generous bite
Out of those miserly, penny-pinching, shriveled,
Avaricious, bloodless old leeches   430
Who lock up the salt cellar along with the salt
And won't let their servants go into the vault.
When you get a chance like this
To do them a disfavor, it's not amiss,
It's actually a virtue, it's not wrong—
But justice, due overlong.
And my master will take it out on me?
Stripped and whipped with stripes; chains applied:
I may take quite a beating
For this cheating . . .   440
But still . . . don't let him think
I'll go crawling to him and ask to be let off.
Heck with him! I've already been punished
In so many ways: there's nothing new in that for me—
I already know what punishment can be.
But look: here comes Toxilus's lad, Paegnium.

Scene 4

(*Enter* PAEGNIUM, *from the house of* DORDALUS)

PAEGNIUM: (*To himself*) I've done the job assigned me, so now
    back home.

SAGARISTIO: (*Hailing him*) Stop, Paegnium! Even if you're in a
    hurry. Wait until you listen to me!

PAEGNIUM: You should buy up a hearer, someone you want to
    have
Listen to you.

(*Keeps moving away*)

SAGARISTIO: Now, hold it right there, I'm telling you.   450

PAEGNIUM: Imagine the trouble you'd be giving me if I owed you
    something.
Now, when I don't, you're giving me such a lot.

SAGARISTIO: You mutt!
    Won't you look back over here?

PAEGNIUM: I know how old I am:
    So you'll get away with this hassle unpunished.

SAGARISTIO: Where is your master, Toxilus?

PAEGNIUM: Wherever he wants to be,
    And in no need of your advice.

SAGARISTIO: You won't tell me where,
    You pain?

PAEGNIUM: I'm saying I don't know, you punching bag.

SAGARISTIO: I'm older, and you're fresh.

PAEGNIUM: As you deserve.
   After all, you started it. My master's orders:
   I work at his command; my tongue is free.   460

SAGARISTIO: Come on, please tell me now: where's Toxilus?

PAEGNIUM: I can only tell you to go to hell and back.

SAGARISTIO: You're in for a good lashing today with a rope end.

PAEGNIUM: On your account, you cuckoo? You hunk of meat:
   I wouldn't worry at all about breaking your head in two.

SAGARISTIO: Oh, now I get it: you've been up to some sexy stuff.

PAEGNIUM: I'll take that lying down. But what does it matter
   To you? I don't, like you, just do it for free.

SAGARISTIO: Pretty sure of yourself, aren't you?

PAEGNIUM: That I am,
   By Hercules. Sure that I'll be free, for example—   470
   Something you can never hope for.

SAGARISTIO: Could you be
   Somewhat less of a bother?

PAEGNIUM: Speaking of which
   Is something you can't do yourself.

SAGARISTIO: Oh, go to hell!

PAEGNIUM: But you'd better head for home. The whole case
   Is prepared for you there.

SAGARISTIO: And I'm prepared to meet
  My bail.

PAEGNIUM: I wish the preliminaries were over with
  And we could cart you right off to jail . . .

SAGARISTIO: . . . about this
      discussion—

PAEGNIUM: Dis'cussin'?

SAGARISTIO: Still tearing strips off me?

PAEGNIUM: You're a slave, and I'm a slave, so I behave
  In character by insulting you.

SAGARISTIO: Oh yeah? Want to knuckle under
  This knuckle sandwich?   481

(*Shaking his fist*)

PAEGNIUM: No food for thought, please:
  You really have nothing to offer.

SAGARISTIO: May all the gods and goddesses
  If I . . .

PAEGNIUM: As your friend I can only express my wish
  That you obtain your heart's desire . . .

SAGARISTIO: If I don't
  Pound you deep underground with my rain of blows.

PAEGNIUM: If you do me in, it won't be long before some others
  Lay you just as low.

SAGARISTIO: You know what I was going to say
   After that, if I hadn't held back my tongue?
   Get out of here!

PAEGNIUM: Nothing could be easier: my shadow   490
   Is already in for a whipping indoors: it's gone on ahead.

(*He exits*)

SAGARISTIO: May the gods and goddesses all crush that character!
   Like a sneaky sliding serpent he's got a double tongue,
   The dirty rat—even if I do mix my metaphors.
   Thank Hercules, he left here. I can be glad of that.
   Ah, ha! The door's opening: here comes another character—
   But this is the one I *wanted* to meet! And here he comes!

Scene 5

TOXILUS: Tell her it's settled where I'll get the money;
   She needn't worry, for I really love her—
   I'm cheerful when she's cheerful. Is that clear?   500
   You've got the message straight?

SOPHOCLIDISCA: Lord, yes.
   I'm solid on the ground as any groundhog.

(*She exits*)

TOXILUS: Get home, and double-quick.

SAGARISTIO: (*Aside*)   Now here's my chance
   To have a little fun with him. Just watch me,
   My elbows out and strutting like a lord.

(*He swaggers*)

TOXILUS: Who's that two-handled jug cavorting here?

SAGARISTIO: (*Aside*) I'll spit the way a lord does.

TOXILUS: Sagaristio!
  How's everything? What about the commission?
  Should I give up my hope in you?

SAGARISTIO: Come on—
  We'll see. I'll do whatever I can.   510
  Come over here and jog my memory.

TOXILUS: (*Seeing wallet bulge*)
  How come your neck's so swollen?

SAGARISTIO: It's a tumor.
  Don't squeeze it; if you're rough you'll make it hurt.

TOXILUS: When did you notice it?

SAGARISTIO: Today.

TOXILUS: I think
  You need an operation.

SAGARISTIO: Not too soon—
  It could make trouble, then.

TOXILUS: I'd like to check it.

SAGARISTIO: Look out! Lay off! And watch out for the horns.

TOXILUS: Horns?

SAGARISTIO: I've got oxen hidden in this wallet.

TOXILUS: Best let 'em out to pasture, or they'll starve.

SAGARISTIO: But they might stray away so far I'd never   520
    Get them back in the barn.

TOXILUS: I'll see to that.

SAGARISTIO: (*Pause*) All right, I trust you. You can have them,
    then.
    Come here; I've got the money that you wanted.

TOXILUS: How?

SAGARISTIO: Master sent me off to Eritrea
    To buy some cattle. For a spell your house
    Is Eritrea.

TOXILUS: Man, you are a marvel!
    I'll see you get your money back at once.
    I'm set to get the pimp's roll—it's all planned.

SAGARISTIO: Better and better!—

TOXILUS: And when I have the girl, I'll
    get some more.
    Come on inside. I need your help.

SAGARISTIO: It's yours.   530

TOXILUS: Well, let's get going, then. Agreed?

SAGARISTIO: Okay.

TOXILUS: Great. Get back home now, and see to it.

(*They exit*)

ACT III

Scene 1

(*Enter* SATURIO *with his daughter in Persian dress*)

SATURIO: God bless this undertaking for us both,
　　And for my belly in particular;
　　Let it have food for ages yet to come—
　　Not just to fill it but to leave it stuffed.
　　Here is the house, dear Daughter. God protect you!
　　I think you know what's to be done, and how—
　　Everything's been explained; you understand it,
　　You know why you are dressed the way you are.　　　　540
　　You're going to be sold today, my dear.

DAUGHTER: I know how fond you are of food, dear Father—
　　If other men supply it—but I can't
　　Believe you'd sell me for your stomach's sake.

SATURIO: Would it be better to sell you for the sake
　　Of Attalus, or King Philip, than for mine?
　　You do belong to me.

DAUGHTER:　　　　　　　I sometimes wonder
　　Whether you think of me as child or servant.

SATURIO: Whichever one does better by my belly.
　　I have the upper hand here, and not you.　　　　　　550

DAUGHTER: Of course it is your right, sir. All the same,
　　Since we're poor people, we should try to live
　　Within our means, and be contented to—
　　For if we compound shame and poverty,
　　Poverty's weight is doubled, and our name
　　Dishonored.

SATURIO: Look here, girl, you're disrespectful.

DAUGHTER: I didn't mean to be—is it insulting
   To tell your father what you feel is right,
   However young you are? Whoever hates you
   Can swell a story out of all proportion.   560

SATURIO: Oh, let them go to hell, whoever hates me—
   I'd pay less heed to them than to a table
   If it was set in front of me this minute.

DAUGHTER: Dishonor doesn't die. It lives long after
   You think it's dead, Father.

SATURIO: Tell me this:
   By selling you—that's frightening?

DAUGHTER: No, Father.
   I want you to be honest.

SATURIO: Your not wanting it
   Is useless. What I intend
   I'll do my way. Why do you act this way?

DAUGHTER: What if a master says he'll whip a slave—   570
   He may not mean to, really, but once the lash
   Is in his hand, and the slave's tunic is off his back
   What tortures he suffers! I'm pretty sure
   That you won't really sell me, but I'm scared.

SATURIO: Any girl's bad if she pretends to know
   More than her parents want her to.

DAUGHTER: Or if
   She won't protest when things are clearly wrong.

SATURIO: Things will be going wrong for you. Watch out!

DAUGHTER: But, sir, it's you I want to watch out for.
　　If you won't let me try, what shall I do?   580
　　No—I shouldn't have suggested it. You see,
　　It's others I want to keep from saying it.

SATURIO: Oh, let 'em talk. I'm doing what I want to.

DAUGHTER: And I must let you—only, if you'd listen,
　　You wouldn't want to do what you think you do.

SATURIO: You going to do as your father says or not?

DAUGHTER: Yes, sir.

SATURIO: You've heard the instructions?

DAUGHTER: Yes, I've heard.

SATURIO: How you were stolen?

DAUGHTER: Yes.

SATURIO: Whose child you were?

DAUGHTER: Yes—but you're making me into a bad woman.
　　You may regret this when I'm asked in marriage.   590

SATURIO: Oh, don't be silly. You know how men are:
　　They'll marry any girl, no matter who,
　　No matter what the scandal, if she's rich.
　　A dowry wipes out all that kind of talk.

DAUGHTER: Should I remind you that I have no dowry?

SATURIO: Hold your tongue, girl. Thanks to the gods above
　　And to your ancestors, you're not to plead
　　That you've no dowry. I've got a box of books—
　　Look, if you'll carry on the job today,

I'll teach you hundreds of bons mots, all Greek,   600
Not one of them Sicilian—with such a dowry
It wouldn't matter if you chose a beggar.

DAUGHTER: O Father, take me anywhere you choose.
Sell me, yes. Have your way.

SATURIO: Good girl!
Come on!

(*Goes toward* TOXILUS's *house*)

DAUGHTER: I hear you, Father. I obey.

(*They exit*)

Scene 2

(*Enter* DORDALUS, *looking sourly at* TOXILUS's *house*)

DORDALUS: What does my neighbor think he's going to do?
I swear he swore to give my money back
Today. If he's not paid me by nightfall,   610
His credit will be gone—and, worse, my cash.
There's some commotion at his doorway now.
Who's coming out, I wonder?

Scene 3

(*Enter* TOXILUS, *speaking to slaves within*)

TOXILUS: Take care of things
In there; it won't be long before I'm back.

DORDALUS: Hello, Toxilus. How's it going?

TOXILUS: (*Turning, shaking wallet*)   Why,
   You rotten pimp, you son of mud and dung,
   You lousy, filthy, double-dealing bastard,
   The shame of Greece, you greedy money-seeker,
   You goddam misbegotten son-of-a-bitch—
   Three hundred lines, three thousand, wouldn't give   620
   Space to describe you, scum. Will you accept
   Your money? Oh, come on, you iron-hearted
   Disgrace to all mankind—here, take your money!
   Take it, away, you dungheap-dweller, take it.
   You guessed I couldn't get someone to lend it
   Because it took my oath to make you trust me.

DORDALUS: (*Gathering himself together*)
   Just let me get my wits together, please,
   So I can answer.
   (*Bellowing*)
              You, the people's idol,
   You, the companion of all slime and filth,
   You freer of whores, you wearer-out of whips   630
   And fetters, you citizen of the mill, you slave for life,
   You goddam drunken thieving good-for-nothing—
   Hand me that money, hear? This very minute
   Give me that money, punk—or must I force you?
   It's mine, you know that. Give it to me, then,
   You impudent reprobate. This is a pimp
   Demanding cash because he freed your mistress,
   You louse—I'll let the whole town hear our quarrel!

TOXILUS: (*Nervously*) Shut up, shut up, man, for the love of
     heaven.
   Nothing's the matter with your lungs, that's clear.   640

DORDALUS: My tongue was born to repay compliments.
   Salt costs me what it costs you, but I'll never
   Take a lick without her as guardian.

TOXILUS: (*Soothingly*) Please don't be angry. It was just that I
    Was angry when you seemed to think I'd cheat you.

DORDALUS: (*Still angry*) Why shouldn't I, when I know you play
      the kind
    Of tricks that bankers love? Trust one of them
    And he'll be out of the forum in a flash,
    Like a rabbit when the door of his cage is opened.

TOXILUS: (*Offering* SAGARISTIO's *wallet*)
    Be good enough to take this.

(*Withdraws it*)

DORDALUS: What are you doing?   650

TOXILUS: Two hundred bucks in here, in cash, none counterfeit,
    Bring the girl around and declare her free.

(*Gives it*)

DORDALUS: (*Opening it*) She'll be here soon enough,
    (*Counts coins*)
                                 But I don't know
    Who's going to tell me this is genuine.

TOXILUS: You don't believe there's anyone you'd trust?

DORDALUS: Bankers, these days, can vanish even faster
    Than wheels can turn.

TOXILUS: Take the back alley there;
    Go to the forum; send the girl to me
    By the same route and through the garden.

DORDALUS: Right.
    I'll see she comes.

TOXILUS: Don't draw attention to her.   660

DORDALUS: My, my, what wisdom!

TOXILUS: She can go to give
   Thanks to the gods tomorrow.

DORDALUS: Certainly.

(*He exits*)

TOXILUS: (*Calling after him*) She could have been back in less
    time than you
   Have spent just standing here and jabbering.

(*He exits*)

ACT IV

Scene 1

TOXILUS: If you give a matter real thought,
   It will go along as it ought.
   Anyone's plans can move
   Smoothly enough to prove
   He's a capable sort of chap,
   And watchful. But if he's a sap,   670
   If he can't keep his mind alert,
   He's likely to lose his shirt.
   Now that's not my way at all;
   I'm in there, right on the ball
   So things will come out all right.
   I've got the pimp tied so tight
   He won't know how to get free.

(Calling indoors)
Sagaristio! Hey, it's me!
Go find the young lady, and get her
Out here, and bring out the letter   680
That you brought in my final version
From the land of the Mede and the Persian.

Scene 2

(Enter SAGARISTIO *and his costumed daughter)*

SAGARISTIO: Man, am I quick!

(Hands letter to TOXILUS*)*

TOXILUS: Indeed! And what a getup!
　　You don't know what that turban does for you—
　　(Looks at girl)
　　And those little sandals—my, how fine they look,
　　And how lovely she is, this lady from far away!
　　You're sure you both know what you're supposed to do?

SAGARISTIO: There'll never have been a performance better than
　　ours.

TOXILUS: You're a real help in a crisis. Get over there
　　Where you won't be seen, and see you keep quiet, too.   690
　　When you notice the pimp and I have begun to talk—
　　But here he comes now. Be off with the two of you.

(They exit)

Scene 3

DORDALUS: (*Not seeing* TOXILUS) Let the gods love a man and
    they reward him.
  Why, look at me—I'll save two loaves a day
  Now that my serving-maid is her own mistress.
  (*Looks at* TOXILUS'*s house*)
  He's paid through the nose; from now on somebody else
  Will feed her, and I won't have to give her a thing.
  (*Dreamily*)
  Today I think I ought to be given a medal
  For being so civic-minded and generous
  And giving the city another citizen,   700
  And furthermore, I've acted nice all day,
  Trusting men right and left, and taking nothing,
  Not even worrying that they'd deny
  Their debts in court. I want so much to be good
  Forever.
  (*Waking up from his dream*)
        But that's the kind of delusion
  That never comes true and never is likely to.

TOXILUS: (*Aside*) So: the trap's ready—let me coax him in.
  I'm good at this, and it's really a first-class snare.
  I'll speak to him now.
  (*Aloud*)
          And how are you doing, sir?

DORDALUS: (*Dreaming again*) Admirably, I trust.

TOXILUS: Where have you been?

DORDALUS: I trust you. May God send you all that you wish.

TOXILUS: So the girl's free?

DORDALUS: I trust so. I trust you.   712

TOXILUS: You're richer by one freed woman; am I right?

DORDALUS: (*Peevishly*) Oh, you're a nuisance. I said I
    trusted you.

TOXILUS: Yes, yes—but is she really free?

DORDALUS: For hours. Go ask the praetor in the forum.
    Get his opinion, if you don't trust me.
    She's free, of course she's free. Are you deaf?

TOXILUS: Well,
    All I can say is, heaven bless you, sir.
    I vow I'll pray your family and you   720
    Be specially blessed.

DORDALUS: Get on with you; no vows.

TOXILUS: Where is she now, the girl?

DORDALUS: She's at your house.

TOXILUS: You mean it? At my house?

DORDALUS: She is indeed
    At your house, now.

TOXILUS: So help me, what rewards
    You're going to reap!
    (*Voice lowered*)
                        See, there was something
    I didn't want to talk about. But now
    You'll hear it all—and then how rich you'll be!
    Why, you'll be grateful all your life for this.

DORDALUS: (*Skeptically*) You'd better be more definite about it.

TOXILUS: Your just deserts, sir—that's what you deserve   730
  And what I'll give. To guarantee good faith,
  Here is a letter.
  (*Holds it out*)
               Take it and read it through.

DORDALUS: (*Declining*) What has that got to do with me?

TOXILUS: Oho—
  A lot. You're going to find it fascinating.
  It came from Persia, from my master.

DORDALUS: When?

TOXILUS: Not long since.

DORDALUS: What does it say?

TOXILUS: It wants to tell you.

DORDALUS: All right, then. Hand it over.

(*Takes it*)

TOXILUS: But you must
  Read it aloud.

DORDALUS: Then keep still while I do.

TOXILUS: Mum is the word.

DORDALUS: (*Reading*)   "If you are well, then I,
  Timarchides, am happy, and I send   740
  Best wishes to Toxilus and the household.
  I'm healthy, busy, and successful—but
  Business will keep me here for eight more months.
  The Persian army's taken an ancient town,
  Chrysopolis in Persia, one of the richest.

There'll be a public auction of the loot—
That's why I'm staying on: I want my share.
This is to tell you that the letter-bearer
Is to be shown all hospitality,
Treated with every kindness, as indeed   750
He treated me when I was at his home."
(*Disgustedly*)
What good does it do me to read about
The Persians, or your master, for that matter?

TOXILUS: (*Eagerly*) Keep still, you fool! Read on! You've no idea
Of what's in store for you, or what a blaze
The torch of Luck will fire to light your way!

DORDALUS: What kind of luck?

TOXILUS: Ask somebody who knows.
(*Points to letter*)
All that I know I learned from that. I read it
Through first, that's all. Now you learn from it.   759

DORDALUS: A good idea. Keep still.

TOXILUS: Here's what affects you.

DORDALUS: (*Reading*) "The man who brings this letter also brings
A girl most beautiful and well-brought-up.
She has been kidnapped from Arabia.
You are to see that she is held for sale,
But warn the buyer he buys at his own risk;
There'll be no warranty given, none at all.
Be sure the bearer's paid in good hard cash.
Watch out for this. Watch out that he's watched over.
And so good-bye."

TOXILUS: (*Excitedly*)You see? Now do you trust me,   770
Now that you've read the letter?

DORDALUS: Where is he,
   The one who brought this?

TOXILUS: Oh, I'm positive
   He'll be here presently. He's only gone
   Down to the ship to fetch the girl.

DORDALUS: (*Shakes head*)   Lawsuits
   Don't interest me—I want no part of such.
   Why should I make such deals without a warranty?

TOXILUS: Oh, knock it off—how stupid can you be?
   What is it you're afraid of?

DORDALUS: I *am* afraid,
   That's true. Those bitten once should be twice shy—
   But I've been bitten often. Why don't I learn?   780
   This kind of sinkhole I've been in before.

TOXILUS: (*Guilelessly ambiguous*) It doesn't seem so dangerous
     to me.

DORDALUS: To you—quite right. I worry for myself.

TOXILUS: (*Shrugs*) It really makes no difference to me, you know.
   It was your good I had in mind—that's why
   I offered you first chance at such a bargain.

DORDALUS: Thoughtful of you. I think it's wiser, though,
   To profit by than *be* a bad example.

TOXILUS: But who is going to try to track her here
   From some Arabian wilderness? You'll buy her?   790

DORDALUS: I shan't decide until I've seen her.

TOXILUS: Right!
   And here he comes, the one who brought the letter.

DORDALUS: That's him? You're sure?

TOXILUS: I am.

DORDALUS: And are you certain
  That she's the girl we mean?

TOXILUS: Oh, as for that,
  I know no more than you do—
  (*Eyeing her*)
                                  though I'd say
  She's no tramp, but a lady, whoever she is.

DORDALUS: (*Hiding delight*) She's a most appetizing dish, indeed.

TOXILUS: (*Aside*) God, what a condescending bastard!
  (*Aloud*)
  Sir, I think we should keep still and just appraise her.

DORDALUS: (*Ogling girl*) The best idea I've heard!
  Congratulations!   800

Scene 4

(*Enter* SAGARISTIO *and daughter, pretending not to see the others*)

SAGARISTIO: Does Athens please you? Is it pleasant? Welcoming?

DAUGHTER: The city, yes—but as for the citizens,
  I haven't had a chance to study their nature.

TOXILUS: (*Aside to* DORDALUS) Pretty well-spoken, and nobody
  coaching her, either.

DORDALUS: (*Aside, to* TOXILUS) You can't really judge good sense
  from the first few words.

SAGARISTIO: How about what you've seen? The walls, for
    instance?

DAUGHTER: A city's protection lies in its citizens.
    If they can rid themselves of bribery, greed,
    Mistrust, and a half-dozen other faults as well—
    Envy, self-seeking, perjury, recrimination,   810
    Injustice, indifference, crime—Oh, Father, a city
    That has conquered those needs, needs only a single wall.
    But if they survive, a wall a hundred feet thick
    Will be as flimsy as reeds.

TOXILUS: (*Aside, to* DORDALUS) Hey!

DORDALUS: (*Aside, to* TOXILUS)   What do you want?

TOXILUS: You're guilty of most of those. Go banish yourself.

DORDALUS: What for?

TOXILUS: You certainly have been a perjurer.

DORDALUS: What she said has some point.

TOXILUS: You'd find her a lot of help,
    I tell you. Buy her.

DORDALUS: The more I consider the matter,
    The more I'm impressed with her.

TOXILUS: Well, if you buy her,
    I swear there'll be no wealthier pimp alive—   820
    You can turn men out of their houses, take their estates,
    Associate with the wealthiest citizens—even
    Have them eating out of your hand. They'll all be coming
    To your house whenever you give a party.

DORDALUS: But I
   Won't be party to such. I won't let them in.

TOXILUS: They'll serenade you, they'll burn your house to the
    ground.
   Better get ready; order new iron doors
   Installed; cover the house with an iron shell—
   Iron doorsteps, a bar, a ring. I beg you, please
   Don't spare it—get some for personal use   830
   In the shape of shackles. Have them riveted on.

DORDALUS: (*Genially*) Oh, to hell with you!

TOXILUS: (*Vigorously*)   You first—but listen to me.

DORDALUS: I only wish I knew what price he has set.

TOXILUS: Shall I call him over?

DORDALUS: I'll go.

(*They advance*)

TOXILUS: (*To* SAGARISTIO) Good-day to you, stranger.

SAGARISTIO: (*Sharply*) I've come to bring this girl, as I said I
    would.
   You know that my ship got into port last night,
   And the girl must be sold at once, if that's possible—
   If not—well, I must be gone as soon as I can.   839

DORDALUS: Good-day, sir.

SAGARISTIO: It will be good if I get the money
   She's worth.

TOXILUS: If you can't do that with this buyer, sir,
(*Winks at* DORDALUS)
I swear that you can't do it with anyone.

SAGARISTIO: You two are friends?

TOXILUS: As true as ever existed.

DORDALUS: (*Aside, to* TOXILUS) Then you must be my mortal
    enemy.
No god would ever give a friend to a pimp.

SAGARISTIO: Well, let's talk business. You want to buy this wench?

DORDALUS: (*Cautiously*) If you're interested in selling, why, I
    might be
Interested in a purchase. Remember, though,
It's no more important to me than it is to you.   849

SAGARISTIO: Make me an offer.

DORDALUS: Put your own price on her.
    She's yours, after all.

TOXILUS: (*To* SAGARISTIO) That's fair enough to ask.

SAGARISTIO: You want to buy her at a good price?

DORDALUS: And you?
    You want a good price yourself, I have no doubt.

TOXILUS: You both want that.

DORDALUS: Put a price on her, like a man.

SAGARISTIO: You understand: there won't be a guarantee.
    You're sure that's clear?

DORDALUS: (*Eagerly*) Yes, yes, of course—just name
    The lowest amount she'll go for.

TOXILUS: (*Aside, to* DORDALUS) Now watch yourself!
    You haven't got the brains of a two-year-old.

DORDALUS: What? What do you mean?

TOXILUS: You should ask some
    questions first
  Of the girl herself.

DORDALUS: Why, that's not a bad idea.   860
    Look at me, will you? Me, the wily pimp,
    About to lose his shirt except for your help.
    A friend you can trust is a great good thing in business.

TOXILUS: Ask her about her family, her country,
    Her history—so that I won't hear you complain
    You bought her because I talked you into it.

DORDALUS: The best advice you could offer!

TOXILUS: (*To* SAGARISTIO)   Sir, may my friend
    Question the girl a little?

SAGARISTIO: By all means.

TOXILUS: (*Back to* DORDALUS) What are you doing, standing
    there, you dope?
    Go up yourself and ask him for permission   870
    To speak to her. I know he said he'd agree,
    But I'd rather you asked for yourself. That way he'll get
    Some notion of you as a person.

(*Goes to* SAGARISTIO, *beckons* DORDALUS)

DORDALUS: Good advice.
   (*Approaches; stops and calls*)
   Stranger, I'd like a word with her.

SAGARISTIO: As you please.

DORDALUS: Have her step over here.

SAGARISTIO: (*To girl*)   Go. Keep him good-natured.
   (*To* DORDALUS)
   Ask anything you choose, sir.

TOXILUS: (*Aside, to girl*)   Come on, young lady!
   Go match your wits with his while fortune's smiling.

DAUGHTER: (*Aside, to him*) I'll do the best that I can to see
      that you
   Go back to camp round-shouldered with your booty.   879

TOXILUS: (*To* DORDALUS) Go back there. I'll bring her to you.

DORDALUS: (*To* TOXILUS)   That's splendid—
   Whatever you feel is best.

(*Steps back*)

TOXILUS: Come here, my dear!
   (*Aside, to her*)
   Remember what you were told to do.

DAUGHTER: (*Aside, to* TOXILUS)   Don't worry.

TOXILUS: (*Aloud*) Follow me.
   (*To* DORDALUS)
                              Here she is, for you to question.

DORDALUS: But I need you with me.

TOXILUS: No. I must obey my master
  And do as this gentleman wishes. Suppose he objects
  To my being with you?

SAGARISTIO: No objection at all.

TOXILUS: (*To* DORDALUS) May I offer my services?

DORDALUS: (*Gratefully*)   You'll be doing
    yourself a service,
  Helping a friend.

TOXILUS: Begin.
    (*Winks at girl*)
                        Now brace yourself.

DAUGHTER: (*Close to tears*) That's enough. I may be a slave, but
    that doesn't mean
  I haven't a sense of duty. I'll tell the truth   890
  As I've heard it told, whatever anyone says.

TOXILUS: Don't doubt that he's honorable.

DAUGHTER: I hope he is.

TOXILUS: And you're not going to be his slave for long.

DAUGHTER: Please God, not if my family does its duty.

DORDALUS: Don't let it surprise you if you hear me asking
  About those parents and your home.

DAUGHTER: Oh sir,
  Why should I? Slavery has made me used
  To any kind of bad luck.

DORDALUS: (*Patting her shoulder*) There, there, don't cry!

TOXILUS: (*Aside, happy*) Oh, she's a pro, she is—sharp as a tack,
    Damn her, she knows exactly what to say!   900

DORDALUS: Your name, my dear?

TOXILUS: (*Aside*)   Here's the first acid test.

DAUGHTER: At home they call me Lucris.

TOXILUS: *Quel nomen!* A lucrative omen!
    That ought to be worth a lot. Come on now, buy her!
    (*Aside*)
    I wasn't sure that she'd get through that one safely.

DORDALUS: Lucris—I hope that the name means *money*
    If I should buy you.

TOXILUS: If you do, by God,
    I'll bet she'll be your slave less than a month.

DORDALUS: That's exactly the way I hope it will come out.

TOXILUS: "We have to work, it seems, to realize
    Our dreams." So far I'd call her letter-perfect.   910

DORDALUS: Where were you born?

DAUGHTER: My mother always told me
    That it was in a corner of the kitchen—
    The left-hand corner.

TOXILUS: Boy, will she bring you luck—
    Born in a nice warm spot, the heart of the house,
    Where all the living is!
    (*Aside*)
        That should teach the pimp—
    Ask her where she was born, and get your leg pulled.

DORDALUS: No, no—I mean what country?

DAUGHTER: This is my land now.

DORDALUS: What did it used to be?

DAUGHTER: All of my past
  Is nothing now—it's all as lost to me
  As breath is to a man who's drawn his last.   920
  Why would you ask him what he was, alive?

(*Sobs*)

TOXILUS: (*Stirred, to* DORDALUS) Lord love us, but she's got the
    gift of words!
  Can't you see how it hurts her to remember?
  You shouldn't make her think of her misfortunes.

DORDALUS: Now tell me, is your father then a captive?

DAUGHTER: No sir, but all his fortune has been lost.

TOXILUS: (*To* DORDALUS) You see? She's far from trash—I'll bet
    she's noble.
  She wouldn't say a word that wasn't true.

DORDALUS: Tell me his name and something of his life.

DAUGHTER: Oh, why should I remember him, poor man?   930
  That is the proper word for both of us—poor, poor!

DORDALUS: How did he stand in his community?

DAUGHTER: No one was more beloved—he was the friend
  Of rich and poor, of slave and citizen.

TOXILUS: I pity him for all that he has lost—
  His home, his wealth, his loving family.

DORDALUS: (*To* TOXILUS) I think I'm going to buy her.

TOXILUS: *Think?* Lord, man,
   Can't you see she comes from a family of rank?
   She'll bring you thousands.

DORDALUS: I certainly hope she will.

TOXILUS: Then buy her.

DAUGHTER: But let me tell you—once my father
   Learns I've been sold, he'll be here as fast as he can,   941
   Or faster, to buy me back from you.

TOXILUS: (*Aside, to* DORDALUS)   How's that?

DORDALUS: What?

TOXILUS: What she said—

DAUGHTER: However much of his wealth
   Is lost—his friends—

(*Breaks down*)

DORDALUS: There, there, my dear, don't cry.
   With a lot of lovers, you'll soon be free. I hope
   It isn't just me that you don't want to belong to.

DAUGHTER: No sir, so long as I needn't belong too long.

TOXILUS: (*To* DORDALUS) See how dear the thought of freedom is
      to her?
   How much your patrons will love! Get on the ball—
   (*Points to* SAGARISTIO)
   I'll go with this gentleman.
   (*To girl*)

Come along with me.   950
(*Nearing* SAGARISTIO)
Here she is, sir.

DORDALUS: (*To* SAGARISTIO) Are you willing to sell this girl?

SAGARISTIO: Well, I'm pretty sure I don't want to throw her away.

DORDALUS: Down to brass tacks, then. What do you want for her?

SAGARISTIO: You may buy her, then, if you wish. For eight
    hundred dollars.

DORDALUS: Too high.

SAGARISTIO: Seven hundred and fifty.

DORDALUS: Still too much.

SAGARISTIO: Well, I'll give you my absolutely lowest figure.

DORDALUS: Come on now, out with it!

SAGARISTIO: You may take her, sir,
    With no guarantee, for just six hundred and twenty.

DORDALUS: (*Aside, to* TOXILUS) Toxilus, what do you think?

TOXILUS: I'm thinking that heaven   960
    Will blast you, you fool, if you don't get on with the deal.

DORDALUS: (*To* SAGARISTIO) Agreed!

TOXILUS: (*Aside, to* DORDALUS)   Oh wonderful! What a
    bargain you've got!
    She would have been cheap at a thousand. This is your day!

SAGARISTIO: Oh, by the way. There'll be fifty dollars added
  For her clothes.

DORDALUS: (*Furious*) You must mean subtracted, you wretch!

TOXILUS:
  (*Aside, to* DORDALUS, *motioning to* SAGARISTIO *not to insist*)
  Shut up—can't you understand? He's doing his best
  To weasel out of the sale. Go along with him now;
  Let him go to hell as he should.

DORDALUS: (*To* TOXILUS)   Keep an eye on him.

TOXILUS: You'd better go in.

DORDALUS: Yes, I'll go and bring back the money.

(*He exits to house*)

Scene 5

TOXILUS: You've helped us out a lot here, young lady.   970
  Indeed, you've done a beautiful piece of work,
  Intelligent and well-concentrated.

DAUGHTER: The good
  You do for good people is usually
  Taken seriously and appreciated.

TOXILUS: Now, Persian, are you listening? When you get
  The money from him, act as though you're going
  Straight to your ship.

SAGARISTIO: No need to tell me that.

TOXILUS: Then double back through the alley to my house
   And enter by the garden here.

SAGARISTIO: You're foretelling
   The future.

TOXILUS: Don't dash right off home with the money,   980
   I'm warning you.

SAGARISTIO: You think that I'm the sort
   To do what you would do?

TOXILUS: Keep quiet now;
   Lower your voice. Our loot is coming out.

                          Scene 6

(DORDALUS *reenters, with the purse*)

DORDALUS: So here they are,
(*Showing the purse*)
                            all six hundred and twenty
   Solid silver, tested coins—minus twenty.

SAGARISTIO: How do you mean that, minus twenty?

DORDALUS: To buy
   The purse, or make sure it comes home again.

SAGARISTIO: As if you weren't quite pimp enough, you have
   To be a dirty, greedy miser and worry
   About the loss of a money bag?

TOXILUS: I say   990
   We forget it. He's not doing anything
   Unusual. He is a pimp, after all.

DORDALUS: Today, according to the auspices,
    Should be a money-making day for me;
    So I don't see that there's any sum so small
    I would not be sorry to overlook it.
    So just take this, won't you?

(*Offers purse to* SAGARISTIO)

SAGARISTIO: (*Bends forward*) Hang it there
    Around my neck, unless you'd be sorry
    For doing that.

DORDALUS: Not at all.   1000

SAGARISTIO: (*Starts to leave*) And now, I guess
    There's nothing else you need from me, is there?

TOXILUS: But why rush off?

SAGARISTIO: Oh, business to attend to.
    I need to deliver some letters I was given.
    Besides, I've heard that my twin brother is here,
    Sold into slavery; so I'd like to look for him
    And redeem him.

TOXILUS: Well . . . I must say I'm glad
    You mentioned that. It seems to me I've seen
    A man looking just like you around here somewhere,
    The same build, the same size.

SAGARISTIO: My brother, no doubt.   1010

DORDALUS: And what would be your name?

TOXILUS: What does it matter
    To you?

DORDALUS: It matters, then, if I don't know it?

SAGARISTIO: Hang on, then, if you'd like to know. Here goes:
    Alibabble Forthieveingofgirls Smalltalk
    Overavitch, Cashgougeroutatheothers,
    Ayatollahso Mohammed over de Monet,
    Ugotitnow and Yul Neverletgoofit!

DORDALUS: Good Lord, a name like yours is bound to need
    A lot of room to write.

SAGARISTIO: Our Persian way
    Is to have long, complexicated names.   1020
    Anything else you want?

DORDALUS: No, just goodbye.

SAGARISTIO: You too. My mind's already on board the ship.

TOXILUS: You could go tomorrow, and have a dinner here
    With us today.

SAGARISTIO: No, I couldn't. Goodbye.

Scene 7

TOXILUS: We can say whatever we please, now that he's gone.
    You should remember this as the day you made
    A fortune. Whatever you pay, you'll get back triple.

DORDALUS: (*Looking after* SAGARISTIO)
    He's a real businessman: sold me a kidnapped girl
    Without a warranty, and made off with the cash!
    For all I know, somebody's around the corner   1030
    Waiting to claim she's free. Should I go to Persia
    To follow him for proof?

TOXILUS: (*Hurt*)   I thought you'd be grateful
  For all I've done.

DORDALUS: (*Repentant*)You know I'm grateful, Toxilus.
  I must admit you've done a lot to help me.

TOXILUS: (*Offguard*) To help you?
  (*Hastily*)
                    Oh yes, of course, of course!

DORDALUS: (*Starting*)   But there—
  I should have given some orders while I was inside.
  Don't let her out of your sight.

(*He exits*)

TOXILUS: (*After him*)   Don't worry, she's safe.

DAUGHTER: Where's Father? He's taking his time.

TOXILUS: Shall I call him?

DAUGHTER: Please do.

TOXILUS: (*Calling at his door*)
  Come out, Saturio!
  It's the chance of a lifetime   1040
  To avenge yourself on your enemy!

(*Enter* SATURIO, *wiping mouth*)

SATURIO: Am I holding you up?

TOXILUS: Get over there where you can't be seen, and stay still.
  As soon as you see me talking to the pimp,
  Let all hell break loose.

SATURIO: That's all I need to know.

TOXILUS: And when I've gone—

SATURIO: Oh, quiet. I know what you want.

(*He exits*)

Scene 8

DORDALUS: I bawled them all out—my house and everything in it
  Is filthy dirty.

TOXILUS: So you're back?

DORDALUS: I am.

TOXILUS: I've brought you luck today, you must admit it.

DORDALUS: I certainly do. Many thanks.

TOXILUS: Nothing more that you'd like?

DORDALUS: Just to see you enjoy yourself.

TOXILUS: (*Turns to go*)   That's the kind of wish
  That I'll see come true before five minutes have passed—
  For by then I'll be in bed with your freedwoman.   1052

(*He exits*)

Scene 9

(*Enter* SATURIO, *roaring*)

SATURIO: May I be damned if I don't ruin that man!
  (*Sees* DORDALUS)
  Ho, fine! He's right in front of his house.

DAUGHTER: (*Rushing up*) O Father darling, God bless you!

SATURIO: (*Hugging her*)   And you, my daughter!

DORDALUS: (*Aside*) Uh-uh! Here's the Persian! Now my luck's
  run out.

DAUGHTER: (*To* DORDALUS) My father, sir.

DORDALUS: (*Pretending surprise*) What? Your father? Oh, this is
  dreadful, it is!
  (*To* SATURIO)
  I suppose I've seen the last of my money now.

SATURIO: (*Leaping at him*) I'll see that your friends have seen the
  last of you,   1060
  You devil!

DORDALUS: Help, help!

SATURIO: Come tell the judge, you pimp.

DORDALUS: (*Innocently*) Why should I have to go to court?

SATURIO: You'll learn
  When you get there. But now come on, come on.

(*Pulling him*)

DORDALUS: You have witnesses?

SATURIO: Should I call any freeman
   To serve as witness for you, you lousy jailbird,
   Who makes your living off freeborn men?

DORDALUS: Now listen—

SATURIO: No way.

DORDALUS: Oh, hear me!

SATURIO: I'm deaf. Come along now,
   You horror, you rapist! And Daughter, you come too—
   We're all going straight to the praetor.

DAUGHTER: Yes, Father, I'm coming.

(*They exit*)

ACT V

Scene 1

TOXILUS: Now that we've conquered all our foes   1070
   And need have no more fear of those,
   Now that our state's at peace, our men
   And all our forts safe—once again
   I offer gratitude, O Lord
   Of all the heavens, who's restored
   Our safety—and the other gods
   I thank as well, for when the odds
   Were great, they brought their generous aid—
   The help for which we all had prayed—

To us, and sent our enemies   1080
To beg for mercy on their knees.
Therefore I call upon my men
To share the spoils.
(*Calls at door*)
                          Out with you, then!
(*Enter* PAEGNIUM *and slaves*)
Here, at our very entrance door
I have all sorts of joys in store.
Put up the couches here, my hearties,
And everything that goes with parties.
But first I want to see this table
Prepared with things to make me able
To cheer the hearts of all of you   1090
Who helped me do what I would do.
If I accept help, I concern
Myself with making some return.

(*Exit slaves, returning with feast. Enter* LEMNISELENIS *at door,
followed by* SAGARISTIO.)

LEMNISELENIS: Toxilus, love, you should be in here with me,
    And I with you.

TOXILUS: Yes, yes—come here and take me in your arms!

LEMNISELENIS: I do, I do.

TOXILUS: Now this is heaven.
    (*They embrace*)
                                              But come,
    Why do we waste time here? To bed, my darling.

LEMNISELENIS: Your wish is mine.

TOXILUS: Mine yours.
    (*They embrace*)
                                        Your place is set

(*To* SAGARISTIO)
There at the head of the table, Sagaristio.   1099

SAGARISTIO: The hell with that. I'm waiting for the partner
 I gave a contract for.

TOXILUS: Presently, presently.

SAGARISTIO: *Presently* is too long.

TOXILUS: (*Pulls him onto couch*)
                               So! On to business.
 Go take your rightful place—let's make today
 My birthday present.
 (*To slaves*)
                     Bring basins full of water
 To wash our hands, boys. Then set up the table.
 (*Crowns* LEMNISELENIS *with wreath*)
 Flowers for my flower! You shall rule us here.

LEMNISELENIS: All right lad, let the games begin, with flagons
 For everyone, beginning with the top man.

TOXILUS: Move it, Paegnium: you're late with my cup. I raise
 A toast: wishing well to myself and to my mistress!   1110
 On this day of days, donated to my desire by the gods:
 I am free to embrace you, a freedwoman.

LEMNISELENIS: But you
 Did the work!

TOXILUS: To everyone's health! And I pass the cup
 On to you, as lover to lover.

LEMNISELENIS: Let me have it.

TOXILUS: Do take it, please. And here's another toast:
 To anyone jealous of me, or happy for me.

Scene 2

(DORDALUS *enters, without at first seeing the others, and solilo-quizes*)

DORDALUS: Of all people living now, wherever they are,
   And all who lived in the past, and are destined to live
   In the future, surely I surpass them all
   At being the most miserablest living human being!
   I'm done for, totally done in! What a deadly day   1120
   Of disaster dawned on me today, when I let Toxilus
   Get around me and make me lose a sackful of money.
   I've overturned a whole wagon load of silver,
   And have nothing at all to show for it. May the gods
   Confound that displaced Persian, and all the other Persians,
   And, while they're at it, every other person they can find!
   It was Toxilus who thought up this intricate move,
   Just because I wouldn't trust him for the money.
   As I live and breathe I'll see him put in chains
   And handed over to torture the moment his master   1130
   Returns, something that I am looking forward to a lot.
   (*Sees the revelers*)
   But what's this I see over there? What kind of a show
   Are they putting on? They seem to be downing drinks
   Right out here in the open.
   (TOXILUS *approaches*)
                    Well, my good man,
   Greetings; and to you, my good—and now, free—woman!

TOXILUS: (*Good humoredly, reeling somewhat*)
   How about that? If it isn't good old Dordalus!

SAGARISTIO: (*Calling across the stage in slightly slurred tones*)
   How about it! Toorific! Have him come right on over.

TOXILUS: (*To* DORDALUS) Won't you join us?

SAGARISTIO: (*To the others*)   All together, now, let's
    have a good big round
Of applause!

TOXILUS: O Dordalus, you delightful specimen   1139
Of the human species, greetings: and here's your place.
(*Points to the couch*)
Just stretch out there.
(*To the slaves*)
                    Hey, lads, bring some water
For this fine man's feet.
(*To* PAEGNIUM)
                  Hither page,
And stand by me! You're bringing the stuff, aren't you?

DORDALUS: (*As* PAEGNIUM *approaches him with a ladle*)
Lay a finger on me and I'll straighten you out on the ground.

PAEGNIUM: Try, and I'll use this ladle to poke your eye out.

DORDALUS: (*To* TOXILUS) And you, you son of a bitch, who knows
    how many lashes you've worn out?
You think you'll get away with that monkey business
You pulled on me—that stuff about the Persian?

TOXILUS: (*Drinking*) Get out. Find somebody else to hear your
    griping.

DORDALUS: (*To* LEMNISELENIS) You knew about this and you
    never told me?   1150

LEMNISELENIS: Silly to let yourself get all stirred up
When you could just relax. Put it off til later.

DORDALUS: (*Furious*) My heart's aflame!

TOXILUS: (*To slave*)   Boy, give him a bottle.
(*To* DORDALUS)

                                                          Try some—
Put out the blaze before it gets to your head.

DORDALUS: Trying to make a fool of me?

TOXILUS: (*To* PAEGNIUM)   Say, Paegnium,
    Want a new partner?
    (*To* DORDALUS)
                            Go on, have your fun—
    Feel free.
    (PAEGNIUM *sidles up to* DORDALUS)
                    Hey, what a come-on! Watch those hips!

PAEGNIUM: They're worth the watching. I'm no amateur—
    I'd love to play with Dordalus. He's a pro, too.

TOXILUS: Keep it up, kid.

PAEGNIUM: (*Pretending to caress* DORDALUS)
                        How do you like that, pimp?   1160

(*Delivers a quick right*)

DORDALUS: Hey, damn it all, he nearly knocked me over!

PAEGNIUM: Once more, with feeling.

(*Repeats performance*)

DORDALUS: (*Shaking fist*)   You—you little bastard,
    So play your games, as long as your master's away.

PAEGNIUM: (*Delivers another punch*)
    That's what I'm doing—just what you tell me to.
    But now it's your turn to take advice from me.

DORDALUS: What is it?

PAEGNIUM: Find a strong rope and go hang yourself.

DORDALUS: Keep your hands off, or I'll thrash you black and blue
    with this cane of mine.

PAEGNIUM: I give you permission. Try it.

(*Hits him again*)

TOXILUS: Ah, that's enough of that, Paegnium.

DORDALUS: I'll wipe out
    The bloody lot of you.

PAEGNIUM: But then the Lord   1170
    In heaven, who hates you and who wants to prove it,
    Will wipe you out as well. And I'm the one
    Chosen to tell you—not these others here.

(*Kicks* DORDALUS)

TOXILUS: (*To* PAEGNIUM) Come on, now, serve the mead, fill up
    the goblets,
    And keep the tankards full. It's a long time
    Since that last drink, and we're so dry we're parched.

DORDALUS: (*Glaring*) I hope those drinks will bloat you till you
    burst.

SAGARISTIO: (*Unsteadily*) I'd like to do a little dance for you
    In honor of my friend, the pimp—a dance
    Hegea used to do.
    (*Prances, with occasional pass*)
                        Wouldn't you call it charming?   1180

TOXILUS: (*Rising*) Oh yes, indeed—and let me show you the
    dance
    Diodorus did once, out in Ionia.

(*Joins* SAGARISTIO)

DORDALUS: (*Backing away*) Get out or take a beating, you swine!

SAGARISTIO: Still sore?
   Don't irritate me any further, or else
   I'll bring that Persian back again.

DORDALUS: (*Looking at him carefully*)
                                        Oho!
   You're that same Persian—you're the one who clipped me!

TOXILUS: Shut up, you fool! This one's his twin brother.

DORDALUS: Oh? So?

TOXILUS: A perfect double.

DORDALUS: May the gods
   Send him and his twin brother to perdition.   1189

SAGARISTIO: Him, yes—not me. I've never done you harm.

DORDALUS: I want to see you pay for what he did.

TOXILUS: (*Taking guests aside*)
   Come on, we're going to have some fun with him.

LEMNISELENIS: (*Shaking head*) That isn't fair at all, unless he's
       earned it,
   And it's no good for me.

TOXILUS: (*Ironically*)   No doubt because
   He didn't try to stop me when I bought you?

LEMNISELENIS: Oh, I don't know—it's just—

TOXILUS: (*Angrily*)   Do you want trouble?
  Listen to me, and see that you remember
  My words: If I'd not been there to protect you,
  You would have been a common whore by now.   1200
  I've seen too many freedmen act like this—
  They must rebel against their patron somehow,
  To prove they're free and equal, must be rude,
  Impertinent, ungrateful, in return
  For all his kindness.

LEMNISELENIS: I never thought—I'll do
  Whatever you say.

TOXILUS: Well, I'm the man who freed you.
  I paid him money for you. What I want now
  Is fun at his expense.

LEMNISELENIS: I'll try to help.

DORDALUS: (*Watching*) I think they've got it in for me.

SAGARISTIO: (*As they all advance on* DORDALUS)
                                        Say, you—

TOXILUS: What is it?

SAGARISTIO: Tell me, is this Dordalus the pimp   1210
  Who deals in freeborn goods? Is this the fellow
  Who talks so big?

(*Hits him*)

DORDALUS: What do you mean? Hey, ow!
  Hit me again like that, and I'll fix you!

(*Waves cane*)

TOXILUS: But you're the one we've fixed and still are fixing.

(*Falls on him*)

DORDALUS: (*To* PAEGNIUM) Stop that! He pinched my ass!

PAEGNIUM: There, there,
    my friend—
  It's been through lots before this.

DORDALUS: No more lip!

LEMNISELENIS: Dear patron, let's go in to dinner now.

DORDALUS: You lazy slut, are you making fun of me?

LEMNISELENIS: Make fun of you, when all I said was just,
  Come and enjoy yourself?

DORDALUS: But I don't want to.

LEMNISELENIS: Don't feel you must.

TOXILUS: (*Hitting him*)   Well now, have you had
  enough?   1220
  See what a lot of trouble money can make?

DORDALUS: (*Aside*) God help me, they wouldn't even stop at
  murder—
  They sure know how to return an enemy's favor.

TOXILUS: (*Final cuff*) Okay. We'll call this quits for punishment.

DORDALUS: Oh, I'll admit I'm guilty—see, I'm praying!

(*Hands clasped*)

TOXILUS: You'll do it better when you're on a crossbar.

SAGARISTIO: (*Winks at* LEMNISELENIS) Let's all go in now and see
  him to the rack.

DORDALUS: (*To the audience as he goes into the house*)
  Those fellows taught me something, wouldn't you say?

TOXILUS: (*After him*) You won't forget that it's Toxilus you met!
  (*To audience*)
  Farewell now, all. You've seen a pimp's end. Cheer us!   1230

THE BROTHERS
MENAECHMUS
(*MENAECHMI*)
Translated by Palmer Bovie

INTRODUCTION

While his plays were based on Greek models and were imitations, Plautus did not simply translate his materials but rearranged and combined them, adding many distinctively Roman touches. As the product of the first Roman artist to devote his work entirely to playwriting, Plautus's comedies were warmly received and constantly reproduced. So many plays were attributed to him (the number reaching as many as 130) that by the time of Varro in the late Republican period it was found necessary to establish a canonical list. Varro did so, listing the twenty-one plays we have today as genuinely from the hand of Plautus. From Horace's severe opinion of Plautus's style and literary aims, it can also be judged that Plautus rated significant consideration among playwrights at the time of the "Golden Age" of Latin literature.

The other writer of Roman comedy always thought of with Plautus is Terence, his immediate successor, as it were, to the mantle of Roman Comedy. The thirty-six years of Terence's life (195– 159 B.C.) saw the composition of the six comedies we still possess, which are often contrasted with the plays of Plautus. Terence himself chides Plautus for *neglegentia* and for arbitrariness in adapting his models. In so doing, he affirms the importance of his predecessor.

The two writers differ in style and mode, Plautus being the noisier and less restrained, Terence the quieter, more deliberate artist; Plautus overflowing the boundaries of his models, Terence finding these limits his best guide to composition. But both men pioneered in a rich and lucrative vein, crossing over from Greek art to Roman experiment and discovering great resources within their own new language for cultivating the sense of humor. Both handed on to later writers and readers a new expression, realized in Latin verse, of man's persistent concern for the bright side of dramatized experience.

The *Menaechmi* ranks among the best work of a self-confident artist with a sharp eye for the stage and a practiced hand in writing for the theater. The profuse Latin verses race forward, beguiling and exciting the ear; the giddy confusions of the plot mount to the head, until by the final scene we are as momentarily dazed as the twin brothers confronting themselves. The lines of the play, the capricious conflicts and uncanny frustrating of communication, have set swirling the age-old problem of identity. A shrewd and practical slave presides capably over the situation caused by the steady accumulation of so many errors within one brief action, and deliberately rehearses the clues like a literary sleuth. As we watch the crafty Messenio fit the pieces together and watch the twins find out who they are, we sense the timeless truth of the theater. Illusion dissolves into reality; distance between the characters changes into proximity; a slave is not only free, but on the verge of becoming rich; two brothers are reunited.

No situation could be more simply farcical to begin with. Each brother sets about managing his own situation competently, gaily, adventurously, playing his satisfactory and amusing role. But gradually, as each character in turn comes forward recognizing Menaechmus II, only to be unrecognized by him—including father-in-law and doctor summoned, if not for this purpose certainly for this effect—the confusion of recognition and nonrecognition becomes a chaos of conflicts ordered by the deft synchronization of exits and entrances. The stubbornness of Menaechmus II in not recognizing his "witnesses" upsets everyone but himself, for he is resourceful enough to pretend not to be, that is, not to recognize, himself. Since Menaechmus I has meanwhile stumbled back into this disturbed and distracted situation he can only add to the trouble by systematically recognizing everyone in sight. But by doing so he meets disaster under the auspices of recognition, where Menaechmus II had triumphed by means of nonrecognition. And he aptly describes himself as "nunc ego sum exclusissumus" ["the most left-out character"] at the end of act 4. The outsider has been taken into the situation; the insider, excluded from it. By the time Menaechmus II is forced to pretend madness as a means of controlling his situation, and Menaechmus I is actually attacked and almost carried off to confinement, the errors in identity have risen to their logical climax. The escape of Menaechmus I, thanks to Messenio's timely intervention, the reappearance of Menaechmus II soon thereafter, and the final triangular confrontation set the stage for a positively Euclidean success of mind over matter.

There is, then, much heart and thought underlying Plautus's mischief. Identity is interesting and elusive, more engrossing perhaps, if less subtle, when it is doubled. Shakespeare increased the number of problems and gained even more violence, melodrama, and threatened punishment; he took measures to offset the added force by contributing romantic and lyric elements not found in Plautus. But the main idea of the confused identities (which Shakespeare derived from the *Amphitryon* as well as from the *Menaechmi*), although more elaborately worked out and more comic in its errors, still provides the main substance of Shakespeare's comedy. When Shakespeare added love interest and pathos and increased the violence, he found occasion not only to compose beautiful lines keyed in the dialectic of love poetry, but also to change over to outrageous puns and obscenities (even adapting Latin to this purpose), to transform the characters of the twins into those of gentlemen with English sensibilities, to turn Plautus's doctor, an authority on madness, into his own Pinch, a schoolmaster, and often to alter and complicate the original play of Plautus beyond easy recognition. But the fundamental interest still derives from the dramatic pursuit of identity, from the discovery of the actual persons responsible for the action, from the reversal of their sad state of affairs to a happy one.

Plautus's technique may, of course, best be studied in the annotated editions of the Latin play and in the extensive critiques of his art written by scholars of the subject. These sources generally award Plautus great credit for inventiveness and facility in language and diction, for mobilizing the powers of Latin for ardent, vigorous expression. It is a daring and exciting sphere, the world of Plautus's language, perhaps reflecting to some extent the state of mind of the new Romans, successful as a nation now having met the challenge of Hannibal and neutralized military rivals in the East. A new sense of dominance in the Mediterranean, unhoped-for signs of commercial prosperity dawned on the Romans after the early centuries of privation and struggle. Plautus seems gifted with an analogous sense of power in his art.

He strikes here and there freely and energetically, Romanizing the Greek externals of his models, adapting, changing, consolidating, claiming the new territory of comedy for his own. As a versifier he gains expert control over the medium while it is still at an early phase of its development, close to the accentual cadence of Latin but capable of being shaped and molded by meter. He builds his verse lines solidly on a twofold base of the trochaic septenarius (seven complete feet and an additional syllable or "half-foot" at the end of each line) and iambic senarius (six complete iambic feet), but handles this pattern with a liberal use of substitution and with an ear for easy and flowing movement.

The lyric songs, in quite different meters, constitute a reworking of the earlier pattern of lyrics in the Greek drama, which had fallen into disuse and are now reintroduced for change of mood and pace. The "song" of either Désirée or Messenio, for example, changes and brightens the scene, momentarily clearing it of the mounting complications of the plot. The intricate metrical structure shows Latin at its most extended power of rhythmic variety, just as the vocabulary and alliterative diction show Latin at an exuberant, flamboyant phase, not unlike the fecundity and verve we can sense in Renaissance English writing. As for the "one-man" chorus, or song-and-dance routine, made possible by the lyric song passages, it should be said that the derivation is from the native Italian as well as the traditional Greek. The chanting buoyance and sprightly meters of these songs owe much to the native country balladry and folksong indigenous to the Italian peasants, the fescennine spirit that preceded the literary arts of comedy and satire. The comedy of Plautus seems to have drawn its inspiration from many different sources, reflecting in temper the bright outlook for a hopeful future, directly incorporating major elements from the traditional Greek reservoir of dramatic models and esthetic practices, while reshaping these into a new medium in a new language, and stemming from the native fescennine raillery and folk poetry written in the Saturnian accentual scheme.

Of as much importance in studying Plautus as the intellectual implications of plot and thought or the specialized techniques of verse composition is the simple matter of his comic attitude. It is readily enough seen that the *Menaechmi* abounds in farce and a kind of hard-headed "fun" that Plautus lets loose on the stage at will. Obviously he means for us to laugh at the predicaments and roar at the characters, not sympathize with them. It is a hard world, he seems to say, and we might as well try to make the most of it and land on our feet if possible. It is a hard world for Désirée and Peniculus, for example; the cliff-hanging statusless woman and the insolvent man-about-town must brazen their way through and manipulate realistically to survive. Furthermore, love affairs are all very well, but they take more money than they are worth. It is a hard world for the indispensable slave, whose gifts and energies sometimes encourage us to laugh with him and at his master. The free and easygoing young men of substance command our interest if not our respect by their near imperturbability. Like the "dramatic street" on which Roman comedy is played with its stage 180 feet long, its standard backdrop of two houses, two exit streets (one leading to the forum, the other to the harbor or country), and its alley for eavesdropping, the comic situation represents a rather open and matter-of-fact way of life. The psychology of its action affords few occasions for soul-searching or remorse, and its busy conduct leads directly to sudden laughter or startled dismay.

Still, there is room for criticism, wry analysis, and considerable, if impulsive and exaggerated, emotional involvement. Peniculus's oration against public orations and Menaechmus I's full cry against the commercial entanglements of the legal process both touch on sensitive areas of Roman sociology. Messenio's successes and the perplexed, unsuitable wife's failures evoke some measure of sympathy, whereas the dense doctor and the hard girlfriend evoke little. Perhaps the most appealing character in this play is the old father-in-law, canny and clear-minded; debilitated as he appears, he makes a most experienced authority on old age. Thrown together in this tough outdoor world, Plautus's band of characters carom off one another, unleashing lines of witty abuse and artful conciliation, bending their whole energies to the solution of a situation that is perfectly real and graspable, and wildly incongruous.

Although there are several passages and lines open to various interpretations, I have not added notes to my translation because the technical consideration of all disputed points is available in the scholarly editions of the play.

In translating into English verse I have relied on a flexible version of the iambic pentameter as the fundamental line rhythm for dialogue where Plautus uses the septenarius or senarius. While trying to preserve the main stress of five beats a line, I have expanded the number of syllables beyond the ten used in strict iambic pentameter, and have occasionally extended the line to a hexameter. I employ rhyme as well, in the hope of registering an English equivalent for Plautus's anaphora, assonance, and alliteration. Plautus's sound effects have encouraged me to try freely for rhyme sounds—initial, medial, and end rhymes—as a means of imitating to some degree the explosive sonority of his amazing ear-filling Latin. I change from rhyme to blank verse and return to rhyme, for the purpose of breaking the monotony of one metrical style. In the lyric passages I have used shorter lines and different rhyme forms in an effort to imitate the lyric shape of the original Latin. Throughout the translation I have tried to reproduce as clearly as I could the temper and spirit of Plautus's comedy wherein, for all the carefree writing and abandonment of exposition to the farcical moment, there persists a steady and generous supply of good humor and good sense.

Palmer Bovie

THE BROTHERS MENAECHMUS

CHARACTERS

PENICULUS [Brush], a parasite
MENAECHMUS I, a young gentleman living in Epidamnus
MENAECHMUS II [Sosicles], a young gentleman of Syracuse
DÉSIRÉE [Erotium], a courtesan
MIXMASTER [Cylindrus], her cook
MESSENIO, slave of Menaechmus II
MAID, in the service of Désirée
WIFE, wife of Menaechmus I
OLD MAN, father-in-law of Mcnaechmus I
A DOCTOR
WHIPSTER I
WHIPSTER II

PROLOGUE

Ladies and gentlemen, and everybody else, I announce
In the first fine foremost and friendly words I pronounce,
Myself! How are you all out there? Do let me greet you.
It's a particular pride and personal privilege to meet you,
And present to you Plautus in person, that is, as he looks
When he speaks in his very own words; I don't mean in books
Where you read what he says, but here on the stage where
   he *is*.

87

Won't you lend us your ears and put yourselves quite at ease,
Tune in on our logic, and turn your minds to the plot
I now go over in a very few words, not a lot?   10
     Oh yes . . . poets often insist, more often than not
In their comedies, "It's an action in Athens," it takes place
Where you're expected to find it most charming, in Greece
    (*Irish pronunciation*).
     But I'm not the underhanded sort who is willing to say
It takes place somewhere it doesn't, or . . . anyway
Nowhere except *when* it does occur there. And today
While I grant that our play bubbles up through Greek grounds,
It's distilled in Sicilian, not acted in Attic towns.
So your Prologue expounds the preface to his foreword. He
    pounds
In the plot now, not a little, but a lot; it's scoops of synopsis   20
To ladle out. I'll shovel on now, and bury my worries,
In view of the generous way you hear out our stories.
     A certain old man was a merchant in Syracuse.
To him twin sons were born, identical youths
So alike in appearance the wet nurse could never get used
To telling them apart when she popped up to offer her breasts;
Their own mother didn't know which was which, she just
    guessed.
Well . . . at least, that's what someone who saw these boys
    once told me:
I don't want you thinking *I* went there and saw them, you see.
Now one day when both boys were seven, their father
    loaded up   30
A huge cargo ship full of goods to be sold, and toted up
One of the boys on the boat. Then off they went
To the market together being held in the town of Tarentum;
The other son, of course, he left back home with the mother.
And when they got to Tarentum, the father and the other,
There was some sort of fair going on, with hundreds of games,
And hundreds of people to watch them, which quickly explains
How the boy wandered off in the crowd, away from his dad.
A merchant from Epidamnus latched on to the lad

And snatched him off home. And then when the father
   discovered   40
He'd lost his son, sick at heart, he never recovered
From the fatal depression that carried him right to his grave
In Tarentum a few days later on. When the messenger arrived
At Syracuse with this grisly news of how the father lay dead
At Tarentum, and twin number one was completely mislaid,
The affectionate grandfather promptly took it in his head
To rename the Syracuse son in honor of the other,
And call him Menaechmus from now on, after his brother—
So dear to the grandfather's heart was that boy and his name:
The grandfather's own, as a matter of fact, was the same.   50
I remember that name *Menaechmus* all right, all the better
Because I'm sure I've seen it stuck up somewhere in *Big
   Letters.*
Isn't that just like us? "Hmmm, *Menaechmus* . . . ," we say,
Funny how it strikes us . . . "Haven't I seen that somewhere
   today?"
But, not to lead you astray,
I hereby officially announce, pronounce, and relay
The fact that both twins henceforth have identical names.
     Now, my feet must head Epidamnuswards, for the claims
Of this complicated plot I must measure by the foot; this
   explains,
I hope, how metricalloused my rhythmic diet may be.   60
To survey this plot I must personally run on and see
Where it happens to be ambling along itself, iambically.
And if any of you out there have something you'd like me to do
At Epidamnus for you, speak up and let me know.
Don't forget what things cost, though; I'll need some dough.
If you don't tip you're bound to be rooked, even though
When you do tip you'll also be had, for the money will flow
Even farther; the less you hold on to, the more you let go.
     Anyway, here I am back where I started. I stand as
I originally did when I came out and ran on. Epidamnus   70
Is the name of the place, you remember, the merchant of which
Kidnapped the other twin brother. Being very rich,
But childless, he adopted the boy to add interest to his life,

And invested as well for his son in a suitable wife
With a juicy dowry, to marry, and arranged his whole life
By making Menaechmus his heir, when he passed away.
Not bad for a lad whose dad was a thief, wouldn't you say?
And curiously enough, that end came around rather soon;
For the merchant was out in the country, not far from town
On a day it had rained very hard, and started across a river.   80
Darned if that body-snatching sliver of a river didn't deliver
The kidnapper himself into the hands of his jailer forever,
And clap the chap off the scene in death's unseen trap.
Menaechmus promptly inherited a fortune; although
    kidnapped,
He is very well off in Epidamnus. He feels quite at ease
And at home with his funds. And guess now, just who would
    breeze
Into town just today with his slave on the run right behind him?
Menaechmus (you like this?) to search for his brother, and
    find him,
Perhaps . . . we'll see about that. *Twins Billed to Appear
At Epidamnus today.* Of course, they wouldn't be here   90
Not a bit of it, if our plot didn't admit of it, but *there*
Wherever the story demanded, and in that case I'd steer
You to the right destination and make the situation clear.
        In the acting profession things tend to change: the town
The play's in, the actor's part, the lines handed down
He has to say. That house front behind me, for instance,
Depends for its very existence on the playwright's insistence
In installing inside it the characters he would provide it
With, and let live a moment; not even reside, it
Appears, but multiply or divide there. Shifty as the truth,   100
It houses an oldster, kings, beggars, gangsters, a youth;
A sharp-witted bellyaching sponger, any kind of quack
You can think of, the real one, the fake. Our profession is kind,
And makes room for all. Like me, the actors will remind
You of the double dealings dwelling anon in our comedy.
I'm off and away now, just going down on one knee
To hope you'll applaud us: smile on poor Plautus
                    And not frown on me!

ACT I

Scene 1

PENICULUS: The boys all call me Peniculus, which may sound
    ridiculous
But just means *Table Duster* and shows *How Able an Adjuster*
I am to dinner and meticulous in clearing off the table: 110
You can call me Soft Hairbrush: It seems to be my fate
To be famous as a famished feaster and wear such a tail plate.
You know, some men chain down their captives, and they
    shackle
The legs of runaway slaves. I think *that's* ridiculous,
To load still worse weight on a badly enough burdened crate.
If you put pressure on him, the underdog *wants* to get up
And take off, and never do another stroke of work.
Somehow, they'll always wriggle loose, file off the link
Or knock the lock to bits with a rock. Are chains worth the
    pains?
If you'd like to rope someone in, so he doesn't feel   120
Like escaping, snare him with wine and a meal!
You're putting a ring through his nose when you take him to
    dinner.
And as long as you keep him well stocked with food and liquor,
Regularly and the way he likes it, he'll stick with you,
Even though he's under heavy sentence. He'll want to serve
    you;
As long as you're bound to give him food, he's bound to eat it.
The nets and meshes of food are remarkably strong
And elastic, and squeeze even tighter when they get long.
I'm off to Menaechmus's at the moment, where I've signed on
To appear for dinner. I volunteer gaily for a jail   130
Like his, especially at meals. He doesn't feed; he deals
With his guests, increasing their status; like a good
    restauranteur
He doesn't diagnose, he offers a cure. This sharp epicure

Puts out a very fine spread; he doesn't spare the courses;
He builds up skyscrapers of dishes—you see something
   delicious
And have to stand up on the couch and stretch out to reach it
Over all the other things that look nearly as luscious.
I've been out of commission for quite a long intermission,
Not in the preferred position at Menaechmus's house, but at
   home,
Domiciled and dominated by my own little sweetmeats. Those
   treats   140
I provide for myself and my near ones have proved dear ones,
Thanks to my expensive tastes—and they all go to waist.
So I'm drumming myself out of those ranks, not burning up
   money
Trooping in with food for the group. Instead, I'm turning
   tummy
To Menaechmus's place. He may just embrace my company.
   Here he comes now
Flouncing out of the house—looks like they've had a row.

Scene 2

MENAECHMUS I: If you weren't such a mean, prying snoop,
   You stoop, you'd see that when I blow up
   It's *your* fault. You'd better stop, or
   I'll pack you right back to your papa,   150
   Drooping out-of-doors, divorced, good and proper.
   Every time I go for a walk, you let go a squawk
   And assault me with questions. Where am I going?
   What's doing? Where? What's *that* I've got there?
   I didn't bring home a wife; I brought home a hawk-
   Eyed customs inspector, an unconscientious objector
   To everything I do. One who makes me *declare*
   Everything I've got in mind. O woemankind!
   Personal effects, you defect detective. Oh, the heck with it!
   I guess I've spoiled you with too much attention   160

And turned this into a house of detention.
From now on, things will be different. I'm here to mention
What I expect or else from your lie detector: shelves full of
    silence;
No more prying, my high-powered Highness; absolute, utter
    compliance.
I gave you money and clothes,
Robes and dresses, domestics;
I've been pretty good and elastic
In meeting your demands.
You keep your hands, and your nose,
Out of my business. That's the best trick   170
To play if you want to stay on good terms with me.
Why look over, inspect, and go right on shaking
The man who's made you a major in his own homemaking?
To prove that you can't fence me in, I've promised today
To take a girl out to dinner and reward you that way.

PENICULUS: Taking it out on his wife? Taking that line
    Won't ruin his wife, but will leave me out on a limb.

MENAECHMUS I: Ah now, by God, and good show! I've finally told
    my wife where to go:
    Inside, and to leave me alone. Now where are you uxorious
    types, all of you
    Out there, you who ought to be oozing up front to shower your
    thanks   180
    On me for fighting the good fight? And look what I've done,
    each and every one
    Of you, my fellow sufferers. I've taken this delicate mantilla-
    dress
    Out of my wife's most favorite chest, to present to my girl.
    An excellent trick, don't you think, to reward the warden
    By stealing something right from under her nose? I propose
    A subject for congratulations: this beautifully planned,
    Charming little crime, dutifully and well carried out:
    Converting a legalized loss to a preferable self-ruination.
    Diverting the loot from the foe's hands to those of our allies.

PENICULUS: I say there, young fellow, what share in the prize
    can I   190
  Hope to realize?

MENAECHMUS I: God! I've dropped into a trap!

PENICULUS: Not at all, a fortified position.

MENAECHMUS I: Who in perdition
  Are you?

PENICULUS: Fine, thanks, who are you? I'm me, as a matter of
  fact.

MENAECHMUS I: Oh, you. My most modern convenience, you
    beautifully timed supergadget!

PENICULUS: Greetings.

MENAECHMUS I: What are you doing at the moment?

PENICULUS: Fervently latching
  Onto the hand of my right-hand man.

MENAECHMUS I: You couldn't be stringing
  along
  At a better time than this that's bringing you on into my orbit.

PENICULUS: That's how I usually time my launching forth in
    search of a luncheon.
  I've studied, got the thing down pat, I don't just play my
    hunches.

MENAECHMUS I: Want to feast your eyes on a sparkling treat I've
    completed   200
  The arrangements for?

PENICULUS: It'll look less crooked to me when I see
  Who's cooked it up. If there's been any slip-up in preparing this
    fête
  I'll know when I see what's left untouched on the plate.

MENAECHMUS I: Say, you've seen the famous painting plastered
    against a wall,
  Showing the eagle ferrying off that handsome sort of fancy-bred
    boyfriend
  To his handler in the sky? Or the one that shows Venus's and
    Adonis's
  Bare . . . ?

PENICULUS: Kneeness? Sure, lots of times, but what do I care
  about art?

MENAECHMUS I: Just look at me? Don't I do that part to
  perfection?

PENICULUS: Cahn't sigh I'm accustomed to a costume . . . what
  the hell is that you're wearing?

MENAECHMUS I: Aren't I the apple of your eye, your Prince
  Charming? Come on, say it.   210

PENICULUS: Not until I know what time dinner is and whether
  I'm invited.

MENAECHMUS I: Why not be so disarming as to admit what I ask
  you to?

PENICULUS: All right, all right, prince, you're charming.

MENAECHMUS I: Anything else
  You'd like to add voluntarily?

PENICULUS: Well, that's a fairily airily merrily
  Wingspread you've got there.

MENAECHMUS I: More, more! Makes me *soar!*

PENICULUS: Damned if I'll say any more, by God in heaven, until
     I get some whiff
Of what my reward will be if. You've had a row with your wife.
I'd better look out warily, carefully; my life is in danger.

MENAECHMUS I: Incidentally, my wife hasn't a clue about where
     we're going, to do
The town today. We're going to set the hot spots on fire.   220

PENICULUS: Well, thank heavens, now you make sense. How soon
     do I light the pyre?
The day's half used up already, dead down to the navel.

MENAECHMUS I: You're slowing up the show, interrupting with
     that drivel.

PENICULUS: Knock out my eye, Menaechmus, dig it into the
     ground, bash it
Back and below til it comes out my ankle, if I ever make a
     sound
From now on, except to say what you order me to.

MENAECHMUS I: Just step over here, away from my door.

PENICULUS: How's this for size?

MENAECHMUS I: A little farther, please.

PENICULUS: It's a breeze. How's this?
     Far enough?

MENAECHMUS I: Now, step out, like a man safe out of reach of the
     lion's den.

PENICULUS: By God in heaven, if you wouldn't make the best
     jockey.   230

MENAECHMUS I: How come?

PENICULUS: You keep looking back over your
    shoulder to see
  If your wife isn't thudding up behind you.

MENAECHMUS I: You're telling me?

PENICULUS: I'm telling you? Well, fellow, I'm not telling you
    anything,
  Let's get that clear; just what you want to hear, or you don't.
  That much I'll say, or I won't. I'm your best yes man yet.

MENAECHMUS I: All right, let's have a guess, then, at what you
    can make of
  This garment I'm exposing to your nose. What sort of scent
  Does it put you on the trail of . . . ? Why get pale and shove it
    out of range?

PENICULUS: Strange, it doesn't put me on the trail of; it pins me
    to the tail of . . .
  Look here, old boy, you know as well as I do, men shouldn't
    try to   240
  Imbibe the fragrance of feminine apparel except from up near
    the top
  Of same dainty. Down lower the unwashed part makes you feel
    fainty.

MENAECHMUS I: All right, Peniculus, try this part over here;
    tickle your nose
  With this wholesome whiff. Aha! Now you make like truffles.

PENICULUS: Sure, it suits my snuffles.

MENAECHMUS I: Oh, puffle, come on and
    say,
  Say what it tells you. What sort of smells you deduce.

PENICULUS: Phew, what a naral escape! I'm glad to produce my
  solution.
  This is my diagnosis: You steal a *jeune fille* for a meal;
  You purloin a *fräulein* for some sirloin; you flirt with a skirt
  And alert your tastebuds to a smorgasbord; a distress   250
  And theft, and this dress is left for your mistress to drape round
  Her; gleaming napery; conjugal japery, all very vapory. The
      whole deal,
  From my point of view, leads straight toward an excellent meal,
      and I'm joining you.

MENAECHMUS I: Don't! I'm not coming apart. But you've hit
  The female suggestion on the head, no question, and orated
      convincingly.
  For I've pretty winsomely sneaked this dress from my wife
  And am spiriting it off to the niftiest mistress of mine,
  Désirée. I'm ordering a banquet, this very day
  For you and me, a treat at her place.

PENICULUS: Oh, I say!

MENAECHMUS I: We'll drink from now til tomorrow's morning star
      puts out   260
  This night so bibulous.

PENICULUS: I say, you *are* fabulous. Shall I knock
  At Désirée's door?

MENAECHMUS I: Sure, go ahead. No, better knock off.
  Hold it! I said.

PENICULUS: You're the one that's holding it: my head
  Wants to get at that bottle, not back off a mile in the distance.

MENAECHMUS I: Knock very gently.

PENICULUS: The door, evidently, 's the
    consistency
Of papyrus.

MENAECHMUS I: Knock off, I insist, do desist! God in heaven!
    Lay off or I'll knock your block off! And besides, rub your eyes:
    Can't you see? Here she comes out, herself, free and easy. Her
      body
    Eclipses the sun. An excellent exit, dancing   270
    Into view like this; she wins more acclaim than the flame
    Of the sun. He goes quite blind, when I find her so entrancing.

Scene 3

DÉSIRÉE: Oh, my dear, *dear* Menaechmus, how *are* you today?

PENICULUS: Hey, say!
    What about me? Don't I rate a greeting?

DÉSIRÉE: Zero, you cipher.

PENICULUS: Well, a soldier has to get used to being a serial
    number, I guess.

MENAECHMUS I: Now darling, look here, I would love to have you
    go and fix up . . .

PENICULUS: Ohhh, fray can you see? Let's have us a mix-up: you
    be the smorgas
    And I'll come aboard you. We'll fight it out all day; ohhh, I
    say . . .
    Til the dawn's early light, which of us battlers is the heavier
    weight
    When it comes to hitting the bottle. Daisy, you can be the
    general,   280

And feel free to choose which company you'll spend the
  duration
Of this dark operation with. Let's hope your proper ration
  is . . . me.

MENAECHMUS I: Sweet and lovely! How loathly my wife appears
  in my eyes
When they light on you.

PENICULUS: Meanwhile you put on her things
And wifey still clings to you.

DÉSIRÉE: What in the world . . . ?

MENAECHMUS I: I'm unfurled.
  My dear girl. Here's the dress I deprive my wife of and provide
  You with. You look better in her clothes than she does without
    them,
  My rose.

DÉSIRÉE: Touché or not touché, I must say I must give way
  To so supersartorial an assault on my virtue. You win the day.

PENICULUS: Listen to the mistress whisper sweet somethings, as
    long as   290
  She sees he's bringing her that gay thing for nothing. Now is
  The time, if you love her, to have what you want of her
  In the form of some toothsome kisses.

MENAECHMUS I: Oh, hang up, Brush Face.
  I've only done just what I swore I would with this garment:
    placed
  It on the altar of her grace.

PENICULUS: By God in heaven, I give in!
  Listen, *twist* in it, won't you? I can see you in the ballet, like a
    fine

Boy, a dear for the dance, with the veil trailing behind your
   tight pants.

MENAECHMUS I: Dance? Me? By God in heaven, you're crazy.

PENICULUS: Me, crazy?
   I'd say, easy does it, you may be *that* way instead, in your head.

DÉSIRÉE: If you're not going to wear it, take it off then. And stop
   saying   300
   "By God in heaven!"

MENAECHMUS I: After all I won this today by playing a
   A pretty dangerous game; I stole it.

PENICULUS: On the whole, it's even
   more fraying
   To the nerves than Hercules (or "heavenly God," if you please)
   Swerving round those curves to steal Hippolyta's girdle and
   sneak off swaying.
   I'd say you were in more mortal danger than that thievish
   stranger
   Ever ran into, even though he was stronger.

MENAECHMUS I: I can no longer
   Hold back this offer I proffer to you, Désirée. So do have it,
   You wonderful girl, sole creature alive sympathetic to my
   wants.

DÉSIRÉE: This is the true-hearted sort of fervor nature should
   always transplant
   In the souls of romancers whose desires are their favorite
   haunts.   310

PENICULUS: Or at least sharp sparks going broke at full speed
   chasing spooks.

MENAECHMUS I: I bought it for my wife last year, $85.00.

PENICULUS: We can close the books on that sum and kiss it
     good-bye.

MENAECHMUS I: And now can you guess what I want to do?

DÉSIRÉE: Yes, I know.
     And what's more I'll do what you want.

MENAECHMUS I: Dinner for three,
     Chez Daisy. Order this done and I'll be pleased.

PENICULUS: And say, see
     While you're at it that whoever goes to buy the food at the
          forum
     Picks out something specially tasty; a perfect little pork filet
     Or savory thin-sliced prosciutto, ham recherché,
     Like a succulent half-section head of a pig—let's do it the
          big way,   320
     And have that ham so well cooked that I can pounce on the
          table like a hawk
     Who knows what he likes, and then strikes. And let's make it
          quick.

DÉSIRÉE: By Jiminy, yes! You're on!

MENAECHMUS I: That's very nice, the way you
          didn't
     Say "By God in heaven." Me and old slothful here, we're
          heading down-
     Town to hang around the forum and see what's up. We'll be
          right back.
     While dinner's cooking, we'll start with the drinking.

DÉSIRÉE: Come on
     Along whenever you want. Things will be ready.

MENAECHMUS I: But do get a
   steady move on.
Now let's go, and let's you keep up.

PENICULUS: By God in heaven, how true!
   I'll follow you all right and I'll slave for you too. If I lost you
Today and got all the wealth in heaven, I wouldn't break even.

(MENAECHMUS I *and* PENICULUS *exit*)

DÉSIRÉE: (Alone) I wonder why they always say "God in heaven"?
   Where else could he be?   333
You, girls in there! Call out Mixmaster, the head cook,
And tell him to come outside here. I need him this minute.

(MIXMASTER *enters*)

DÉSIRÉE: Take this shopping basket, my man, and, yes, here's
   some money;
Let's see . . . $9.63.

MIXMASTER: Right you are, miss.

DÉSIRÉE: Now scoot, sonny-boy,
   And get on with your catering. Buy enough for three people
   only,
No more, no less.

MIXMASTER: Who's coming?

DÉSIRÉE: Menaechmus, and that lonely
   Crowd of his, Soft Hair, the never-to-be-brushed off, plus me.

MIXMASTER: Well, miss, that's three *times* three plus one,
   actually:
Peniculus eats enough for eight, and you both make two.

DÉSIRÉE: I've given out the guest list. The rest of this is up
    to you.

MIXMASTER: Right you are, miss. The dinner is as good as all
    done.
  You can all take your places. Won't you all please sit down?

DÉSIRÉE: Get going now, you fix-faster, and hurry right back from
    town.

MIXMASTER: I'll be back here so soon you won't even know I've
    been gone.

ACT II

Scene 1

(*Enter* MENAECHMUS II *and* MESSENIO, *accompanied by several
crew members*)

MENAECHMUS II: Messenio, I tell you, there's no greater source
    of delight
  For sailors than to look out across the deep water and sight
  The land they're heading for.

MESSENIO: I couldn't be more   350
  In agreement, provided the land you refer to is home.
    Therefore,
  Why in hell, I implore you, are *we* in Epidamnus?
  Do you plan to act like the ocean and noisily slam us
  Against every damned piece of land we can touch?

MENAECHMUS II: As much
  As I need to cover to locate my own twin, my brother.

MESSENIO: But how much longer do we have to keep looking for
    him?
  It's six years now since we started. When we departed
  You didn't say we'd try everywhere, moseying to Marseilles,
  Skirting around Spain, bounding back to menace Venice,
  And do the whole coastal *bit* from Trieste to Dubrovnik to
    Split,   360
  Or skim the whole rim of Italy, littorally. As the sea
  Goes, that's where we rows. My point is—a haystack
  With the well-known needle in it . . . you'd have found it. But
    we lack
  The object to bring our search to a head. He's quite dead,
  The man you're after, while you ransack the land of the living
  If he were anywhere around you'd have found him.

MENAECHMUS II: I won't give in
  Until I've found out for sure from someone I have to believe in
  Who'll say that he knows that my brother is dead. And when
    that day
  Arrives, our travels are over. But I *won't* stop pursuing
  My other half, and I know what I'm doing: he means   370
  Everything to me.

MESSENIO: You're looking for a knot in a marshmallow
  reed.
  We won't go home until we've gone round the world, then, as
    fellow
  Travelers, and written a book about what it looks like?

MENAECHMUS II: I doubt it.
  But see here, my boy, you just do as you're told; don't be too
    bold;
  Eat your food; be good; don't be a bother. It's not your good
  That matters in this expedition.

MESSENIO: Take that definition
  Of a typical slave's condition. I know who I am now, all right.
  He couldn't have put a bigger proposition in many fewer words,

Or in so clear a light. Still and all, I just can't keep stalling
Around; I can't just stop talking. You listening, Menaechmus?
My purse, I mean, our purse, now that I look at it,   381
Has too much vacation space; our wardrobe there looks quite
    scanty,
Are we going in for summer sports? By God in heaven, you'll
    groan,
Exhausted by the search for your twin, unless you turn back
    home.
They'll *wham* us in Epidamnus, positive; Dubrovnik us to
    clinkers.
The town's chock full of nuts, fast-living long-range drinkers,
Go-between wheedlers, middlemen who take you, the stinkers,
In to be cleaned and doused by the masters of the house,
I mean mistresses, who whisper sweet slopniks to you,
And profit from your losses in the process. That's what they do,
Damn us strangers in this town. No wonder it's called, up and
    down,   391
Epidamnus; every damn one of us innocents in Greece
Gets introduced here to the golden fleece, before he's released,
Enormously decreased in value.

MENAECHMUS II: Take it easy. Hand me that greasy
    Wallet.

MESSENIO: What do you want with it?

MENAECHMUS II: Your speech has haunted
    Me. I'm panicked by your frantic appeal to the facts of life.

MESSENIO: Afraid, why afraid for me . . . ?

MENAECHMUS II: You'll whammy us both
    in Epidamnus.
You're a great lady's man, Messenio: I know you. And I?
I'm a man of many moods, all of which prompt me to fly
Off the handle in a hurry. And since I'm the furious sort,
And you the luxurious sport, always in pursuit of a skirt,   400

I'll manage both crises nicely, and simply divert
The money into my control. Then you won't waste the whole
Thing on women; and I won't get mad when you do; or even
    peeved.

MESSENIO: Take it and keep it then, do. I'm somewhat relieved.

Scene 2

MIXMASTER: I've shopped very shrewdly and well, if I say so
    myself:
I'll spread a fine feast in front of these dauntless diners.
Oh, oh, Menaechmus, already! I'll bet I'm in for a beating:
The guests have arrived and here I've just gotten back
From the market. They're walking around in front of the house;
I'll go up and greet them. Menaechmus, good afternoon!   410

MENAECHMUS II: Best wishes, old chap, whoever you happen
    to be.

MIXMASTER: Whoever I'm . . . ? You don't say, Menaechmus, you
    don't know?

MENAECHMUS II: Oh God in heaven, you know I don't.

MIXMASTER: But where
   Are the rest of our guests?

MENAECHMUS II: What guests?

MIXMASTER: Your parasite, for one.

MENAECHMUS II: My parasite? Obviously this fellow is quite off
    his nut.

MESSENIO: Didn't I tell you this town was lousy with scroungers?

MENAECHMUS II: Which parasite of mine did you mean, young
    man?

MIXMASTER: Why that peachy little Peniculus, the fuzzy table
    duster.

MESSENIO: Oh *him,* peenie brush? He's safe all right, here in
    our bag.

MIXMASTER: Menaechmus, you've come along a bit soon for
    dinner: 420
I'm just getting back from buying the food.

MENAECHMUS II: Listen here,
How much does a good box of sure-fire tranquilizers cost
In this town?

MIXMASTER: $1.98 for the economy size.

MENAECHMUS II: Here's $3.96. Get yourself a double
    prescription.
I can see you're quite out of control, making trouble like this
For someone like me you don't even know, whoever *you* are.

MIXMASTER: I'm Mixmaster: that's not complicated, and don't say
    you don't know it.

MENAECHMUS II: You can be Mixmaster, or Sizzling Ham Steak
    with Cloves en Brochette,
I couldn't care less. I've never seen you before today   429
And now that I have, I'm not at all very pleased to meet you.

MIXMASTER: Your name's Menaechmus.

MENAECHMUS II: You seem to be talking sense
At the moment, since you call me by name, but where did you
    learn
Who I am?

MIXMASTER: Who you are? When I work for your mistress right in
   this house?
Désirée?

MENAECHMUS II: By God, she's *not* my mistress and I *do not*
   Know you.

MIXMASTER: Don't know *me*, who pours you out drink after drink
   when you come here
For dinner?

MESSENIO: I wish I could lay hands on something to bat this nut
   with.

MENAECHMUS II: *You* mix drinks and pour them for *me*, for *me*,
   Who never even came this way, much less saw Epidamnus
   Bcforc today?

MIXMASTER: Never even saw it, you say?

MENAECHMUS II: Yes; I mean *no*, dear God in heaven, so help
   me, *no!*   440

MIXMASTER: I suppose you don't really live in that house over
   there?

MENAECHMUS II: May the gods cave the roof in hard on whoever
   does!

MIXMASTER: Stark, raving loony. Wishing himself such bad luck.
   Can you hear me, Menaechmus?

MENAECHMUS II: Depends on what you're
   saying.

MIXMASTER: Now look, take my advice. Remember that $3.96
   You offered to give me a minute ago for the pills?
   Go spend it on yourself; you're the one who needs it the most,

And the soonest, calling down curses, by God in heaven,
On your very own head. You're just not *all there*, Menaechmus.
If you've any brains left you'll send out at once for the
    medicine;   450
There's a new triple dose thing out, The Three Little Big
    Tranquilizers,
Frightens off all kinds of weird wolves.

MENAECHMUS II: He sure talks a lot.

MIXMASTER: Of course, Menaechmus always teases me, like this;
    he's a joker
When his wife's not around. What's that you're saying,
    Menaechmus?

MENAECHMUS II: I beg your pardon, Mixmaster, did you say
    something?

MIXMASTER: How does this stuff look? Like enough for dinner for
    three?
Or shall I go out and buy more for the girlfriend and you
And your parasite pal?

MENAECHMUS II: Women? Parasite? Pals? What women,
    what parasites, pal?

MESSENIO: Look here, old boy, what terrible crime is weighing on
    your mind
And making you pester him so?

MIXMASTER: Stranger boy, you stay out   460
Of my business; I'll conduct that with the person I know
And am talking to.

MESSENIO: Oh God in . . . I give up; except for the fact
That I'm sure as can be that this cook is completely cracked.

MIXMASTER: Well, now, I'll just get busy with these things. I can promise you
  Some succulent results, very soon. You'll stay around the house,
  Menaechmus, I hope. Anything else you can think of?

MENAECHMUS II: I can think of you as one real upside-down cake. You're baked.

MIXMASTER: Oh by God in . . . somewhere or other, I could swear it's you
  Who are the mixed-up master. I wish you would go . . . lie down
  Somewhere until you feel better, while I take this stuff   469
  And commit it to the fire-breathing forces of Vulcan. I'll tell
  Désirée you're out here. She'll want to ask you in, I feel sure.

(*He goes into the house*)

MENAECHMUS II: Gone, has he? God, how right I see your words were
  When you talked about this place.

MESSENIO: Mark my words further.
  One of those fast-working, loose-jointed women lives here, you can bet,
  As sure as that crackpot cook who went in there said she did.

MENAECHMUS II: I do wonder, though, how he came by my name?

MESSENIO: That's easy.
  Why, that's a cinch. The women have it all worked out.   478
  They send their slave boys or housemaids down to the docks.
  When a strange ship comes in, they ask the passenger's name,
  And find out where he's from. Later on, they pick him up casually

And stick close to him. If their charms have the right effect
They ship him back home plucked quite clean of his money.
(*Pointing to* DÉSIRÉE's *house*)
And right over there rocks a fast little pirate sloop at anchor:
We'd better look out for her, and look sharp, commander.

MENAECHMUS II: Damned if I don't think you're right.

MESSENIO: I'll know what
    you think
For sure when I see what preeeeecautions you're taking.

MENAECHMUS II: Just a moment.
    I hear the door swinging open; let's see who comes out.

MESSENIO: I'll drop our seabag right here. Heave ho, my
    bellboys!
You fleet runners, shift this gear into neutral for a while.   490

Scene 3

DÉSIRÉE: (*Singing gaily*) Open the doors, open wide: I don't want
    them shut.
    You in there, look to it, come here and do it,
    What has to be done:
    Couches to be hung with fine drapes;
    Tables adorned; some incense burned;
    Lights set blazing; the place made amazing.
    To dazzle and delight your bright lover's heart
    Is to play with skill your gay charming part,
    And importune at his expense while you make your fortune.
    Where is he though? A moment ago, my cook said I'd find him
        standing   500
    Around by the door . . . oh there he is, the one I adore when
        he's handing

His money over freely. I'll ask him in now for the meal he
    wanted made ready
And get him started on the drinks, to keep him from staying
    too steady.
I'll just slip over and speak to him first.
O my favorite fellow, my poor heart will burst
If you keep standing here outside
When the doors to our house are open wide
To take you in. It's much more your place,
This house, than your own home is, an embrace,
A bright smile on its face just for you, and a kiss   510
On that most generous of mouths. This really is your house.
And now all is prepared just the way you wanted
And shortly we'll serve you your dinner and pour out the wine.
(*Pause*)
I said, the meal's all in order, just as you commanded;
Whenever you're ready, come on in now, honey, any time.

MENAECHMUS II: Who in the world does this woman think she's
    talking to?

DÉSIRÉE: To you, that's who.

MENAECHMUS II: But what business have I with you
    At present, or what have I ever had to do with you up to now?

DÉSIRÉE: Heavens! It's you that Venus has inspired me to prize
    Over all the others, and you've certainly turned out to be
        worth it.   520
    Heavens above! You've set me up high enough with your
        generous gifts!

MENAECHMUS II: This woman is surely quite crazy or definitely
    drunk,
Messenio, talking such intimate stuff to me,
A man she doesn't even know.

MESSENIO: I told you so!
  And now, it's only the leaves that are falling. Just wait;
  Spend three more days in this town and the trees themselves
  Will be crashing down down on your head. The women are
     biased,
  Buy us this, buy us that, and buzzing around for your money.
  But let me talk to her. Hey, sweetie, I'm speaking to you.

DÉSIRÉE: You're what?

MESSENIO: No, I'm not, I'm who. And while I'm at it,
    just *where*   530
  Did you get to know the man here who's with me so well?

DÉSIRÉE: Why, right here in Epidamnus, where I've been for so
    long.

MESSENIO: Epidamnus? A place he never set foot in before today?

DÉSIRÉE: A *delicious* joke, you rascal. Now, Menaechmus,
    darling,
  Won't you come in? You'll feel much cozier and settled.

MENAECHMUS II: By God, the woman's quite right to call me by
    my own name.
  Still I can't help wondering what's up.

MESSENIO: She's got wind of your
    money-bag,
  The one you relieved me of.

MENAECHMUS II: And damned if you didn't alert me
  To that very thing. Here, you'd better take it. That way,   539
  I can find out for sure whether she's after me, or my money.

DÉSIRÉE: *Andiam', O caro bene!* And we'll tuck right into that
    meal;
  Mangiamo, igitur, et cetera.

MENAECHMUS II: Music to my ears,
  And you're very nice to sing it, my dear. I only regret
  I cannot accept.

DÉSIRÉE: But why in the world did you tell me, a short
      while ago,
  To have dinner ready for you?

MENAECHMUS II: *I* told *you* to have dinner ready?

DÉSIRÉE: Of course, dinner for three, you, your parasite, and me.

MENAECHMUS II: Oh hell, lady, what the hell is all this parasite
      stuff?
  God, what a woman! She's crazy as can be once again.

DÉSIRÉE: Cookie duster Peniculus, C. D. Peniculus, the crumb
      devourer.

MENAECHMUS II: But I mean what kind of a peniculus? We all
      know that's a soft hair   550
  Brush, but I don't know anyone *named* that. You mean my
      ridiculous
  Little thing, the traveling shoebrush I carry for my suede
      sandals,
  The better to buff them with? What peniculus hangs so close
      to me?

DÉSIRÉE: You know I mean that local leech who just now came by
      with you
  When you brought me that sweet silk dress you stole from your
      wife.

MENAECHMUS II: I gave you a dress, did I? One I stole from my
      wife?
  You're sure? I'd swear you were asleep, like a horse
      standing up.

DÉSIRÉE: Oh gosh, what's the fun of making fun of me and
    denying
Everything you've done?

MENAECHMUS II: Just tell me what I'm denying.

DÉSIRÉE: That you gave me today your wife's most expensive silk
    dress.   560

MENAECHMUS II: All right, I deny that. I'm not married. And I've
    never been married.
And I've never come near this port since the day I was born,
Much less set foot in it. I dined on board ship, disembarked,
And ran into you.

DÉSIRÉE: Some situation! I'm nearly a wreck. What's
    that ship
You're talking about?

MENAECHMUS II: Oh, an old prewar propeller job,
    Wood and canvas, patched in a million places; transportation,
I guess, runs on force of habit. She's got so many pegs
Pounded in now, one right up against the next, she looks like
    the rack
You see in a fur-seller's store, where the strips are hung all in
    a row.

DÉSIRÉE: Oh, do stop now, please, making fun, and come on in
    with me.   570

MENAECHMUS II: My dear woman, you're looking for some other
    man, not me.

DÉSIRÉE: I don't know you, Menaechmus? The son of Moschus,
    Born at Syracuse in Sicily, when Agathocles ruled,
And after him, Phintia; then Leporello passed on the power
After his death to Hiero, so that Hiero is now the man in
    control?

MENAECHMUS II: Well, that information seems certainly accurate,
    miss.

MESSENIO: By God Himself! Is the woman *from* Syracuse to have
    This all down so pat?

MENAECHMUS II: By the various gods, I don't see
    How I can now really decline that offer she's making.

MESSENIO: Please do, I mean *don't* step over that doorstep!
    You're gone if you do.

MENAECHMUS II: Pipe down. This is working out well.
    I'll admit to anything she says, if I can just take advantage
    Of the good time in store. Mademoiselle, a moment ago   582
    I was holding back on purpose, afraid that my wife might hear
    About the silk dress and our dinner date. I'm all set
    Now, anytime you are.

DÉSIRÉE: You won't wait for Soft Hair?

MENAECHMUS II: No, let's brush *him* off; I don't care a whisker if
    he never, . . .
    And besides, when he does, I don't want him let in.

DÉSIRÉE: Heavens to Castor!
    I'm more than happy to comply with that one. But now,
    Just one thing, darling, you know what I'd like you to do?

MENAECHMUS II: All you need do is name it.

DÉSIRÉE: That sweet silk dress:
    send it over   590
    To the Persian's place, the embroiderer's shop. I want
    It taken in, and a pattern I've specially designed added to it.

MENAECHMUS II: What a good idea! It won't look at all like
  the dress
I stole, if my wife should happen to meet you in town.

DÉSIRÉE: Good. Take it with you, then, when you go.

MENAECHMUS II: Yes, of course.

DÉSIRÉE: And now let's go on in.

MENAECHMUS II: Right away. I've just got to speak
  To him for a minute. Hey, Messenio, hop over here!

MESSENIO: What's cooking?

MENAECHMUS II: Jump, boy.

MESSENIO: What's all the hurry?

MENAECHMUS II: We're all the hurry, that's what. I know what
  you'll say.

MESSENIO: You're a dope.

MENAECHMUS II: Nope, I'm a fiend. I've already stolen
  some loot.   600
Real loot. This is a big deal: Operation Mix-up.
And I'm one up already without even throwing up earthworks.
Race off, fast as you can, and drape all those sea troops
(*Points to the sailors*)
In the local bar, on the double. Stay where you are then,
Until just before sunset, when it's time to come pick me up.

MESSENIO: Really, commander, you're not *on* to those call girls.

MENAECHMUS II: You manage your affairs, I'll handle mine,
  and you
Can hang up and stay there. If I get into trouble, it's me

Who'll suffer for it, not you. That girl isn't crazy; she's dumb
And doesn't know what's up, at least as far as I can see,   610
Or where could this high-priced, pretty little dress have come
    from?

(*He exits*)

MESSENIO: I give up. You've gone, have you? In there? You're
    gone,
And done for. The pirate ship's got the rowboat on the run,
And you'll end up in the drink, *Menaechmus on the rocks.*
But who am I, a dumb slave, to try to outfox
That woman, with my hopes of showing Menaechmus the
    ropes?
He bought me to listen to him: I'm not in command.
Come on, kids, let's do what he says. But I'll be on hand
Later on, as he wanted, and drag him out to dry land.

ACT III

Scene 1

PENICULUS: In all my born days—and it's more than thirty years'
    worth—I've never   620
Pulled a boner like this. I'm a treacherous fiend, and this time
I guess I've really transgressed. Imagine my missing a meal!
And why? I got involved in listening to a public speech
And while I stood around gawking, all open mouth and ears,
Menaechmus made his getaway and got back to his girl,
And didn't want *me* along, I suppose. May the heavenly gods
Crack down on whoever it was that thought up public speeches,
That invented this out-of-doors way to use up people's good
    time
Who haven't any. Shouldn't the audience consist only of those

With time on their hands? And shouldn't they perhaps be fined
If they fail to attend those meetings where someone gets up
In public and starts sounding off? There are people enough
With nothing much to do, who eat only one meal a day,   633
Never dine out, or have guests in, and it's to them the duty
To show up at meetings or official functions should be assigned.
If I hadn't stuck around today to listen, I wouldn't
Have lost out on the dinner Menaechmus invited
Me to come to—and I do think he meant it, as sure as I can see
I'm alive. I'll show up, anyway, on the off-chance
There's still something left; the mere hope makes my mouth
    water.   640
What's this I see? Menaechmus *leaving*, well looped?
That means *dinner's over:* by God, my timing is perfect.
I'll hide over here and watch a bit to see what he does
Before I go up to my host and give him a buzz.

Scene 2

MENAECHMUS II: Calm down in there, woman! I'll bring the dress
    back soon enough,
Expertly, so charmingly changed you won't even know it.

PENICULUS: Dinner's done, the wine's all gone, the parasite's lost,
And *he's* off to the couturier, with that dress in tow.
Is *that* so? I'm not who I am if I take this last bit
In my stride, lying down. Watch how I handle that garment
    worker.   650

MENAECHMUS II: I thank you, immortal gods, each and all of you.
On whom have you ever showered so many good gifts
As you have on me today? And who could have hoped for them
    less?
I've dined, I've wined, I've reclined, and at very close quarters,
With one of the most delicious daughters . . . well, I've had it
    in the best sense

Of that past tense. And here I am at present, still gifted
With a precious piece of silk. No one else will inherit
These convertible goods, much less wear it. How high am I, its
Heir—Oh!

PENICULUS: Hell, I can't hear from over here—did he say "hair,"
   though?   659
That's my cue to brush in, isn't it, and sweep up my share?
Hair today and bald tomorrow . . . Drink to me only with
   mayonnaise . . .
I'll demand redressing . . . I'll scrape something out of this
   mess yet.

MENAECHMUS II: She said I stole it from my wife and gave it
   to her.
When I realized how wrong she was, of course I began
To agree with everything she said, as if we agreed
On whatever it was we were doing. Need I say more?
I never had so good a time for so little money.

PENICULUS: Here I go; I'm raring to get in my licks.

MENAECHMUS II: Well, well, who's this comes to see me?

PENICULUS: What's that you say,
You featherhead, you worst of all possible, good-for-nothing
   . . . man?   670
Man? You're not even a mistake, you're a premeditated crime,
That's what you are, you shifty little good-for-nothing . . . I just
   said that . . .
So-and-so. And so you spirited yourself away
From me at the forum a while ago, and celebrated my funeral
At this cheerful dinner your friend just couldn't attend?
Some nerve, when you said I was invited to share it with you.

MENAECHMUS II: Look, kiddo, what's with it, with you and me,
   that can make

You curse out a man you don't even know? Would you like
A nice hole in the head in return for turning loose your lip?

PENICULUS: God damn it to God damn. That hole's already in my
    stomach;   680
You gave my mouth the slip.

MENAECHMUS II: What's your name, kid,
    Anyway? Spit that much out.

PENICULUS: ·   Still being funny,
    As if you didn't know?

MENAECHMUS II: As far as I know, no.
    God knows I never saw you before today, never knew you,
    Whoever you are. I do know, though, if you don't
    Get funny with me, I won't make it hard for you.

PENICULUS: For heck's sake, Menaechmus, wake up!

MENAECHMUS II: For Hercules' sake,
    I'm up and walking around. I'm completely convinced of it.

PENICULUS: But you don't recognize me?

MENAECHMUS II: If I did, I wouldn't say I
    didn't.

PENICULUS: You don't know your old parasite pal?

MENAECHMUS II: It's your old
    paralyzed dome   690
    That's slipped, or cracked. You'd better have it patched up and
    fixed.

PENICULUS: All right. Here's a question for you. Did you, or did
    you not,

Sneak a dress out from under your own wife's nose today,
And give it to dear Désirée?

MENAECHMUS II: For Hercle's sake, no.
   I don't happen to be married, and I didn't happen to
   Give it to Désirée, and I didn't happen to fasten onto
   A dress. Are you quite sure you've got it in the head, enough?

PENICULUS: Well, that's that, I guess. *Caput! E pluribus* be none.
   Of course I didn't meet you coming out of your house and
      wearing
   The dress, just a while ago?

MENAECHMUS II: Ohhhhh for *sex'* sake!   700
   (*Very effeminate sibilants*)
   You think we're all fairy fine fellows just because you're such
   A *native* dancer, in a perfect fright at what's under our tights?
   You say I put on a dress, and I wore it?

PENICULUS: Could of swore it, on Hercules' head.

MENAECHMUS II: Don't bring him up,
   He was a he-man, but you aren't even a me-man:
   You don't even know who you are or I am, you absolute nut.
   You'd better take the cure; you're asking for trouble from the
      gods.

PENICULUS: Yeee gods, that's it! Now nobody's going to stop me
      from going
   Straight to your wife to spill the beans about you and your
      schemes
   You've creamed me, and I'm whipped. But banquet boy, just
      you wait   710
   Until this stuff starts coming back at you. That dinner you ate
   And I never got to, is going to give you bad dreams.

MENAECHMUS II: What's going on around here? Is everyone I see
    Planted here on purpose to make fun of me? And what for?
    And here comes another, whoever it is, out that door.

Scene 3

MAID: Menaechmus, Désirée would like you to take
    This bracelet to the jeweler's, as long as you're going downtown
    With the dress, and have this piece of gold worked into it.

MENAECHMUS II: Oh, glad to take care of both things, of course,
    and anything
    Else you want done along those lines; you only need
    mention it.   720

MAID: You remember the bracelet, don't you?

MENAECHMUS II: It's just a gold
    bracelet.

MAID: But this is the one you sneaked out of your wife's jewel box
    And stole from her.

MENAECHMUS II: I don't do things like that, I'm damned
                       sure.

MAID: Well, if you don't recognize it . . . look, you'd better give it
    back to me.

MENAECHMUS II: Hold on . . . I think I do remember it now. . . .
    Yes, that's the one I gave her, that's it all right.
    But where are the armlets I gave Désirée when I gave her
    The bracelet?

MAID: You never gave her no armlets at all.

MENAECHMUS II: Oh yes, that's right, it was just the bracelet,
   come to think of it.

MAID: Can I tell her you'll have this fixed up?

MENAECHMUS II: Yes, I'll take care of it.

MAID: And look, be a dear, and have him design me some
      earrings,   730
   Won't you, teardrop-style, six dollars of gold work in each?
   If you do, you'll be *persona* terribly *grata* to me, your
   Obedient, cooperative servant, the next time you visit.

MENAECHMUS II: Why of course. Just give me the gold, and I'll
      stand the cost
   Of having it set.

MAID: Oh, you furnish the gold, why don't you?
   And I'll pay you back later.

MENAECHMUS II: No, no, after you, my fair lady.
   You let me pay you back later, and I'll pay twice as much.

MAID: I don't have the gold at the moment.

MENAECHMUS II: When you get it, I'll
      take it.

MAID: Is there anything else, kind sir?

MENAECHMUS II: No, just say I'll handle this.
   (MAID *exits*)
   And make a quick turnover on the market value of the stuff.
   She's gone in? Yes, I see she's closed the door.   741
   The gods must be on my side the way they're helping me out,
   Enriching me, and doing me favors. But why hang around
   When now is my chance to get away and out of reach
   Of these foxy, and I must say, sexy, confidence women?

Come on, Menaechmus, my boy, my own likeness, enjoy
Your rapture; and pick up your feet, old chap, let those sandals
    slap.
Here goes the laurel lei for today.
(*Throws it right*)
But I think I'll go this way,   749
In case they come looking for me; they can follow this lead
In the wrong direction. I'll dash off and make enough speed
To head off my slave, I hope, and tell that good lad
The good news about the goods we've acquired. Won't he be
    glad?

ACT IV

Scene 1

WIFE: I suppose I'm supposed to submit to total frustration
    Because I married a man who steals everything in the house
    He can lay hands on and carts it off to his mistress?

PENICULUS: Not so loud, please. You'll catch him with the goods,
    I promise.
    Come over here. Now look over there. He was taking
    Your dress to the couturier; he was well looped and weaving
    Downtown with the same dress he snuck from your closet
        today.   760
    And look, there's the laurel loop he had on, lying on the
        ground.
    Now do you believe me? He must have gone in that direction.
    If you'd like to follow up his tracks. Hey, we're in luck:
    Here he comes back, just this moment; but not with the dress.

WIFE: What should I do?

PENICULUS: Oh, what you always do, start nagging,
    Nag him to pieces; don't take it, let him have it, I say.
    Meanwhile, let's duck over here on the sly and not let him
    See us. He'll tangle himself in the birdcatchers' net.

                              Scene 2

MENAECHMUS I: This is some social system we've got going here,
    The troublesome custom of patrons and clients: 770
    Bothersome clients, and jittery patrons, who fear
    They may not have a big enough following. Compliance
    And conformity to habit require even the best of us
    To just make the most of it; and as for the rest of those
    Trapped in place in the status race, let's face it,
    They're coming at us, pushing forward from the ends
    To swell out the middle. And it isn't *fides*, it's *res*
    That matters in the clientele deal, which depends,
    Not on the client's value as man and as friend,
    But simply on his assets. Money is what he's worth   780
    And you must amass it to show off less dearth
    Of a deficit than the next aristocrat. You give a wide berth
    To the poor man who needs you, however fine he may seem,
    But if some rich bastard shows up and wants you to use
    Your influence, you're ready to go to any extreme
    To hang onto him. That's the scheme, and does it confuse
    Us poor patrons with a gang of fast-breaking scofflaws
    To stand up for in court? Thereby hang the loss
    And the profits for us poor patricians. The client's position
    Is: pressure on the middle. He's got the money,   790
    We've got the rank; we need his dough, he needs our thanks.
    It's only lucky the prolies don't rate either of any;
    Thank heavens, they're not powerful, just many.
        I'm from a good family and entitled to go into court
    And represent as I wish some client who's short
    Of the necessary social credentials. And, confidentially,
    I say a lot that I wish I didn't have to. A lawyer can manage

To do this pretty well if he concentrates on it; and damages
Are his principal concern: to collect for, to sue for, to affirm
What is said to be false, and to deny what is said to be true for.
On behalf of some client whose character makes him squirm
He will bribe the witnesses or rehearse them in what to do.
When the client's case comes up on the calendar, of course
That's a day we have to be on hand too, and be resourceful
In speaking up professionally in defense of his actions, awful
And impossible to defend though they are.   806
It's either a private hearing at the bar;
Or a public proceeding before a jury with people in the
    congregation;
Or a third form it takes is what you would call arbitration,
When a mediator is appointed to decide this special situation.
        Well, today a client of mine had me right on the ropes;
His case came up as a private hearing, and my hopes
Of doing what I'd planned to today, and doing
It with the person I wanted to, have drooped and dropped near
    to ruin;
He kept me and kept me; there was angle after angle.
He was obviously at fault, with his wrong, tangled,
Illegal action, and I knew it when I went in.
So in arguing the case I laid it on pretty thin,
And pleaded *extenuating circumstances;* that's a logical maze
And a judge's jungle, but a lawyer's paradise.   820
I summed up the case in the most complicated terms
I could summon up, overstating, sliding words like worms
Off the track, leaving a lot out when the need
Of the argument indicated, and the magistrate agreed
To drop the proceedings; he granted permission
For a settlement by *sponsio.*
There's a legal ounce for you, of the words we pronounce in due
    process,
Full of awful, responsible-sounding phrases like: I promise
You this *sponsio* I owe you, et cetera. What it comes down to
Is that a civil hearing can be brought to an end by payment
Of a fixed fee known as a forfeit or *sponsio,* a defrayment
Of the expenses plus a sum added on: call it "costs   832

And considerations" if you will, in consideration for the lost
Time and money involved. What happened today was that I
Had worked hard and fast to convince the judge that my
Client should be allowed to settle for costs and considerations.
The judge came around; and I was set to leave for the
   celebration
Of a good time at Désirée's party, when what did my other
   smarty party
Of a client pull but an "Oh, well . . . I don't know about that
   sponsio . . .
I don't think I ought to flounce in with a lot of money all at
   once   840
You know . . . I'm not so sure I've even got it. Are you sure
That's the way we want it to go, the case, et cetera?" The totally
   pure
Imbecile, caught redhanded, absolutely without a legal leg to
   stand on
And three unimpeachable witnesses were waiting just to get
   their hands on
Him and wring his neck! He nearly let it come up for trial.
And that's where I've been all this while.
      May the gods, all the gods, blast that fool
Who wrecked my beautiful day
And they might as well, while they're at it, lay
Into me for thinking I could steal   850
Off to town and look the forum over that way
Without being spotted and tapped for something dutiful.
No doubt, I've messed up a day
That promised to be quite alluring
From the moment I told Désirée
To set things up nicely for dinner. All during
The time I've been detained, she's been waiting for me
And here I am at last, the first instant I could break free.
If she's angry, I suppose she has some reason to be.
But perhaps the dress I purloined from my wife won't
   annoy her   860
In the least, and I'll win this one too, as my own lawyer.

PENICULUS: What do you say to that?

WIFE: That I've made a bad
     marriage
  With an unworthy husband.

PENICULUS: Can you hear well enough where
     you are?

WIFE: All too well.

MENAECHMUS I: The smart thing for me is to go on in there
  Where I can count on a pretty good time.

PENICULUS: Just you wait,
     Bad times are just around the corner.

WIFE: (*Confronting him*)   You think you got away
  With it, do you? This time you'll pay up, with interest.

PENICULUS: That's it, let him have it.

WIFE: Pulled a fast one on the sly,
     didn't you?

MENAECHMUS I: What fast one are you referring to, dear?

WIFE: You're asking me?

MENAECHMUS I: Should I ask him, instead?

WIFE: Take your paws off
     me.   870

PENICULUS: That's the way!

MENAECHMUS I: Why so cross?

WIFE: You ought to know.

PENICULUS: He knows, all right, he's just faking.

MENAECHMUS I: With reference
   to what?

WIFE: To that dress, that's what.

MENAECHMUS I: That dress that's what what?

WIFE: A certain silk dress.

PENICULUS: Why is your face turning pale?

MENAECHMUS I: It isn't.

PENICULUS: Not much paler than a thin silk dress,
   it isn't.
   And don't think you can go off and eat dinner behind my back.
   Keep pitching into him.

MENAECHMUS I: Won't you hang up for a moment?

PENICULUS: God damn it, no, I won't. He's shaking his head
   To warn me not to say anything.

MENAECHMUS I: God damn it, yourself,   879
   If I'm shaking my head, or winking or blinking or nodding.

PENICULUS: Cool! Shakes his head to deny he was shaking his
      head.

MENAECHMUS I: I swear to you, wife, by Jupiter, and all the other
      gods—
   I hope that's reinforced strong enough to satisfy you—
   I did *not* nod at that nut.

PENICULUS: Oh, she'll accept that
   On good faith. Now let's return to the first case.

MENAECHMUS I: What first case?

PENICULUS: The case of the costly couturier's
      place.
   The dress-fixer's.

MENAECHMUS I: Dress? What dress?

PENICULUS: Perhaps I'd better bow out.
   After all, it's my client who's suing for redress of grievance
   And now she can't seem to remember a thing she wanted to
      ask you.

WIFE: Oh dear, I'm just a poor woman in trouble.   889

MENAECHMUS I: Come on, tell me,
   What is it? One of the servants has upset you by answering
      back?
   You can tell me about it; I'll see that he's punished.

WIFE: Don't be silly.

MENAECHMUS I: Really, you're *so* cross. I don't like you that way.

WIFE: Don't be silly.

MENAECHMUS I: Obviously, it's one of the servants you're mad at?

WIFE: Don't be silly.

MENAECHMUS I: You're not mad at me, are you?

WIFE: Now you're not
      being so silly.

MENAECHMUS I: But, for God's sake, I haven't done anything.

WIFE: Don't start being silly all over again.

MENAECHMUS I: Come on, dear, what is it that's wrong
And upsets you so?

PENICULUS: Smooth husband, smooths everything over.

MENAECHMUS I: Oh, hang up, I didn't call you.

WIFE: *Please* take your
      paw off me.

PENICULUS: That's the way, lady, stick up for your rights. We'll
      teach him   900
To run off to dinner and not wait for me, and then stagger out
Afterwards and lurch around in front of the house still wearing
His wreath and having a good laugh on me.

MENAECHMUS I: Dear God in heaven,
If I've even eaten yet, much less gone into that house.

PENICULUS: You don't say?

MENAECHMUS I: That's right, I don't say, you're damned right I
      don't.

PENICULUS: God, that's some nerve. Didn't I see you over there
      just now,
In front of the house, standing there with a wreath on your
      head?
Didn't I hear you telling me I was way off my nut, and insisting
You didn't know who I was, and were a stranger here yourself?

MENAECHMUS I: But I left you some time ago, and I'm just
    getting back.

PENICULUS: That's what you say. You didn't think I'd fight back,
    did you?   910
    Well, by God, I've spilled the whole thing to your wife.

MENAECHMUS I: Saying what?

PENICULUS: How should I know? Ask her.

MENAECHMUS I: How about it, dear?
    What all has this type told you? Come on, don't repress it;
    Won't you tell me what it is?

WIFE: As if you didn't know.
    You ask me?

MENAECHMUS I: If I knew, for God's sake, I wouldn't be asking.

PENICULUS: This is really some man the way he fakes out. Look,
    you can't
    Keep it from her, she knows all about it. By God in wherever
    he is,
    I practically dictated it.

MENAECHMUS I: Dictated what?

WIFE: All right. Since you seem not to have an ounce of shame
    left,   919
    And you won't own up, give me your undivided attention.
    This is why I'm upset and this is what he told me. I repeat,
    I'm not really "cross"; I'm double-crossed, and doubly upset.
    Someone sneaked one of my very best dresses right out of my
    house.

MENAECHMUS I: A dress? Right out of my house?

PENICULUS: *Listen* to that louse,
Trying to scratch his way into your affections. Look, Menaechmus,
We're not playing matched towels in the doctor's bathroom
Marked "Hisia" and "Hernia"; we're discussing a valuable dress,
And its *hers* not yours, and she's lost it, at least for the time being.
If *yours* were missing, it would really be missing for good.

MENAECHMUS I: Will you please disappear? Now dear, what's your point of view? 930

WIFE: The way I see it, one of my best silk dresses is not at home.

MENAECHMUS I: I wonder who might have taken it?

WIFE: I'm pretty sure
I know a man who knows who took it, because he did.

MENAECHMUS I: Who dat?

WIFE: Welllll . . . I'd like us to think of a certain Menaechmus.

MENAECHMUS I: Some man, just like us! Isn't that the fancy one, that man?
But he's a mean man. And who the hell are all the men you mean
Named Menaechmus?

WIFE: You, that's what I say, you.

MENAECHMUS I: Who accuses me to you?

WIFE: I do, for one.

PENICULUS: I do too. And I say you gave it to a dear little Daisy.

MENAECHMUS I: I? Me? I'm that mean aechmus who . . .

WIFE: Yes, you,
     that's who,   940
  You brute, *et tu*.

PENICULUS: You who too too too . . .
  What is this, the Owl Movement from the Bird Symphony?
  My ears are feeling the strain of that to-who refrain.

MENAECHMUS I: I swear, Wife, by Jupiter, and all other gods
     within hearing distance—
  And I hope that's a strongly enough reinforced religious
     insistence—
  That I did not *give* . . .

PENICULUS: But *we* can appeal to Hercules and he's
  Even stronger, that we're not exactly not telling the truth.

MENAECHMUS I: That technically I did not *give* it, I only
     conveyed it
  To Daisy today; you see, she doesn't have it, she's just using it.

WIFE: I don't go around lending out your jacket or cloak.   950
  A woman ought to lend out women's clothes, a man men's.
  You'll bring back the dress?

MENAECHMUS I: I'll see that that's done.

WIFE: If you know what's good for you, you will, I'm here to
     assure you.
  You won't get back in this house unless you're carrying that
     dress.
  I'm going in.

PENICULUS: What about me and my work?

WIFE: I'll pay you back when something is stolen from your
    house.

PENICULUS: Oh God, that means never. There's nothing in my
    place worth stealing.
  Well, Husband and Wife, may the gods do their very worst for
    you both!
  I'll run along now, to the forum. It's quite plain to see
  I've lost out, and lost my touch, with this family.   960

(He exits; never returns)

MENAECHMUS I: My wife thinks she's making life hard for me,
    shutting me out
  Of the house. As if I didn't have a much more pleasant place
  To go into. Fallen from your favor, have I? I imagine
  I'll bear up under that and prove pleasing to an even more
    desirable
  Favorite. Désirée won't lock me out; she'll lock me in.
  I guess I'll go in there and ask her to *lend* back the dress
  I *conveyed* to her this morning, and buy her something much
    better.
  Hey, where's the doorman? Open up, somebody, and tell
  Désirée to come out; there's someone to see her.   969

Scene 3

DÉSIRÉE: Who's calling me?

MENAECHMUS I: A man who'd be his own enemy
    Before he'd be yours.

DÉSIRÉE: Menaechmus, *dahling*, come in!
    Why stand out there?

MENAECHMUS I: I bet you can't guess why I'm here.

DÉSIRÉE: Oh, yes I can. You want something sweet from your
     honey,
And what's more you'll get it, you naughty little tumblebee.

MENAECHMUS I: As a matter of fact, or thank heavens, or
     something . . .
   What I have to have is that silly dress back I gave you
   This morning. My wife's found out all about it.
   But I'll buy you one worth twice as much, whatever kind you
     want,
   So be a good girl and romp in there and get it, won't you?

DÉSIRÉE: But I just handed it over to you to take to the Persian's,
   Just a while ago, and gave you that bracelet to take to the
     jeweler   981
   And have the gold added to it.

MENAECHMUS I: The dress and a bracelet?
   I think you may find you did no such thing. I gave
   The dress to you and then went to the forum, and here
   I am looking at you for the first time again since I left you.

DÉSIRÉE: Don't look at me, I'll look at you. I see
   Just what you're up to, and what I'm down to, for that matter.
   You take the stuff off my two trusting hands and then
   Do me out of it and pocket the cash for yourself.

MENAECHMUS I: I'm not asking for it to cheat you out of it, I
     swear.   990
   I tell you, my wife's cracked the case.

DÉSIRÉE: Well, I didn't ask
   For it in the first place. You brought it of your own free will,
   And you gave it to me as a gift; you didn't *convey* it, you
     shyster.
   Now you want it back. I give up. You can have the stuff;
   Take it away, wear it yourself if you want,
   Or let your wife wear it, or lock the loot in your safe.

You're not setting foot in my house from this moment on,
Don't kid yourself about that. I deserve better treatment
From you than being jerked around and laughed at like a
    clown.
I've been your friend, lover boy—but that's at an end.   1000
From now on, it's strictly for cash, if and when.
Find some other doll to play with and then let her down.

MENAECHMUS I: God damn it, don't get so God damn mad. Hey,
    don't go
Off like that. Wait a minute! Come back here. You won't?
Oh, come on, Dee. Not even for me? You won't? So I see.
She's gone in and locked the door too. And I guess that
    makes me
Just about the most locked-out fellow in this town today,
Most unwanted man, most unlikely to get in, much less to say
Anything that a wife, or a mistress, might take to be true
I'll go ask my friends what they think I ought to do.   1010

ACT V

Scene 1

MENAECHMUS II: It was really pretty dumb of me to put that
    purseful of money
In Messenio's hands, the way I did. He's probably holed up
In some dive, drinking it down, and looking them over.

WIFE: I think I'll just take a look and see how soon Husband
Wends his way home. There he is now. And all's well for me:
He's got the dress with him.

MENAECHMUS II: Where in hell has Messenio
    wandered off to?

WIFE: I'll go up and welcome him now in the terms he deserves.
Aren't you ashamed to show up in my sight, you mistake
Of a man . . . I mean, you deliberate premeditated crime,
Tricked out with that fancy gown?

MENAECHMUS II: I don't get it, do I?   1020
What's on your mind, my good woman?

WIFE: How dare you address me?
How dare you utter a single slimy syllable, you snake?

MENAECHMUS II: What have I done that's so bad I don't dare
address you?

WIFE: You must have cast-iron nerves to inquire about that.

MENAECHMUS II: I don't know if you read much, lady, but
Hecuba,
The Greeks always called her a bitch. I suppose you know why?

WIFE: As a matter of fact, no. I don't.

MENAECHMUS II: Because she acted the way
You're acting right now. She kept dumping insults and curses
On everyone she met, and snarling at, pitching into everyone
Her eyes lighted on. No wonder they called her a prime bitch.

WIFE: I really can't take this kind of abuse any longer.   1031
I'd much rather never have been married, than submit to
The kind of dirt you shovel on me the way you do now.

MENAECHMUS II: What's it to me whether you like being married
or not,
Or want to leave your husband? Do all the people around here
Tell their stories to every new man that blows into town?

WIFE: What stories? I simply won't take it any longer, I tell you.
I'd rather live all alone than put up with you.

MENAECHMUS II: For God's sake, then, live alone, as far as I care,
  Or as long as Jupiter may decide to grant you the option.

WIFE: A few moments ago you were insisting you hadn't
    sneaked off   1041
  That mantilla-dress of mine, but now you're waving it
  In front of my eyes. Aren't you a tiny bit conscience-stricken?

MENAECHMUS II: God only knows what kind of a squeeze play
    you're pulling,
  You whack, you brazen. . . . How dare you say I took this,
  When another woman gave it to me to take and have altered?

WIFE: By God (my God, this time), a statement like that
  Makes me want to . . . and I'm going to send for my father,
  And tell him every single horrible thing you've done,
  That's what I'll do. Hey, Decio, in there, come out,   1050
  And go find my father and ask him to come here with you.
  Tell him please to come quickly, I simply have to see him.
  I'll show him every single horrible thing you've done to me.

MENAECHMUS II: Are you feeling all right? What single horrible
    thing?

WIFE: You housebreaker-into! You steal my dress and my jewels
  From my house and rob your wife of her goods to throw at
  The feet of or load in the arms of your girlfriend as loot.
  Have I rehearsed the story accurately enough for your ears to
    take in?

MENAECHMUS II: Lady, you ought to watch your prepositions; and
    while you're at it
  Could you mix me a sedative of half hemlock, half lime juice?
  You must have some hemlock around here. I must be kept
    quiet   1061
  If I'm meant to sustain your attacks. I'm not sure I know
  Exactly who you think I am. I may have known you
  Long ago in the days of Hercules' father-in-law's father.

WIFE: Laugh at me all you want, but your father-in-law
   Won't stand for that. Here he comes now. Take a good look,
   Won't you? Recognize somebody?

MENAECHMUS II: Oh, him? I may have known
      him . . .
   Yes, I did . . . oh sure, I remember old George from the Trojan
      War:
   He was our chaplain, bless his old heart. No. I guess not.
   I've never seen him before, just as I've never seen   1070
   You before either, either of you, before today.

WIFE: You say you don't know me, and you don't know my father?

MENAECHMUS II: You're right. And actually, if you produced your
      grandfather,
   I'd say the same.

WIFE: One joke after another. What a bother!

Scene 2

OLD MAN: Here I come, pushing one foot after the other,
   As fast and as far as my age allows, and to meet
   This crisis at my own pace, pushing these pedals, progressing
   As best I can. Papa isn't planning to pretend,
   Though, to anybody, that it's easy. He's not so spry anymore.
   I'm pretty darned pregnant with years, that's a fact; planted
   With a crop of them, if you conceive of me carrying the burden
   Of this body. And there's precious little power left. Oh, it's a
      bad deal,   1082
   This business of being old. We're stuck with the bulk
   Of our unwanted goods. Maybe we get more than we
      bargained for
   Out of life. Old age brings the most of the worst when it comes,
   To the ones who want it the least. If I named every pain

It bestows on us oldsters, I'd be drawing up a long, long list,
And you'd have too much to listen to.
                                        I wonder why my
    daughter
Sent for me all of a sudden? It weighs on my mind   1089
And tugs at my heart to know what's afoot that can bring me
Running over here to see her. She didn't say why she sent
    for me,
Or tell me what's up. I can figure it out pretty well,
Of course. A quarrel with her husband has sprung up, I bet.
That's the way wives behave who bring a big dowry,
Coming loaded into the marriage and expecting their husbands
To love, honor, and slave away for them. They can be rough.
Of course, the husbands are at fault themselves, every now and
    then.
But there's a point at which it's no longer dignified
For the husband to take it any longer. That dear daughter of
    mine,
Darn her, never sends for me unless they've both of them been
    doing   1100
Something wrong and a quarrel has started or is definitely
    brewing.
Whatever it is, I'll find out. *Yup!* I'll get brought up on the
    news.
Here she is now in front of the house. I see how aroused
They both are. She must have lashed into him; he looks
Pretty dashed. *Yup!* Just as I thought. I'll go call to her.

WIFE: I'll go greet Father. Good afternoon, Dad. How are you?

OLD MAN: Fine, thank you dear, and you? I hope everything's all
    right.
    You didn't send for me because you're in trouble? But you look
    Pretty peaked. And why's he standing over there looking mad?
    You both look as if you've been trading punches, exchanged a
        few blows   1110
    Just for size, to see how it goes. Fill me in on the facts.
    Tell me who's to blame, and explain the whole situation.

But briefly, I implore you. Let's not have even one oration,
Much less two.

WIFE: I didn't do anything, Father,
  Don't worry. But I can't live here any longer, I can't
  Stick it out. Please take me back.

OLD MAN: How did this happen?

WIFE: I've become someone just to be laughed at.

OLD MAN: By whom?

WIFE: By him,
  The man, the husband you conferred me on.

OLD MAN: .   A fight, eh?
  That's it, eh? How many times have I told you both of you
  To watch out you don't come whining to me with your troubles?

WIFE: How could I watch out, Father dear?   1120

OLD MAN: You really ask that?

WIFE: Only if you don't mind my asking.

OLD MAN: How often have I told you
  To put up with your husband? Don't watch where he goes;
  Don't see what he does; don't pry into what he's engaged in.

WIFE: But he's crazy about this daisy of a flower girl; and she lives
    right next door.

OLD MAN: That's perfectly natural, and in view of the way you're
    so busy
  Keeping an eye on his business, he'll get even dizzier about
    Daisy,
  I just bet you.

WIFE: But he goes over there for drinks all the time.

OLD MAN: What's it to you whether he drinks over there? If he
    drinks,
    He'll have to do it somewhere. And what's so terrible about
        that?   1130
    You might as well ask him to stop having dinner in town,
    Or never bring anyone home for a meal. Are husbands
    Supposed to take orders from you? Let them run the house
        then,
    And order the maids around, hand out wool to be carded
    And get on with their spinning and weaving.

WIFE: But Father, I ask you
    To represent *me*, not to be *his* lawyer in this case.
    You're standing here on my side, but you're taking his.

OLD MAN: Of course, if he's misbehaved, I'll get after him as
    much
    As I've lit into you—in fact, more so. But he seems to be taking
    Pretty good care of you, giving you jewels, clothes,
    Your servants, furnishing the food. You ought to take a
        practical,   1140
    More sensible view of the thing.

WIFE: But he's rooked me by stealing
    Jewels and dresses from my closet at home to sneak off with,
    My clothes, my jewels, to dress up that girl he calls on on the
        sly with.

OLD MAN: That's some prep . . . I mean proposition, I mean
    some imposition.
    I mean, that's terrible if that's going on—if it isn't
    Your supposition's as bad, putting an innocent man under
        suspicion.

WIFE: But Dad, he's got them there with him, the dress and that
    sweet

Gold flexible bracelet. He took them to her
And now, since I've found out about it, he's bringing them back.

OLD MAN: Well, now, we'll see about that. I'm going to find out
About that. I'm going right over there and ask him, I am.   1151
Oh say, Menaechmus, would you mind telling me, if you don't
Mind, about the matter you've been . . . discussing with her?
I'm curious to know. And why are you looking so down
In the mouth, old fellow? Why's my girl standing over there
By herself, all alone and so cross?

MENAECHMUS II: I summon all the gods,
And Jupiter Himself Supreme, as they are my witnesses. . . .
Old boy, whoever you are, whatever your name
May happen to be.

OLD MAN: As they are your witnesses to what?   1159
Why do you need such a cloud of high-ranking witnesses?

MENAECHMUS II: That I have not done anything wrong to this
   woman
Who claims that I surreptitiously deprived her
Of this dress and carried it off under suspicious circumstances.

WIFE: Well, that's a clear enough lie. He's perjured himself for
   sure.

MENAECHMUS II: If I have ever even set foot inside her
   house
May I be of all men the most terribly tremendously miserable.

OLD MAN: That's not a very bright thing to wish for, is it? You
   don't say
You've never set foot in the house there you live in, do you,
You stupid goop?

MENAECHMUS II: What's that you're saying about me
Living in that house, you goofy duffer? *I* live *there?*   1170

OLD MAN: You deny it?

MENAECHMUS II: Oh for Hercle's sake, of course I deny it.

OLD MAN: Oh, for Hercle's sake right back, you lie if you do
  Say you don't, I mean deny it. Unless you moved out last night.
  Come here, Daughter, listen: You two haven't moved
  Recently, have you?

WIFE: Heavens! Where to? Or why should we
  have?

OLD MAN: Well, of course, I couldn't know about that.

WIFE: Don't you
  get it?
  He's joking around with you.

OLD MAN: All right, Menaechmus, I've taken
  Enough of your joking now. Come on, boy, let's get down to
  business.

MENAECHMUS II: *Je vous en prie!* What the hell business have you
  got with me?
  In the first place, who the hell are you? And, in the second
  place,   1180
  I don't owe you any money. Nor her, in the third place.
  Who's giving me all this trouble, in the next few places?

WIFE: Look, do you notice how his eyes seem to be going all
  green
  All of a sudden? And there's a green tinge developing on the
  skin
  Around his temples and forehead. Look at his eyes glowing red,
  Or is it green?

MENAECHMUS II: I wonder if I'd better not pretend I *am* crazy
And scare them away by throwing a fit? They're the ones
Who seem to be insisting on it.

WIFE: His arms twitch, his jaw drops.
Oh, Father, what shall I do?

OLD MAN: Come here to your father,
My girl, stay as far away as you can from him.   1190

MENAECHMUS II: *Ho yo to yo! Tobacco Boy! Take me back to ya!*
I hear ya callin' me out to that happy hunting ground
Deep down in desegregated Damnasia (that's in the Near East),
Callin' your boy to come on out huntin' with his hound dogs!
I hear ya, Bromie Boy, but I jes' cain come near ya.
They won't let me loose from this toothpickin' witch-
    huntin' northland.
They's an old foam-covered bitch and she's keeping watch
On my left. And right behind me here they's a goat,
An ole toothpickin' garlic-stinking but I mean old goat,
Who's been buttin' down innocent citizens all of his life   1200
By bringing up things that ain't true against them
And then rounding up people to come listen to them refute
    them.

OLD MAN: I'm afraid your mind's been affected.

MENAECHMUS II: I've just swallowed
    an oracle
Of Apollo that orders me instantly to start setting about
Finding two red hot searchlights to put her eyes out with.

WIFE: Goodness, what a prepositionous preposterous proposition,
Father. He's threatening to burn out my eyes in.

MENAECHMUS II: Touché, for me. They say I'm raving, but they
Are rather wild at the moment. The straitjacket's on the other
    foot.

OLD MAN: Oh, my poor girl.

WIFE: Yes, Father?

OLD MAN: What shall we do?
  Suppose I send for the slaves in a hurry; I'll go   1211
  And bring them myself, to take him away and chain him
  Safely at home before he starts getting more destructive.

MENAECHMUS II: Trapped! Strung up by my own guitar! If I don't
  Improvise something soon they'll come on and cart me away.
  Yes I hear you, sugar Radiant Apollo! I'll follow through
  With my fists (you insist?) and spare not the laying on of
    hands.
  Punch that woman in the jaw, you say, according to your law,
  Unless she disappears from my view and gets herself gone
  The holy hell and crucified crutch of a cross   1220
  Out of my way? Apollo, I'll do what you say!

OLD MAN: Scoot into the house, fast as poss, or he'll slug you.

WIFE: Scoot I go,
  Father, *ergo*, soon I'll be out of the way. But please, Father,
  Keep stalling him, don't let him slip out of reach. Don't you
    agree,
  I'm a most put-upon specimen of woman to put up with that?

MENAECHMUS II: I've got rid of her: not bad. Now for Dad. You
    slob,
  Listen, you baggy bearded, quavering long-since-past father,
  You shriveled old, dried-up grasshopper—and besides your
    voice's changed,
  Singing your Glorias Swansong soprano in your second
    childhood   1229
  What's that, Apollo? Thou sayest I should smashest his frame,
  His bones, and the joints that hook them to same? I'm game.
  Smashomin, you say, with his owncluboff? Use his cane?

OLD MAN: There'll be trouble for you if you lay a finger on me,
  Or move any closer.

MENAECHMUS II: *Oh sir, Apollo? The following*
  Changes in wording? Take one each two-headed ax
  And split right down through the frame, through the guts to the
    bones,
  And hack his back to bits and make slivers of his liver and his
  Whole intestinal tract, don't just cudgel the codger?
  Roger to tower. Look at that geezer cower and run for cover.

OLD MAN: I suppose I'd better look to my laurels, what's left of
    them, withered   1240
  As an old man's may be. I'll look after me. He's a menace,
  That's clear enough. He just may decide to take it out on my
    hide.

MENAECHMUS II: For God's sake, Apollo, what's this? Another
    message? The traffic's
  Getting heavy. Take four wild bucking broncos and hitch
  Them up to a buckboard, and climb aboard and drive them
    over
  This lion, this bearded biped, this antique toothless
  Gumclicking biped with bad breath? Roger, I'm mounted,
    oh joy
  To Yoy, King Roy Apolloy. I'm holding that wagon's reins
  And flicking the whip already. Up there, you double pair
  Of quadruplets. Drum it out on the ground when you trample
    him down.   1250
  Bend your knees, noble steeds, be nimble as the breeze.
  Pound you there, pound.

OLD MAN: He's coming at me with two pairs
  Of horses?

MENAECHMUS II: Whoa there! *Yes, Apollo, of course I hear you*
  Telling me to launch my attack against him, yes, him

Over there, and murder him. Whoa there! Who's hauling me
   back
By the hair, and pulling me out of the chariot? Who does this
Reverses the very command and eeeeeeedict of Apollo.

OLD MAN: It's really this poor fellow who's having the attack, I
   would say.
And he's really having one, the full-scale deluxe one with nuts
   in it,   1259
God save us all. Well, that's how it is, by God. Here's a fellow
Completely crackers, and a minute ago he was perfectly rational.
When that mad stuff hits you it lands hard all of a sudden.

(*He exits*)

MENAECHMUS II:
   (*Alone, faces audience and addresses them across the
   stagefront*)
Now I ask you, have those two at last gotten out of my sight,
Who forced me to play this mad role, when, as *you* know,
I'm perfectly well? This is my chance to pick up and go
Winging back to my ship, don't you think, quick as a wink,
While I'm still safe and sound? Listen, if you're still around
When the old man comes back, you won't tell—he'll be in a
   rage—
Where I went when I left the stage? You won't say where I can
   be found?

(*He exits*)

Scene 3

OLD MAN: My back's stiff with sitting, my eyes nearly worn out
   with looking,   1270
Hanging around waiting for God darn that darn medicine man
To finish with his patients and meet this emergency.

Well *finally* he's pulled himself away—not much urgency
Either, from his victims. He's his own worst pain in the neck!
Such a specialist, in name-dropping at least, of who's on his list
Of big shots with big troubles only he can fix. When I insisted
He hike over here, he said, "Right away," but first he must set
This broken leg, to the Greater Glory of Aesculapius,   1278
And then put an arm back in place, On Behalf of Apollo.
Which half of Apollo beats the Belvedere out of me: but I see
Him racing over now, weaving down the track like an ant
With lumbago. It's just his ego slows him down, the hot
     airman.
Putting those pieces together! What is he, a repairman,
A tinker, a joiner at heart? Are his patients all coming apart?

DOCTOR: Now let us see, my man. . . . You described the case of
     the diseased
As *larvated, id est*, he sees actual, live, dead ghost spooks?
Or *cerebrated, id est*, perturbated footzled left lobar cavity?
Which is of course only a false hallucination and would show
Some degree of mental inquietude. Would you be so good
As to describe the condition again, so I can decide   1290
What to prescribe or proscribe, indeed just how to proceed?
Did you mention a species of *Hibernating* coma, a kind of
Tendency to feel sleepy all the time? Or did you more
     plainly see
A subaqueous subcutaneous *slurpation*, like say, water on the
     knee?

OLD MAN: The reason I've brought you in on the case is to
     find out
From you just what's wrong and ask you to cure it.

DOCTOR: How true,
     And I'll do it to perfection, never fear; upon my profession
     I assure you he'll be quite well again.

OLD MAN: You'll give him
     The most careful attention?

DOCTOR: First-class care, rest assured.
  My word, Deluxe! Private room; personal visits from me.
  I'll see him daily and ponder him most thoughtfully,   1301
  Heave hundreds of luxury sighs. He'll rate a thrill
  Being ill; and so will you when you see the bill.

OLD MAN: Shh. Here's our man. Let's watch and see what he
  does.

Scene 4

MENAECHMUS I: By God in heaven, if this hasn't been the worst
  Of all possible days for me! Everything's gone blooey.
  What I planned to do on the sly, that particular parasite,
  Peniculus, brought to light, and flooded me with shame and
    remorse
  In the process. Some Ulysses type, doping out this dirty deal
  For his own best protector and patron. Why that . . . sure as I
    live,   1310
  I'll do him right out of his ensuing existence, I'll unroll
  His scroll for him. *His* existence? I'm a fool
  To call *his* what's actually mine. I'm the one who brought
    him up
  By wining and dining him. It was my subsistence he lived on:
  All he ever managed was coexistence. I'll snuff out
  That half of his light by cutting off the supplies.
  As for that mercenary Daisy, all I can say is she
  Acted quite in keeping with the character of a kept woman,
  And I suppose that's human, if meretricious. A very
    meretricious   1319
  And a happy new year to her. When in doubt, just give money.
  All I did was ask her for the dress to return to my wife
  And she claimed she'd already handed it over. Turned it over,
  I bet, to some dealer for cash. Crash! Oh God in heaven,
  Did any man ever let himself in for this big a cave-in?

OLD MAN: You hear that?

DOCTOR: He says he's unhappy.

OLD MAN: Go on up to him.

DOCTOR: Meeeeenaechmus, *ciao!* How are you? Why expose
  your arm
That way? Exposure can aggravate your serious condition.

MENAECHMUS I: Why don't you go hang up, yourself, on the
    nearest branch?

OLD MAN: Notice anything peculiar?

DOCTOR: Anything? The whole thing,
    That's what I notice. This case couldn't be kept under control
    By a peck of Prozac. Menaechmus, just a word with
        you, please.   1331

MENAECHMUS I: What's up, doc?

DOCTOR: You are. Answer a few questions,
        please,
    And take them in order. First, what color wine do you drink?
    White wine, or red?

MENAECHMUS I: Oh, my crucified crotch!
    What's that to you?

DOCTOR: I seem to detect a slight tendency
    To rave here.

MENAECHMUS I: Why not color-quiz me on bread?
    Do I take purple, cerise, or golden red? As a rule,
    Do I eat fish with their feathers or birds with their scales
        and all?

OLD MAN: I win! Ill, eh? Pu! Can't you hear he's delirious?
    Hurry up   1339
  With that sedative, can't you? Why wait for the fit to come on?

DOCTOR: Just hold on a bit. I've a few more questions to ask.

OLD MAN: You'll finish him off with the questions you keep
    inventing.

DOCTOR: Do your eyes ever feel like they're starting out of your
    head?

MENAECHMUS I: What do you take me for, you seahorse doctor, a
    lobster?

DOCTOR: Do your bowels rumble powerfully, as far as you can
    tell?

MENAECHMUS I: They're perfectly still when I'm full; when
    hungry, they grumble.

DOCTOR: Well now, that's a perfectly straightforward, digestible
    answer,
  Not the word of a nut. You sleep until dawn, and sleep well?

MENAECHMUS I: I sleep right through, if I've paid all my bills.
    Listen, you
  Special investigator, I wish to heaven the gods would crack
    down on you.   1350

DOCTOR: Ah, now, to judge from that statement, he's being
    irrational.

OLD MAN: Oh no, that's a wise saying, worthy of Nestor,
    compared
  To what he was saying a while back, when he called his own
    wife
  A stark raving bitch.

MENAECHMUS I: What's that you say I said?

OLD MAN: You're out of your head, that's what I say.

MENAECHMUS I: Who's out of
     what? Me?

OLD MAN: Yes, you, that's who. Boo! Threatening to flatten me
     out
   With a four-horsepower chariot. I can swear to it.
   I saw you with my own eyes. I charge you with it.

MENAECHMUS I: Ah, but here's what I know about you. You
     purloined the crown
   Of Jupiter, his sacred crown, and were locked up in jail.   1360
   That's what I know about you. And when they let you out,
   It was to put you under the yoke and whip you in public,
   With birch rods. That's what I know about you. And then, too,
   You killed your own father and sold off your mother as a slave,
   That's what I know about you. Don't you think that might
     possibly do
   As a reasonably sound reply to the charges you're letting fly?

OLD MAN: Oh hurry up, doctor, for Hercle's sake, and do what
     you ought to.
   Can't you see, the man's *off*?

DOCTOR: You know what I think is best?
   Have him brought over to my place.

OLD MAN: You're sure?

DOCTOR: Sure, why not?
   I'll be able to treat him there by the very latest methods.

OLD MAN: Good. You know best.

DOCTOR: I assure you, Menaechmus,
  you'll lap up   1371
  Super tranquilizers for twenty days.

MENAECHMUS I: Is that medicine,
  Your madness? I'll gore you, hanging there, for thirty days.

DOCTOR: (*Aside*) Go call the help, to carry him over to my house.

OLD MAN: (*Aside*) How many men do we need?

DOCTOR: (*Aside*)   At least four, to judge
  From the way he's raving at present.

OLD MAN: (*Aside*)   They're practically here.
  I'll go run and get them. You stay right here, doctor, do,
  And keep a close eye on him.

DOCTOR: (*Aside*)   No. As a matter of fact,
  I think I'll be off for home, and make the preparations
  To receive him. There's quite a lot to do. You go get the help;
  Have them bring him to me.

OLD MAN: (*Aside*)   He's as good as carried there
  already.   1381

DOCTOR: I'm off.

OLD MAN: So am I.

MENAECHMUS I: Now I'm alone. That father-in-law
  And that doctor have gone, somewhere or other. But what in
     God's name
  Makes these men insist I'm insane? I've never been sick
  A day in my life, and I'm not ailing now. I don't start fights,
  Or dispute everything that comes up. I wish others well
  When I meet them, quite calmly, I recognize people I know,

And speak to them civilly enough. I wonder if they,   1388
Who absurdly declare that I'm mad, since they're in the wrong,
Aren't in fact crazy themselves? I wish I knew what to do.
I'd like to go home, but my wife won't allow it—as for that
     place,
(*Points to* DÉSIRÉE's *house*)
No one will let me in there. Well, it's all worked out
All right; worked me out of house and home. So I guess
I'll stick around here. I imagine, by the time night comes,
I'll be welcome to enter the right one of these two homes.

Scene 5

MESSENIO: God slave the king!
     And of me I sing.
     Or rather, the slave's the thing
     I present and I represent.
     The good slave, intent   1400
     On making his master content,
     Looks after his master's affairs.
     Arranging and planning, he never spares
     Any effort in lavishing cares
     On everything that needs being done.
     When the master's away, he handles all alone
     Problems that keep coming up, and he solves them
     As well as the boss could, himself, all of them;
     And sometimes manages the whole business better than
          Master.
     You need a good sense of balance, to fend off disaster   1410
     From your legs and your back. And you've got to remember
     That your throat and your stomach are not the most vital
          members.
     If you go off guzzling and eating, instead of performing,
     When you come back you're in for a beating and a good body-
          warming.

May I remind all the shiftless delinquents who keep hanging
    back
From doing their work, of the price all masters exact
From good-for-nothings, men they can't count on, in fact?
Lashes and chains;
Turning those wheels at the mill
Until you begin to feel   1420
Your brains churning loose and writhing like eels.
You'll be starved and left out to sleep in the cold open fields.
That's the wages of laziness.
Not to fear earning—that would be the worst sort of craziness.
Therefore, I've decided, for once and for all, to be good
And not bad. I'd rather be lashed by the tongue than the wood.
As for meal, I find it more pleasant to eat than to grind it.
Therefore, I always comply with the will of my lord
Calmly, and well I preserve it; and I can afford
To deserve whatever I get by way of reward.   1430
Let others look after their interests; they'll find a good way.
But this is how to serve your man best. That's what I say.
Let me always be careful, and pretty darn prayerful
Not to get in any trouble, so that I'll always be there, full
Of energy, coming in on the double where he needs me most,
His assistant host. Slaves who keep themselves good and scared
When they're not in the wrong usually find that they are
    declared
Highly usable by their owners. The fearless ones are the
    goners;
When it comes time to face the music, these singsongers
Will be cheeping like jailbirds and wishing they weren't such
    gone-wrongers.   1440
But I don't have to worry much longer, not me.
The time's almost here now when he promised to set me free.
That's how I slave and work well, and how I decide
To do the best thing and take the best care of my hide.
Sooooo . . . now that I've seen all the baggage and the porters
    in their bedding
In the tavern downtown, as Menaechmus instructed, I'm
    heading

Back to meet him. Guess I'll knock on the door
So he'll know I'm out here and get up off the floor
Or at least let me pull him outside
From this den of iniquity, now that he's tried   1450
To have a good time, and probably found out the cost.
I hope I'm not too late and that the battle's not already lost.

Scene 6

OLD MAN: Now I tell you, by all that's human or holy, make sure
    You carry out my orders just right as I ordered you to
    And order you now. You're to heft that man on your shoulders
    And hustle him off to the clinic, if you don't want your legs
    And your back pounded in. And don't pay the least attention,
    Any one of you, to anything he says. Well, don't just stand
        there.
    What are you waiting for? You ought to be after him, lifting him.
    I'll trot on over to the doctor's and be there when you pull in.

MENAECHMUS I: Well I'll be *God* damned! What's on the schedule
        now?   1461
    Why are these men rushing at me, what in the name of . . . ?
    What do you guys want? What's all the racket about?
    Why are you closing in on me all of a sudden? What's the
        hurry?
    Where we going? Some rumble. Creepers! They're giving me
        the tumble
    God *damn* us! Citizens all, of Epidamnus! To the rescue!
    Save me, my fellow men! Help! Let go me, you whipster
        bastards.

MESSENIO: Holy smoke! Creepers! What's this bunch of gypsters
        think
    They're gonna get away with? My master? Why those hijacking
        lifters,

They've got him on their shoulders. Let's see who gets the
   most blisters.   1470

MENAECHMUS I: Won't *anyone* lend me a hand?

MESSENIO: I will sir, at your
   command;
You brave captain. Boy, this is gonna give Epidamnus a
   black eye,
A mugging like this, right out in the open. *Epidam-nee-ee-ee-I!*
My master's being towed away in broad daylight, a free man
Who came to your city in peace, attacked on the street. *Can*
Anybody help us? Stay off, you lugs. Lay off.

MENAECHMUS I: Hey, for God's sake, whoever you are, help
   me out,
Won't you? Don't let them get away with murder. You can see
I'm in the right.

MESSENIO: Quite. Of course I'll pitch in   1479
And come to your defense and stand by you with all might.
I'd never let you go under, commander, I'd sink first.
Now you sink your fist in that guy's eye . . . No, not that one,
The one who's got you by the shoulder. That's it. Now a bolder
Swipe at the ball, gouge it out for him. I'll start distributing
A crack in the puss here, a sock in the jaw there. I'm at liberty
To do so? By the heavyweight Hercules, you thugs are
   gonna lug
Him away like a carload of lead, today. You'll pay by the ounce
When you feel my fists bounce all over your faces. Let go his
   grace.

MENAECHMUS I: I've got this guy's eye.

MESSENIO: Make like it's just a hole in
   his head.
You're a bunch of bums, you body-snatching, loot-latching
   whipsters.   1490

WHIPSTER I: Hey, this wasn't what the doctor ordered, was it, or
the old mister?

WHIPSTER II: They didn't say we'd be on the receiving end, did
they . . . ouch!
Gee Hercules, Jerkules, that hurt!

MESSENIO: Well, let him loose, then.

MENAECHMUS I: How dare this ape lay hands on me? Bongo him,
jungle boy.

MESSENIO: Here we go, kids, you too; take off, fade out, monkey
face;
Get the crucified cross of a holy hell and gone out of here.
You too, take that, you vandal. Get a lift from my sandal.
You're the last one, might as well get what's left behind.
Well . . . Phew . . . ! Say, I made it, didn't I? Just about in
time.

MENAECHMUS I: Young man, whoever you are, may the gods
always shine   1500
On your face. If it hadn't been for you I wouldn't have lasted
Through sunset today.

MESSENIO: By all that's holy, if you wanted
To reward me, O Master, you could free me.

MENAECHMUS I: Me liberate you?
I'm afraid I don't follow, young fellow. Aren't you making some
mistake.

MESSENIO: Me make a mistake?

MENAECHMUS I: By our father Jupiter, I swear
I am not your master.

MESSENIO: Don't talk that way.

MENAECHMUS I: I'm not lying.
  No slave of mine ever helped me as you did today.

MESSENIO: Well, then, let me go free, even if you say you don't
      know me.
  Then I won't be yours.

MENAECHMUS I: But of course! Far as I'm concerned,
  Thou art henceforth free—and thou mayest go wherever thou
      wantest to.

MESSENIO: You say that officially?

MENAECHMUS I: By Hercules, yes. In my official
      capacity,   1510
  Insofar as that governs you.

MESSENIO: Thanks very much.
  And greetings, dear patron! Now that I'm free to be your client
  And depend on you on equal terms.

(*Turns to audience*)

      Gaudete! He's free today!
      Good show for Messenio!
      Aren't you all glad he's let go?

(*Audience cheers and applauds—and that is* some *stage direction*)

(*Still to audience*)

  Well, I guess I'll accept it from you; thanks for the
      congratulations.
  You've all given me quite a hand. I feel *man you mitted*.
  But, Menaechmus, my patron, I'm just as much at your service
  As I was when I used to be your slave. I want to stay by you.
  And when you go home I want to go with you too.   1521

MENAECHMUS I: (*Aside*) God, no! Not another client.

MESSENIO: I'll ankle downtown
  To the tavern and bring back the baggage and cash. That purse
  I hid away and locked in the trunk with the traveler's checks.
  I'll go get it now and deliver it all back to you.

MENAECHMUS I: Oh yes, do bring that.

MESSENIO: I'll bring it all back intact
  Just as you handed it over. You wait here for me.

(*He exits*)

MENAECHMUS I: There's a bumper crop of miracles manifesting
        marvels by the millions   1528
  Around here today: some people saying I'm not who I am
  And keeping me out from where I belong; then comes along
  This slave who says he belongs to me, whom I've just set free.
  Now he says he'll go bring me back a purseful of cash;
  And if he does that I'll insist he feel perfectly free
  To take leave of me and go where he wants, just in case   ·
  When he comes to his senses he begins asking back for the
        dough.
  The doctor and my father-in-law, though, claim I'm out of my
        head.
  At least, that's what they said. It's all very hard to get hold of,
  Like a dream you dream you're having or are just being told of.
  Oh well, I'll go on in here to visit my mistress, even though
  She's provoked at me, and do my best to prevail   1540
  On her to give back the dress. I can certainly use it as bail
  To get off the street and into my house, *id est*, my jail.

Scene 7

MENAECHMUS II: You have the nerve to be telling me you
    reported back to me
  Since the time I sent you away and told you to meet me?

MESSENIO: Exactly. Only a moment ago I saved you from
    destruction
  At the hands of those four whipsters hoisting you on their
    shoulders
  And carting you off, right in front of this house. You were
    letting out
  Loud shouts, calling on all the gods and on men,
  When I roared in and pulled you loose by sheer brute strength
  And knocked the block off them all, much to their surprise.
  And for the service I rendered in saving you, you set me free.
  Then I told you I'd go get the baggage and our cash—and
    then *you*   1552
  Doubled round the corner as fast as you could, to meet me
  And deny the whole thing.

MENAECHMUS II: I told you you could be free?

MESSENIO: Positive.

MENAECHMUS II: I'm more positive still that before I'd see
  You turned free man I'd turn into a slave, yes me, man.

Scene 8

MENAECHMUS I: (*Coming out of* DÉSIRÉE's *house*) You can swear
    by your two jaundiced eyes if you want, that won't
  Make it any more true that I took away the dress and bracelet
    today,
  You whole bunch of blue-eyed, organized man-eaters for pay.

MESSENIO: Heavens to . . . let's see . . . What's this I see?   1559

MENAECHMUS II: So, what
   Do you see?

MESSENIO: Your looking glass, boss.

MENAECHMUS II: You mean to say what?

MESSENIO: I say I see your reflection over there. I could swear
   It's your face exactly.

MENAECHMUS II: God, if it isn't like me,
   When I stop to consider how I look.

MENAECHMUS I: Oh boy, there, whoever
    you are,
   You saved my life. Glad to see you.

MESSENIO: Young man, I wonder
   If you'd mind telling me what your name is, by God in heaven?

MENAECHMUS I: Heavenly God, no, of course I don't mind. The
    favor
   You did me rates in return my nonreluctant behavior: 1568
   After all, you're my savior. I go by the name of Menaechmus.

MENAECHMUS II: So do I, for God's sake.

MENAECHMUS I: I'm Sicilian, from Syracuse.

MENAECHMUS II: And my native city is the same.

MENAECHMUS I: What's that you claim?

MENAECHMUS II: Only what's the truth.

MESSENIO: I can tell you which is
    which easily.
I'm his slave,
(*Points to* MENAECHMUS I)
       but I thought all along I was his.
And I thought you were him. That's why I talked back that way.
Please excuse me if I've spoken too stupidly for words to you.

MENAECHMUS II: You're raving right now. Think back. Remember
   how
You got off the ship with me today?

MESSENIO: A fair enough question.
    I'll change my mind. You're my master and I am your slave.
So long, you. Good afternoon, again, to you. And I mean you.
I say, this one's Menaechmus.

MENAECHMUS I: I say that's me.   1580

MENAECHMUS II: What's the story, you? Menaechmus?

MENAECHMUS I: Yep. Menaechmus.
    Son of Moschus.

MENAECHMUS II: You're my father's son?

MENAECHMUS I: No, fellow, *my* father's.
    I'm not
After yours. I don't want to hop on yours and take him
   from you.

MESSENIO: By all the gods, all over heaven, can my mind
   Be sure of what it hopes for so desperately? *I've got 'em
    untwined:*
   These men are the two twins who separately now are combined
   To recall the same father and fatherland they shared in their
    likeness.
   I'll speak to my master. Ahoy there, Menaechmus.

MENAECHMUS I and MENAECHMUS II: (*Together*) What is it?

MESSENIO: No, no, not both. I only want my shipmate.

MENAECHMUS I: Not me.

MENAECHMUS II: But me.

MESSENIO: You're the one I must talk to.
     Come here.

MENAECHMUS II: Here I am. What's up?

MESSENIO: That man's either your
     absolute brother   1590
  Or an absolute fake. I never saw one man look more like
     another.
  Water's no more like water, or milk more like milk
  Than you two drops of the same identical ilk.
  Besides, he cites the same fatherland and father.
  Don't you think investigating further might be worth the
     bother?

MENAECHMUS II: Say, that's very good advice you're giving me.
  Thanks very much.
  Keep boring in, I implore you, by Hercules' knee.
  If you come up with my brother, I fully intend to see
  That *thou shalt go free.*

MESSENIO: I hope I come out right in the end.

MENAECHMUS II: I hope the same thing for you.   1601

MESSENIO: (*To* MENAECHMUS I) Now, fellow, what do you say?
  Menaechmus, I believe that is what you said you were called.

MENAECHMUS I: Right you are.

MESSENIO: Now this fellow here has the name of Menaechmus,
  Just like you, and you said you were born at Syracuse.
  So was he. Now both of you pay close attention to me,
  And see if what I work out doesn't prove well worth it.

MENAECHMUS I: You've already earned the right to whatever you
    want   1609
  From me. You've only to ask and you'll gain it. If it's money
  You want, I'm ready to supply it. Just ask. I won't deny it.

MESSENIO: I am hopeful at the moment of setting about to
    discover
  The fact that you two are twins, born for each other
  And on the same day to the very same father and mother.

MENAECHMUS I: That sounds miraculous. I wish you could keep
    that promise.

MESSENIO: I'll come through all right. Now listen here, each one
    of you
  To just what I say. And answer my questions in turn.

MENAECHMUS I: Ask what you will. I'll answer and never keep
    back
  Anything I know.

MESSENIO: Is your name Menaechmus?

MENAECHMUS I: I admit it.   1619

MESSENIO: Is that your name too?

MENAECHMUS II: So it is.

MESSENIO: You say that your father
  Was Moschus?

MENAECHMUS I: So I do.

MENAECHMUS II: Me too.

MESSENIO: You're from Syracuse?

MENAECHMUS I: That I am.

MESSENIO: How about you?

MENAECHMUS II: Naturally, me too.

MESSENIO: So far, it all checks perfectly. Now let's forge ahead.
    Tell me, how far back do you remember having been in your
        country?

MENAECHMUS I: Well, I remember the day I went to Tarentum,
    to the fair
    And wandered off away from my father among some men who
        took me
    And brought me here.

MENAECHMUS II: Jupiter One and Supreme, that can only
    mean . . . !

MESSENIO: What's all the racket? Can't you pipe down? Now,
    how old
    Were you when your father took you with him from Sicily?

MENAECHMUS I: Seven. I was just beginning to lose my first
    teeth,   1630
    And I never saw my father again.

MESSENIO: Here's another question:
    How many sons did your father have?

MENAECHMUS I: Two, to my knowledge.

MESSENIO: Were you the older, or was the other?

MENAECHMUS I: Both the same age.

MESSENIO: That's impossible.

MENAECHMUS I: I mean, we were twins.

MENAECHMUS II: The gods are
    on my side.

MESSENIO: If you keep interrupting, I'll stop.

MENAECHMUS II: No, no. I'll be quiet.

MESSENIO: Tell me, did you both have the same name?

MENAECHMUS I: Not at all. I had
    The name I have now, Menaechmus. They called him Sosicles.

MENAECHMUS II: The lid's off! I just can't keep from hugging him
    hard.
    My own twin brother, *ciao!* It's me: Sosicles!

MENAECHMUS I: How come you changed your name to
    Menaechmus?   1640

MENAECHMUS II: After they told us how you had been taken away
    From our father, and carried off by strangers, and Father died,
    Our grandfather gave me your name. He made the changes.

MENAECHMUS I: I bet that's just how it happened. But tell me
    something.

MENAECHMUS II: Ask me something.

MENAECHMUS I: What was our dear mother's
    name?

MENAECHMUS II: Henrietta Battleship.

MENAECHMUS I: That's it, all right. Never
    on a diet.
Oh, *Brother*, this is a riot. I just *cain't* keep quiet.
Imagine meeting you here after all these years, I mean,
I never thought I'd ever lay eyes on you again, much less
Wring your neck, you old numero *uno*, I mean *duo*.   1650

MENAECHMUS II: Oh, you big beautiful brute, you. *Et ego et tu.*
    You know
How long I've been hunting for you, and how much trouble
I've gone to to locate my double! I'm glad to be here, lad.

MESSENIO: You see, Boss, that's why that mercenary much of a
    wench in there
Called you by his name. She thought he was you when she
    hauled
You in to dinner.

MENAECHMUS I: As a matter of heavenly fact, I did order dinner
    set up
Behind my wife's back, right here today, and sneaked out a
    dress,
And gave it to Désirée.

MENAECHMUS II: Wouldn't be this dress, Brother,
    Would it?

MENAECHMUS I: That's it, Brother. But how did you happen to
    come by it?

MENAECHMUS II: I just happened to come by and the girlfriend
    pulled me in to dinner   1660
And said I'd given her the dress. I dined very well,
I wined like a lord, I reclined with my refined escort.
Then I took away the dress, and this gold bracelet too.

MENAECHMUS I: Good for you.
    Old boy, Because of me, you've at least enjoyed

Your day in Epidamnus. I'm glad of that. Now, when she
Called you in, she of course thought sure you were me.

MESSENIO: Ahem! Need I wait much longer to be free as you
   commanded?

MENAECHMUS I: Brother, he's asking for only what is his just due.
   Just do it
   For my sake, won't you?

MENAECHMUS II: *Thou art henceforth free.*

MENAECHMUS I:
   Gaudete! He's free today!   1670
   Good show for Messenio!
   Aren't you all glad he's let go?

MESSENIO: Congratulations are all very fine, but perhaps
   something more *exchangeable*
   Like, say, money, will make a free future not only assured but
   manageable.

MENAECHMUS II: Now, brother, everything's finally worked out so
   well,
   Let's both go back to our homeland.

MENAECHMUS I: I'll do anything you wish,
   Brother. I'll have a big auction here and sell all I own.
   Meanwhile, temporarily, here we go home rejoicing.   1679

MENAECHMUS II: I'm with you.

MESSENIO: I've a favor to ask.

MENAECHMUS I: Don't hesitate.

MESSENIO: Appoint me auctioneer.

MENAECHMUS I: Sold! To the former slave!

MESSENIO: Well, shall I announce the sale then?

MENAECHMUS I: Sure, for a week
    from today.

MESSENIO: (*To audience*) Big auction at Menaechmus's house a
    week from today!
  Must sell slaves, furniture, town house, country estate!
  Everything's going, everything, for whatever you can pay!
  He'll even sell the wife to any buyer willing to try her.
  We'll make a million dollars and we may even go higher
  If you count my commission. All invited! It ought to be great!
  —But, oh, wait, spectators! Don't forget the theater's laws.
  We'll leave you first, on a burst of good loud applause!   1690

THE LITTLE BOX

(*CISTELLARIA*)

Translated by R. H. W. Dillard

INTRODUCTION

The *Cistellaria* is for any translator what is usually termed a "problematic" play. This is not because it is over two thousand years old and written in a "dead" language. The language is actually quite alive and well in the tongues of its linguistic progeny all over this planet and even, briefly, on the moon. And the concerns and behavior of its characters are quite familiar and up to date; after all, love and foolishness will, I hope, never be outdated. And besides, if those were problems, they would be problems facing the translators of all of Plautus's plays, and there would be no need to single this one out as problematic.

No, what gives the *Cistellaria* its problems is that so much of it is missing, maybe as much as a fourth (?) of it, act 2 being especially riddled with lacunae. Earlier translators have either translated the isolated bits and pieces—a word here, half a line there, sometimes even a sentence or two, a whole speech—and nestled them in clusters of annoying or frustrating asterisks, late-blooming blossoms of time and loss. Others have simply skipped all of the most difficult passages, either indicating in a footnote that certain actions seem to have occurred in an unspecified hiatus in the action, or simply pressing on in the hope that no one will notice that the play is making less sense by the minute.

Rather than use either of these methods of presenting this damaged play, I have resorted to my own method of plugging the lacunae. I have faithfully translated all of Plautus's words, but I have also allowed two rather intrusive and often objectionable characters of my own devising to interrupt Plautus's characters, to comment on them and the action of the play, and to engage in certain doings of their own when they're not needed on stage. Thanks to the faulty hearing and memories of two of my old friends and fellow transla-

177

tors, Henry Taylor and Kelly Cherry, I came by the names Lacuna
and Hiatus for my two characters; I wish here to thank Henry and
Kelly for their advertent and inadvertent help, and to say that I think
Plautus might well himself have approved of the names, if not the
violence that the named, abetting the depredations of time, do to his
play. Then again, he might appreciate that even Hiatus and Lacuna
are better for the good health of his work than all those weedy
asterisks. I hope so.

My Latin teachers of too many years ago, Isabel Brown and
Rhoda Noell, figured out early that while I was sorely deficient in
vocabulary and syntax, I had a good ear for the language, so that
while I labored and fell to ruin in the dangerous thickets of Cicero's
prose, I could scan Virgil like a bandit. Enough of that skill still
remains to enable me to realize that, while I might successfully fill
the lacunae, there was no way I could capture in English the remark-
able extravagances and subtleties of Plautus's use of Latin metric
verse. I, therefore, chose to render his disciplined lines in a loose
five-beat accentual English verse that enabled me to indicate something of the poetic movement of his Latin lines while at the same
time catching as much as I could of his whacky wordplay and distinctive sound.

Which leads me to my overall method of translating what I feel
to be the distinctive tone of Plautus's writing into a modern English
play. Since this is the 1990s and postmodernism is in flower, it is at
least arguable to see Plautus himself as a forerunner and ancient
father of much that is labeled postmodern today. Whether you call it
appropriation or, like Kathy Acker, more honestly call it plagiarism,
Plautus did steal most of his plays from the Greeks. The *Cistellaria*
may well, from some minimal internal evidence, have been lifted
from a lost play by Menander. Many of his plot situations and gags
were already ancient when he used them. His characters break out
of the mise-en-scène for a chat with the audience whenever they feel
like it. The play was apparently written during the closing years of
the Second Punic War, and Auxilium (the god of helpfulness) gives
the audience a little patriotic pep talk at the end of the first act that
has absolutely nothing to do with the action of the play. The play,
then, for all its freshness and distinctively Plautine quality, steals the
past blind, refuses to conform to stage conventions, totally ignores

(when it sees fit) any illusion of reality, and subverts everything in sight; in other words, it's thoroughly postmodern. Right?

To catch that unbuttoned and subversive quality of the *Cistellaria*, I have not only stolen my *Little Box* from Plautus (and Menander secondhand), but I have filled it with toys of my own, many of them also stolen, from everyone from William Shakespeare to the Platters to Walter Pater to Billy Ray Cyrus. Like Plautus, I have no shame. I have changed names of certain of his characters, given names to those who previously had no name, put in terrible puns and awful alliterations, and given an obscene spin to words and lines that were once upon a time almost as pure as the virtue of the whore Selenium, one of the young lovers of our tale. All this I have done in an effort to breathe comic life back into a very funny play that has become nearly comatose from centuries of dry, literal translations, renderings by Latinists more interested in the ablative absolute than in the absolute ablation of the humor in this play over all those years.

Lest this brief preface become exclusively an extended *apologia pro translatione sua*, I should conclude by saying that, except for the lacunae, *The Little Box* needs no apologies. Here human folly and vice are revealed with comic clarity and something approaching grace. The speech by Alcesimarchus that opens the second act is as accurate an expression of the anguish of love-sickness as you'll find anywhere. And love does, as it must in a comedy, despite greed and price and lust and selfishness, conquer all.

I hope that you will find some pleasure examining the toys in this little box, and that your problems while playing with them will be few, and that you will join me at the end in giving Titus Maccius Plautus, that grand Roman clown, after all these centuries, a very big hand.

R. H. W. Dillard

5/ too many characters
/ missing parts

THE LITTLE BOX

CHARACTERS

LACUNA, an interested bystander
HIATUS, a less interested bystander
SELENIUM, a "prostitute"
GYMNASIUM, a prostitute
ARENA, a madam and mother of Gymnasium
AUXILIUM, the god of helpfulness
ALCESIMARCHUS, a young man of Sicyon
ANONYMOUS, a slave, belonging to Alcesimarchus
TERTIUS, the third man
PATER, father of Alcesimarchus
LAMPADIO, slave of Demipho
MELAENIS, a madam and supposed mother of Selenium
PHANOSTRATA, wife of Demipho
HALISCA, maid to Melaenis
DEMIPHO, an old man of Sicyon

ARGUMENT

Lemnian teenager wrongs girl of Sicyon, goes home,
Is married, fathers a daughter. But in Sicyon
The girl also bears a daughter. Young slave
Takes this child away, leaves her, but lurks around,
Learns what happens. Whore picks her up, gives her
Early to another whore. Later Lemnian goes back, marries

 * wronged woman, betroths his Lemnian daughter *
 * to young man who loves the other daughter. *
But slave searches and finds the girl he left behind.
Once her identity and citizenship are legally proven,
X on the dot, she gets to marry her lover, Alcesimarchus.

ACT I

Scene 1

LACUNA: (*Alone, addressing the audience*)
  Let's get this straight from the start. First thing,
  You know? This is sure enough the same old story,
  The one you've heard before so many, many times.
  Not necessarily love and glory, but close enough.
  You'll recognize it as soon as it begins, or sooner
  Maybe. I mean, Plautus stole it flat-footed himself
  From the Greeks, right? And he wrote it,
  For God's sake, in Latin, and any schoolboy knows
  What's killing the Romans. (Do girls know better?)
  But, anyway, as the butcher says in the joke,   10
  At this price, you were expecting maybe fresh?
  There are the usual mistaken identities, lost
  And found loves, bad dads, broken-hearted moms;
  But it does have its points: a high-class whore
  Named Gymnasium right off the bat, and that's
  Not bad for openers, and her drunken mom (her madam),
  And another "prostitute" to boot. They're coming now,
  About to enter, although usually they're entered
  Before they come—if you get what I mean. You do?
  But that's another story, and this one's complicated   20
  Enough as it is. I'll step aside and let you watch,

But I have a feeling I'll be back before this play
Is through. We'll see, but for now, enough's enough.

HIATUS: (*Enters and speaks to* LACUNA)
Enough *enough's* is more like it. You've said *enough*
Enough times to stuff a whore's mattress, enough
For a whole play much less to fill a little hole in this one.
Come on, Lacuna. I'll buy you a drink or two, or enough
To make it more than likely you'll get stuffed yourself
Before enough of this play's passed to interrupt us
When it's time (soon enough) to plug yet another breach!   30

(HIATUS *and* LACUNA *withdraw as two prostitutes,* SELENIUM *and*
GYMNASIUM, *enter along with* GYMNASIUM's *mother,* ARENA)

SELENIUM: I always knew you were my friend, and I've always
    loved you,
My Gymnasium, and your mother, too—but today . . . today
I really know how much you mean to me. The both of you.
Even if you were my very own sister, you couldn't love me
More. No, I know you couldn't have loved me more.
Just put everything you were doing down—to help
Me. I love you for it, and I'll love you two forever, too.

GYMNASIUM: Oh come on, you make it easy to care for you
And take care of you, too, at the price you pay:
A lunch at your house so good we'll never forget it!   40

SELENIUM: My pleasure, my dears, and it always will be, too,
To do things for you that I think will please you.

ARENA: As the man shed, his bark borne by a breaking wind
Over the tranquil she, "I rejoice that we blew
Your way." The wonderful way you treated ush today,
Everything perfect, exshept you don't dish-
Cipline your help, didn't like that a little bit.

SELENIUM: Why, love, how so?

ARENA: No one pashed . . . passed the wine
   Or when they did, it was shpoiled . . . wash spoiled!

GYMNASIUM: Darling, is this the place to say such things?   50

ARENA: Divinely lawful and just it is. There's not
   A shingle stranger in hearing or in shite.

SELENIUM: What's right is that I love you two, you who
   Are so good to me, who treat me so fine.

ARENA: Oh come on, my own Selenium, people in our business
   Had better treat each other well and keep the faith;
   Just think of those snobs, those high-born rich bitches,
   How they take care of each other and make sure
   That they're friends (*hic*) only with their shelves.   60
   If we do the shame thing, follow their example,
   Even when we scarcely make ends meet, they hate us so.
   They want us (*haec*) at their beck and call, totally
   Dependent, dishempowered on our own, always having
   To come (*hoc*) to them for everything. And when
   You do go to them, you wish you'd only come to say
   You really must be going, the way they gush so warm
   All over us in public, but behind our backs—
   Brrrr!—nothing but cold water. They claim   70
   We latch onto their husbands as their mistresses,
   And they try to put us down. Since we were freed slaves,
   Both your mother and I, we became prostitutes.
   She reared you, and I reared thish girl, both your fathers
   Being cash . . . casual acquaintances. So it wasn't
   My pride that led to her fall into a life of whoring,
   Just the fact that I need food, you she, to shurvive.

SELENIUM: But wouldn't it have been better to have married
    her off?

ARENA: Hey, wait! She's married every day, one man today,   80
   Another one tonight. I never let her sleep alone.

If she didn't marry morning and night, you'd be
Mourning our little family, dead of starvation.

GYMNASIUM: I'll always be just the way you want me, Mother.

ARENA: I won't regret that, for sure, as long as you keep
Doing it. As long as you do what I say,
You'll never lose your youth even if you grow old,
Taking from the men and giving to your mom,
And without costing me a thing.

GYMNASIUM: Gods willing.

ARENA: Jusht remember: gods help those who help their
shelves.   90

GYMNASIUM: By God, I vow I'll part my . . . I mean, do my part.
But enough of this talk; look at my Selenium, I've never
Seen her look so sad. Dear, where has your happiness gone?
And you're not as chic as usual either—just look,
That's a major sigh—and you're pale, too!
Tell us, dear girl, what's the matter, and how
Can we help you—we need to know. Please don't cry.
You're breaking my heart, darling.

SELENIUM: I'm in torment, Gymnasium, I hurt all over, my eyes
ache,
Even my soul is sore, I feel so bruised! What can I say?   100
It's my own dumb foolishness that makes me feel this way.

GYMNASIUM: In the same place you found this foolishness, you
should
Take it and stick it!

SELENIUM: I should do *what?*

GYMNASIUM: Put it, my dear,
   Where the sun don't shine—deep in your heart. And don't
   Let anyone see it. Just keep your foolishness to yourself.

SELENIUM: But I'm so heartsick.

GYMNASIUM: What? Where, pray tell,
   Did you get a heart to be sick? According to men,
   That's something neither you nor any woman even has.

SELENIUM: If I have one to be sick, it's sick; if I am heartless,
  It hurts here anyway.

GYMNASIUM: This woman is in love.   110

SELENIUM: Indeed. Does love, then, begin by being bitter?

GYMNASIUM: Oh come on, surely you know love is rich with
    honey and gall:
   A taste of the sweet, and tastes and aftertastes of bitterness
   Till they fill you up brimful and flowing over.

SELENIUM: The soreness torturing me is just like that, dear
    Gymnasium.

GYMNASIUM: Love is, the song cries out, perfidia.

SELENIUM: It sure is cheating me.

GYMNASIUM: Chill out. This illness won't kill you. You'll survive.

SELENIUM: I believe you, but only if the right doctor comes,
   The one who has the right cure for the disease.

GYMNASIUM: He's sure to come.

SELENIUM: To someone in love, "He's
   sure to come,"   120

Is a hard comfort indeed, unless he sure enough comes.
But it's my own fault, my own foolishness, that makes my cause
The worse, for he's the only one I want to spend my life with.

ARENA: That is more appropriate for a married woman, dear
    Selenium,
    To love just one man for the rest of her life once they're wed,
    But a whore is like a major city: she can't improve
    Her infrastructure without the investment of a lot of men.

SELENIUM: Dears, lend me your ears, and I'll explain why I sent
    for you,
    Asked you to come to me. My mother, knowing I don't take
    kindly
    To being called a whore, obeyed me as I always
        obeyed her,   130
    And allowed me to live alone with the man I love.

ARENA: By gods, she was shtupid! But you've never shlepped . . .
    Slept with any men?

SELENIUM: With no one, no one but Alcesimarchus.
    No one else has ever even laid a finger on my virtue.

ARENA: You've got to tell me, just how did this one insinuate
    Himself into your good graces . . . and secret places?

SELENIUM: At the Festival of Dionysus, Mother took me to see
    The procession. On the way home, he tailed me
    All the way to our door. And then he made friends
    With Mother—and with me—with sweet words   140
    And even sweeter presents and gifts.

ARENA: If such a man should be offered to me,
    I'd know how to work him for real.

SELENIUM: No words are needed. Bodies talk together;
    We were together, and I loved him, and he loved me.

ARENA: O dear Selenium . . . you ought to just pretend
  To be in love. Once you really are in love,
  You pay too much attention to your lover's needs
  And forget your own.

SELENIUM: But he swore on a stack of books
  To my mother that he would marry me. And now   150
  His father's making him take another woman home,
  Some cousin from Lemnos who lives next door here.
  And now Mother is mad at me because I didn't go
  Home to her after I found all this out,
  Found out he was going to marry someone else.

ARENA: Nothing's unfair in love.

SELENIUM: Now I beg you to let
  Gymnasium stay here for the next three days
  To house-sit for me. Mother is making me go home.

ARENA: Although this will be a burdensome three days for me,
  To say nothing of lost cash flow, I'll agree to it.   160

SELENIUM: You are so friendly and kind. But, dear Gymnasium,
  If Alcesimarchus comes while I'm gone, don't really
  Give him grief or let him have it—no matter
  What he's done to me, I still care for him. Please
  Be gentle; don't say anything to hurt his feelings.
  Here are the keys; if you need anything, it's yours.
  I've got to go now.

GYMNASIUM: Now I'm crying, too!

SELENIUM: My Gymnasium, good-bye.

GYMNASIUM: Take care of yourself, dearest.
  But are you really going in such a mess?

SELENIUM: A messy fate deserves a messy dress.   170

GYMNASIUM: At least, don't let your hem drag behind you.

SELENIUM: Let it drag just like I'm dragging, too.

GYMNASIUM: Whatever. . . . Good-bye and watch out for
    yourself.

SELENIUM: If I could, I would.

(*She exits*)

GYMNASIUM: Is there anything you want,
    Mother,
  Before I go inside? Wow, she sure does
  Have it bad, or so it seems to me.

ARENA: Now you know why I'm constantly filling your ears
  With: DO NOT FALL IN LOVE WITH ANY MAN. Go on inside.

GYMNASIUM: You're sure there's nothing else you want with me?

ARENA: Take good care of yourself.

GYMNASIUM: You, too.   180

(*She exits*)

                          Scene 2

ARENA: (*Alone, addressing the audience*)
  I've got the shame problem as most of the women
  In my profession: once we've taken on a full load
  At the table, we're just as filled up with words,
  And we talk too much. Take me, for instance.
  Now that I'm fully laden with my choice of wines,
  I've suddenly decided to be a bit more free

With my own tongue; I just can't decide to keep
What ought to be kept to my shelf to my . . . self.
You know that girl who just went weeping away?
I found her years ago—she was just a tiny thing—   190
Found her on a side street—she'd been abandoned.
I gave her to a friend of mine, a whore who,
You know, had always begged me to find her anywhere
A little boy or girl, newborn, so that it
Could pass as her own. So this gave me my chance.
I gave her what she had so often asked for.
After she got this girl from me, she gave birth
To this shame girl (the one she got from me)
without troubling a midwife and without a shingle pain
Like those other women suffer who have babies   200
And bring trouble on their shelves. She shed,
She said her lover was from out of town, and that
That was the real reason for the trick and the baby.
Only we two know the story—I, who gave
The child to her, and she, who took the child from me.
Except for you, of course. Anyway, that's how
It went, and I want you to remember all this
In case we need it. But now—I want to go home.

(*She exits*)

Scene 3

AUXILIUM: (*Entering abruptly*) Now there's an old woman who
      drinks and talks too much.
   She's scarcely left room for a god to say a word   210
   In her rush to tell everything about this substituted
   Girl. But even if she had managed to bite her tongue,
   I'll admit I would have told you the same story,
   But, as a god, I would have told it more clearly.
   For my name is Auxilium, the god of helpfulness!
   Now pay attention, and I'll make the whole plot

Plain and simple for you: It all began a long time
Ago in Sicyon at a Festival of Dionysus.
A Lemnos businessman came here for the festivities,   220
And, drinking wine as only a young man can,
In the dead of night, he did it in the road
With an underage virgin. When he sobered up
And remembered the punishment for rape, he let
His feet do their stuff and headed for Lemnos,
Where he was then living. And nine months later,
The girl he had raped gave birth to a baby girl.
Since she didn't know the identity of the perpetrator,
She turned to one of her father's slaves for advice
And gave the baby to him to abandon, exposed   230
To die. He abandoned it; that old woman
Found it. The slave who had left it watched in secret
To see where, to what house, she took it. As you
Just heard her admit, she gave the baby
To the whore Melaenis, who raised her modestly
And as well as her own daughter. In Lemnos, the man
Married the girl next door, his cousin.
Then, just once, she was compliant to her husband: she died.
After he had properly buried her, he moved here.
And here he married again—the same woman   240
Whom he had raped when she was a girl! When they
Finally recognized each other, rapist and victim,
She told him that, because of that night, she had borne
A daughter and had given her to a slave to expose.
He immediately ordered the same slave to play
The detective to see if he could find again
The woman that he saw pick the baby up.
And now that slave is spending night and day
On the case, trying to find the whore
He saw from hiding so long ago, picking   250
Up the child that he had just abandoned.
Now for all the rest that remains, I want
To pay in full, so that you'll scratch my name
From your ledger and close my account. Here in Sicyon
There is a young man whose father is still alive,

And he, the son, is desperately in love with her,
The abandoned girl, the one who just left here
In tears to see her mother. And she loves him,
Too—the sweetest love of all. But then,
They *are* human, and for humans, nothing lasts   260
Forever. The young man's father wants
To give him a wife. When the girl's adopted mother
Heard, she told her daughter to come home.
And that's the way things are.
(*Adopting a godly tone*)
                              Farewell, and (some advice)
Prevail by your innate valor, as you have done
Before; support your allies, old and new;
Increase your resources by your fair laws;
Destroy your enemies, earn praise and laurels,
And give the defeated Carthaginians what they deserve!   270

ACT II

Scene 1

ALCESIMARCHUS: I believe it was Love itself that first created
    The torturer's trade among us. I figured this out
    Right here by myself, no need to open the door
    And leave home, for who can lay a finger on me
    Among all men for putting my soul through the wringer?
    I am shaken, rattled and rolled, done to a turn
    On the rotisserie of love, poor me! I'm blown
    This way and that, torn to pieces, riven, driven,
    With my head all groggy and my thoughts all foggy.
    Where I am, there I am not; where I am not,   280
    There my soul is sure to be—an omniplex
    Of conflicting desires! What pleases me, pleases me
    Not (and just as much!); Love mocks my achy breaky heart,

Pushes it away, chases after it, lusts for it, kidnaps it,
Holds it prisoner, seduces it, and ravishes it with gifts;
But what it gives, it takes away. It deludes me.
It persuades me, then dissuades me; it dissuades me,
Then urges me on. I toss in the sea of love,
Which is breaking up my heart, and my only hope's
That it doesn't swamp it totally, the only thing   290
That doesn't make my ruin complete. This is the way
My father has kept me tied up at his country house
For six whole days, unable to sail off to my love.
Isn't this an awful thing to have to tell?

(ALCESIMARCHUS *keeps muttering to himself, but he is drowned out
by the noisy entrance of* HIATUS *and* LACUNA, *both disheveled and a
little the worse for wear. They are positioned such that they are able
to block or drown out the action of the play and the words of the
other actors.*)

HIATUS: Who is this wimp, and what's he going on
    About?

LACUNA: His name's Alcesimarchus, if I remember right,
    But I'm not sure. The wine I've drunk is making
    My head thump about as hard as you were thumping
    Me before you came, I mean, became a drunk
    Yourself, a boob sagging on my shoulders, sodden   300
    On my boobs, and three boobs is more than enough
    For any woman, if I remember right. And that reminds
    Me, Alcesimarchus is his name, and he's no wimp,
    He's just in love.

HIATUS: Love! And you say he's not
    A wimp? Say, can't we skip this part? What's he
    Doing anyway?

(ALCESIMARCHUS *goes to his door, where he speaks to the slave who
stops him at the threshold*)

LACUNA: He's talking to a slave,
   His slave, who is telling him that Selenium
   Left his house in a snit.

ANONYMOUS: . . . six days ago.

LACUNA: And now, he's so worried—look at him sweat—
   That he scarcely notices the slave leave.   310
   (He's going inside to tell Gymnasium the news.)
   Look at that face! Look at him knot his fist!
   I'll bet he's planning to bring her back by force,
   A typical man's solution to most problems of the heart.

HIATUS: You're pretty good at figuring these things out.
   I'm so pissed I can barely see, much less hear.
   What's happening now?

LACUNA: The slave's come back,
   And it looks like he's trying to calm the boy down.
   But I don't think he's succeeding at all.

ALCESIMARCHUS: Man, are you bad enough to do something
      bold?   320

ANONYMOUS: There are plenty of other bold types around.
   I myself am not particularly "bad," I must confess.

(HIATUS *farts very noisily*)

ANONYMOUS: But what does *that* mean?

ALCESIMARCHUS: I want to be punished—badly.

ANONYMOUS: For what?

ALCESIMARCHUS: For being alive.

ANONYMOUS: I'm easily "bad" enough
   For that, by God . . . if, of course, you wish.

ALCESIMARCHUS: I wish.

ANONYMOUS: On the other hand, there's always the chance
   You'll fist me one in the mouth and send me off
   Into my own private place.

ALCESIMARCHUS: Why, I would never do that!   330

ANONYMOUS: Do you promise?

ALCESIMARCHUS: I promise not to do it.
   In the first place, because I was able to stay
   Away from my girl all these days, I'm a nothing.

ANONYMOUS: Yes, by God, you are a real nothing!

ALCESIMARCHUS: When I loved her desperately, she loved me
      back.

ANONYMOUS: Dammit, you deserve every single thing you get!

ALCESIMARCHUS: So often I did so much that made her heart
      sore.

ANONYMOUS: You'll never be any good!

ALCESIMARCHUS: Especially since
   She made her promise to me in all good faith . . .

ANONYMOUS: From neither gods nor men do you deserve   340
   Anything good after this!

ALCESIMARCHUS: . . . when she was going
   To pass the rest of her days married to me . . .

ANONYMOUS: You ought to be chained up and never let loose!

ALCESIMARCHUS: . . . when she was entrusted to me and trusted
    me . . .

ANONYMOUS: Shit, I think you ought to be beaten with a stick!

ALCESIMARCHUS: . . . when she called me "little honey" and
    "deep-kiss"!

ANONYMOUS: For that word alone, you deserve ten lashes!

ALCESIMARCHUS: Oh, gladly! But what should I do right now?

ANONYMOUS: I'll tell you: make it up to her—
    Hang yourself, so she won't be angry with you!   350

HIATUS: Aren't these guys ever going to get it on—
    Either start the spanking or get on with the plot?
    Can't we fast-forward and see what happens?

LACUNA: Let me try to get you on . . .

HIATUS: Not that! Not now!

LACUNA: No, no, not that indeed. I know *that's* hopeless.
    What I was trying to say was let me try
    To get you on in the plot a bit, to get
    You straightened out . . .

HIATUS: No, not that, not again!

LACUNA: Get you straightened out about the plot,
    You numskull. Get your mind out of the gutter!   360

HIATUS: My mind's about to gutter out from all
    The getting on and out that's going on
    Around here.

LACUNA: Then get this straight, pal,
  Either you shut up or we go right back to the boy
  And the slave.

HIATUS: I'll be good. I'll be quiet.

LACUNA: I think I've got this straight now—not you,
  Not you—it's this way: Alcesimarchus
  Decides that Selenium will forgive him. The slave
  Of course, continues to crack wise—no cracks
  From you, Hiatus—and then Gymnasium comes out   370
  Of the house and tells Alcesimarchus just why
  Selenium actually left. She leaves, and just now
  There's a mysterious third man, Tertius,
  Who's just arrived. He tells the boy that he
  Ought to go see the girl, but this upsets him.

HIATUS: A "just" account.

LACUNA: I warned you . . . no cracks.

HIATUS: One crack was more than enough for me today.

ALCESIMARCHUS: Because . . .

LACUNA: What was that crack?

HIATUS: Mum's the word.

ANONYMOUS: Well, what are you . . .

(HIATUS *snorts loudly with muffled laughter*)

ANONYMOUS: . . . with her sleeve?

ALCESIMARCHUS: What if I'm in love?

(HIATUS *begins to laugh out loud*)

TERTIUS: . . . love is . . .

(HIATUS *howls with laughter*)

TERTIUS: . . . and that girl   380
   I understand you're in love with . . .

LACUNA: Will you
   Be quiet?

TERTIUS: . . . let me have you both thrown in jail . . .

HIATUS: Oh God, I can't help it. This third man's so hard to
   follow.

TERTIUS: Nothing but love, night and day . . .

LACUNA: You are the one,
   The only one that's making him so hard to follow.

TERTIUS: Unless dead . . .

HIATUS: *Me?* This guy makes no sense at all!

TERTIUS: Never anyone to me . . .

LACUNA;   Just be quiet,
   And give him a chance. He'll make a lot of sense.

TERTIUS: No indeed, the greatest. For those whose love
   Is silly, excessive, and downright shameless . . .   390

HIATUS: This guy's going to be promoting family values next.

TERTIUS: Ought not love at all.

LACUNA: For once, you're right.
   What a jerk!

ALCESIMARCHUS: Where are you?

ANONYMOUS: I'm here!

ALCESIMARCHUS: Go, bring me arms and a cuirass, too.

ANONYMOUS: Bring him a queer ass?

ALCESIMARCHUS: Go! Run!
   Get a horse!

ANONYMOUS: Oh, God! The poor man's insane!

ALCESIMARCHUS: Go on! And lots of spearmen, lots of
      skirmishers,
   Lots of lots—and no backtalk either!
   Where is what I ordered?

ANONYMOUS: This man is nuts!   400

TERTIUS: I believe the old dame has really hurt him
   From the way he's acting.

ANONYMOUS: Please I'm begging, are you
   Crazy or dream-walking—to order me to get
   A horse, to bring a queer ass, and lots of spearmint,
   And then lots of scrimmagers, lots with lots? That
   Is the crazy stuff you've been saying to me!

ALCESIMARCHUS: I said *that?* Please.

ANONYMOUS: By God, of course
   You said it, just here, just now!

ALCESIMARCHUS: Not in person, surely.

ANONYMOUS: You are a real trickster, if you're both here
   And not here!

TERTIUS: I see Love's slow poison your whole   410
   Bloodstream fills, young man, so I must warn
   You all the more.

ALCESIMARCHUS: Warn on.

TERTIUS: Make love, not war
   With Love, I'm warning you.

ALCESIMARCHUS: What shall I do?

TERTIUS: Go to her mother's house; spit it all out,
   Give her your word, flatter her, beg her, convince
   Her not to be mad at you.

ALCESIMARCHUS: By God, I'll let it all
   Hang out until I talk myself hoarse!

(ALCESIMARCHUS, ANONYMOUS, *and* TERTIUS *exit*)

HIATUS: Who's that?

LACUNA: Who? Oh, I see, that old gentleman,
   The one whose gleaming bald pate glows
   Like a hard, gemlike flame. I think   420
   He's Pater, the father of Alcesimarchus,
   The twitterpated young man who just left.

HIATUS: I do notice some things, then. For instance,
   I notice that bawdy babe with the funny name
   Has just come out of Alcesimarchus's door,
   But that the old man hasn't yet seen the whore,
   He's so busy talking to himself.

PATER: The amount
   Of money, the big dowry she's standing in the way of!

LACUNA: Don't you think that in his greedy rage, he's just
   About to mistake one whore for another?

HIATUS: You surprise me.   430

PATER: Now there's a well turned-out little babe! By God,
   A real looker! Even if I am an old gelding,
   I still believe I might manage a whinny or two
   To a little filly like her, if we could go one on one.

GYMNASIUM: (*To herself*) How lucky for me that Alcesimarchus
    has returned;
   There's no one who hates being alone more than I do.

PATER: (*To himself*) All you've got to do is call, and I'll be there.
   I guarantee you'll never walk alone:
   I'll come up with something to keep you stepping.

GYNMNASIUM: Too much! The way Alcesimarchus has fixed up
   this house!   440

PATER: When Venus steps in, of course it's swell; isn't love
   Always lovely?

GYMNASIUM: This house smells like Venus's spirit,
   Just because a lover furnished it.

PATER: It's not only
   That's she's so good-looking, but the lovely way
   She says the things she says! But not just how she says
   Them, but what she says. . . . By God, she's the one,
   The one who is corrupting my son! That's my opinion!
   Of course, I've never seen her, but it's my suspicion.
   And my suspicion is my belief! For this is the house
   My son rented, right there where she's standing.   450
   She's the one; I know it. And she mentioned his name.
   What if I just walk up and speak to her? Greetings,
   You damned, depraved jailbait!

LACUNA: Did you hear
  What that old fart is calling her?

GYMNASIUM: . . . will beat you up!

HIATUS: That's telling him, girly!

PATER: . . . at your house, eh?

GYMNASIUM: I'm going in; a call girl who stands alone
  On the street might be taken for a common whore.

HIATUS: She's wise for her years.

LACUNA: Hush.

GYMNASIUM: . . . what you want.

PATER: I want you to tell me whatever . . .

HIATUS: Whatever what?

PATER: What harm have I or my family ever done to you,   460
  Please explain, that you are being such a predator
  And terminator to my son and his mother and all we have?

GYMNASIUM: (*To herself*) I knew it! The poor thing is totally
    mistaken.
  What an elegant chance to have some fun with him
  Now that I see the occasion.
  (*Aloud*)
                Won't you stop
  Being so mean to a perfectly innocent girl?

PATER: But I implore you, haven't you got another lover
  Besides my single only son?

GYMNASIUM: I certainly do not.
   Not a single other one.

PATER: But I . . .

HIATUS: Butthead, he means.

GYMNASIUM: I have nothing to say to you.   470
   You are nothing but trouble to women like me.

PATER: What . . .

HIATUS: Can't we fast-forward this guy?

LACUNA: Not for years . . . but he might make more sense
   Right now if you'd just let him say his piece.

HIATUS: I want nothing to do with his piece.

GYMANSIUM: Is this what he thought?

HIATUS: Give me a break. I can't bear to listen to this
   Any longer. I promise to straighten up my own piece
   If you'll get me through all this more quickly.

LACUNA: Just stand up and do your part when I tell you to again
   And I'll straighten you out in more ways than one.

HIATUS: A deal's a deal, but delete the dull parts.   480

LACUNA: Okay, look. I'll help things along. The old man's
   Not so upset about the bleak future of his lone son
   That he doesn't compound his boner with another boner,
   Both having to do with Gymnasium: first, who she is,
   And then, just look at the size of that thing!
   Who would have thought the old man to have
   So much blood in him?

HIATUS: Not me, that's for sure.
But what's happening now?

LACUNA: He's propositioned her,
I think, and she's responding professionally to it.

GYMNASIUM: You old gentlemen usually give the loveliest   490
Little rewards.

LACUNA: And now she's called out her mother
To make the necessary financial arrangements.

ARENA: You want my word of honor? The nerve! The thing
I do is to get my agreements *from* men—
That's how I get my money—not from making promises
To men.

LACUNA: She's blunt but very smooth, it seems to me.
But what's she saying now?

ARENA: . . . that is, should you
Make requests according to your riches, or according to
The small means you have . . .

HIATUS: It's getting kinky.

LACUNA: And from the looks of his equipment, I don't think   500
His means are small. They've cut the deal. They're leaving.
She's forgotten all about her promise to Selenium.

ARENA: Go on, go on if you are going! You're just shuffling along.

GYMNASIUM: It's the gods' truth, Mother, that I've had more
exercise
On my back than up and running. No wonder I'm so slow.

LACUNA: And off they go, leaving Alcesimarchus's house all alone,
But Demipho's slave Lampadio (remember him?)

Shows up, snooping around and mumbling to himself,
Making no sense to me at all.

LAMPADIO: They remember their duty . . . um, um . . . how
    the scent   510
Of new wine reached my nose . . . um, um . . . with chopped
Hair and clipped ears . . . cleaning out these mean streets
Like an executioner's . . . not the sort that are here now:
Slugs; bruised, feverish, miserable women;
Bony, penny-a-tumble, cheap-perfumed monstrosities
With swollen ankles, with thighs like a bird . . . um, um.

HIATUS: That's plain talk!

LACUNA: Pig talk, you mean, but he's not
    Totally pig-stupid. He's recognized Arena as the woman
Who found Selenium, and off he goes after them
Like a bloodhound. But here comes everybody!   520
It's Alcesimarchus with Selenium and Melaenis, her mom,
In tow, and she's clearly gotten to her daughter's ear.
Listen.

SELENIUM: You bother me.

ALCESIMARCHUS: My house wishes for its little mistress.
    Let me take her home.

SELENIUM: Don't touch me!

ALCESIMARCHUS: My own little sister!

SELENIUM: I reject you as my little brother.

ALCESIMARCHUS: Then, *you* then,
    My little mother.

MELAENIS: I reject you as my little boy.

ALCESIMARCHUS: I beg you . . .

SELENIUM: Good-bye.

ALCESIMARCHUS: to allow me . . .

SELENIUM: I'm not listening.

ALCESIMARCHUS: To clear myself.

HIATUS: What will she say?

LACUNA: She said it while you were asking.   530

ALCESIMARCHUS: Let me make my plea.

MELAENIS: I've had my fill of your perjuries.

HIATUS: What? Is this citizens' court now?

LACUNA: If it is,
    I'm hauling you up for contempt if you don't shut up.

MELAENIS: . . . But now it's impossible.

ALCESIMARCHUS: I want to fall on my knees to you.

SELENIUM: That's one prayer I don't care to hear.

ALCESIMARCHUS: See!
    I'm undergoing every known punishment. Poor me!

SELENIUM: Rightly so, and you deserve no pity either.
    (*Begins to mumble*)
    Although a man . . . to tell lies . . . not those things . . .
    Who break promises . . . them.

HIATUS: Excuse me,
But are we having problems with the sound here? 540

LACUNA: She's just upset, and, see, there she goes away.

SELENIUM: . . . You will give.

ALCESIMARCHUS: But I won't, and I won't let you go
Today unless you will listen to what I have to say.

MELAENIS: Can't you stop yourself from molesting people?

ALCESIMARCHUS: Why not!
It's my name; all living beings call me that: Molester!
Please!

MELAENIS: Don't "please" me! Because without all . . .

ALCESIMARCHUS: I swear to you . . .

MELAENIS: But I've come to beware the
sworn oaths
Of people like you; lovers' most serious pledges
Are nothing but total confusion.

ALCESIMARCHUS: Those who don't know . . . 550

MELAENIS: You are being completely silly!

ALCESIMARCHUS: I'll take my punishment . . .
In the way I . . .

HIATUS: In the way you make no sense at all.
Am I sobering up or getting drunker? This stuff
Makes no sense to me at all.

LACUNA: My love!
You are coming to your senses, and soon you'll get

Your just reward. But first let's listen to these two
Trying to get their problems straightened out.
You see, Alcesimarchus does love Selenium
And wants to marry her, but her mother doesn't trust
Him or his motives one little bit. Why should she?   560
She's been around.

HIATUS: Around the world more than once,
   I'd say.

LACUNA: Now you stand up straight and bear with me
   While I hear this part, and then I'll let you get bare
   With me in that lovely house just across the way.

HIATUS: I'm all ears.

LACUNA: I hope not.

MELAENIS: . . . because you've found
   Another girl who . . . a girl who . . . you know.

ALCESIMARCHUS: May the gods destroy her, too . . . if I am ever
   Untrue in this.

MELAENIS: I have nothing to say . . .

HIATUS: You said
   A mouthful there!

LACUNA: You'd better shut your mouth
   If you want me to shut mine on something soon.   570
   Know what I mean?

HIATUS: More than I know what they mean,
   But mum's the word, although mumble's more like it.

MELAENIS: You're a false cheat, so you . . . faith doesn't even
   know.

Let's put it this way: you may fool me
But you'll never fool the gods.

ALCESIMARCHUS: But I swear
By the gods that I will marry her.

MELAENIS: Marry, if . . .
Now if it suits you, sure . . .

ALCESIMARCHUS: I covered her
With jewels and clothes.

HIATUS: I'll bet he covered her.

MELAENIS: If you were in love . . . to cover her.

HIATUS: What say?

MELAENIS: But never mind.

HIATUS: Thanks.

MELAENIS: Just answer this one question   580
I'm going to ask: you covered her just as you wished?

HIATUS: Lacuna, I've heard enough.

ALCESIMARCHUS: . . . what I wish.

HIATUS: What I wish is to leave these bores to themselves.
They're on their own. The time has come for us
To go. We've covered for them enough already.
Let them seek the aid of Auxilium, god of helpfulness,
Or just let them take in each other as they will.

LACUNA: You've certainly straightened up your act.
Your whole demeanor's changed. I think I'll take
You in again.

HIATUS: I stand ready.

LACUNA: Then, lay on   590
    And damn'd be him that first cries, "Hold, enough!"

(LACUNA *and* HIATUS *exit*)

MELAENIS: You speak so easily only because you're engaged to
        another,
    A rich girl from Lemnia. Keep her! We aren't upper class
    Like you, nor are we so rich, but still I have no fear
    That anyone will doubt our word. You, however, if you
    Do suffer, you will know just why you are in pain.

ALCESIMARCHUS: God damn me . . .

MELAENIS: Whatever you wish, may it happen.

ALCESIMARCHUS: . . . If I ever marry the woman my father has
        engaged me to.

MELAENIS: And me as well, if I ever let you marry my daughter.

ALCESIMARCHUS: You'll permit me to perjure myself?

MELAENIS: I surely will,   600
    And more easily than I'll permit my business to go to hell
    And my daughter to be made into a joke. Look somewhere
    Else for someone to believe your promises. With us,
    Alcesimarchus, you've already torn up your ticket
    Of admission.

ALCESIMARCHUS: Try me just once.

MELAENIS: I've tried you more
    Than once, and I didn't like it.

ALCESIMARCHUS: Give her back to me.

MELAENIS: To give an old proverb a new job: "What I gave, I
     gave;
   What I didn't give, I won't give."

ALCESIMARCHUS: Then you're not
   Going to return her to me?

MELAENIS: You said it for me.

ALCESIMARCHUS: You're not going to give her back?

MELAENIS: You already know   610
   The answer to that one.

ALCESIMARCHUS: It's already settled in your heart?

MELAENIS: If you've heard it, I've said it.

ALCESIMARCHUS: By God, my ears have caught
   Not a single one of your words.

MELAENIS: No? What are
   They catching then? You'd better spread them and catch
   What you're doing now.

ALCESIMARCHUS: And so may all the gods and goddesses,
   Superior, inferior, and mediocre, and so may Juno,
   The wife and daughter of Supreme Jove, so may
   Saturn, his uncle . . .

MELAENIS: His father, you mean.

ALCESIMARCHUS: . . . so may
   Opulent Ops, his grandmother . . .

MELAENIS: No, she's his mother!

ALCESIMARCHUS: Juno, his daughter, and Saturn, his father's
    brother,   620
And Jupiter above. . . . You put a spell on me;
You're the cause of all these mistakes.

MELAENIS: Tell me
  About it.

ALCESIMARCHUS: Aren't you going to tell me? Tell me
  What you're thinking now?

MELAENIS: I definitely will not
  Send her back.

ALCESIMARCHUS: To be sure, so may Jupiter, so may Juno,
  So may Janus, so may . . . I don't know what to say.
  Now I know! Yes, lady, listen, so that you may know
  What I mean. May all the gods, big ones and little ones,
  Even the platter gods, keep me from living long enough
  To kiss Selenium again, unless I slaughter you   630
  And your daughter and myself this very day, and then
  Unless, at dawn's early light, I kill you both tomorrow,
  And, by God, unless, on my third attack, I kill everybody—
  If you don't send her back to me! I have spoken! Farewell!

(*He exits into the house*)

MELAENIS: Gone indoors in a rage! What shall I do now?
  If she goes back to him, we'll be in the same fix
  As before; once he gets bored with her, he'll dump her
  And marry that Lemnian woman. But still, I'll keep on the
    chase.
  I've got to be careful that he doesn't do anything foolish.
  And, since justice is for the rich and it's the poor who get   640
  The blame, I'd rather lose some time than lose my daughter.
  But who's that coming down the street in such a rush?
  I'm afraid of what's going to happen, but this really scares me!
  I'm such a poor thing, afraid from head to toe!

Scene 2

LAMPADIO: (*Entering on the run*)
  I clambered and clamored after the old broad
  Through streets and alleys. Really worried her. She fought
  Hard not to remember that most immemorial year.
  How many blandishments, how many good things I promised,
  How many fabrications, how many lies as I grilled her!
  I just barely managed to get her tongue swinging   650
  By promising to present her with a whole cask of wine.

Scene 3

PHANOSTRATA: (*Entering from her house*)
  I thought I just heard the voice of my servant Lampadio
  From out here.

LAMPADIO: You aren't deaf, mistress. You heard me.

PHANOSTRATA: What are you doing here?

LAMPADIO: Something to delight you

PHANOSTRATA: What is it?

LAMPADIO: A little while ago, I saw a woman
  Leaving that house.

PHANOSTRATA: The one who carried off my baby?

LAMPADIO: You've got it!

PHANOSTRATA: What happened?

LAMPADIO: I told her how I saw
Her pick up my mistress's daughter at the Hippodrome.
That really scared her!

MELAENIS: I'm shaking all over!
My heart just skipped a beat! Because I remember   660
That it was from the Hippodrome that the little girl was
    brought
To me, the one I reared as my own.

PHANOSTRATA: Go on, go on,
Please! My very soul is yearning to hear how things
Turned out.

MELAENIS: Would that you couldn't hear a thing!

HIATUS: (*Enters, adjusting his clothing*)
Anything for a break, even listening to all this gossip!
That Lacuna is the abyss of women, the ocean floor.
She cannot be filled up even after you've shifted
Your whole load into her. I told her I had to take
A piss, although I'm too sore even to try to try.
What I need is a bowl of Wheaties or something.   670
But anyway, she told me not to interrupt these two,
And now I've gone and done it. But they're too occupied
With each other to notice. What you couldn't hear
Is that the slave followed the old woman home
Where he met Gymnasium, but he thought she was Selenium.
He's telling this other old lady that now.

LACUNA: (*Offstage*) Are you talking to someone out there? I told
    you to be quick.
The river of my love is in full flood, high water.
Come back to the raft, Hiatus honey.

HIATUS: (*Exiting*)   Although I may
Never come again, I'm coming, dear.   680

LAMPADIO: So I say to her: "That old dame is inviting you
   To follow her from riches to rags. She's not your mom;
   She's only your foster mother. Let me return you
   And restore you to super riches, to your proper place
   In a fancy family where your father will surely give
   You an enormous dowry. For this is not a place
   Where you'd have to follow the Tuscan habit
   And earn your dowry on your back."

PHANOSTRATA: Is she, dear man,
   The woman who stole her, is she then a prostitute?

LAMPADIO: Not now, but she was. Let me go on with
      the story.   690
   I was just winning the girl over, very persuasive,
   When the old woman grabbed her around the knees, teary
   And begging her not to desert her. She swore
   To me that she was her child and that she herself
   Had given birth to her. "She's not," she said, "the one
   You're looking for; I gave that one to a friend of mine
   To rear as her own daughter. And she's alive,"
   She says. And, quick as a wink, I say, "Where is she?"

PHANOSTRATA: God save me, I beg you.

MELAENIS: But me, you're destroying!

PHANOSTRATA: You should have asked to whom she
      gave her.   700

LAMPADIO: I did ask, and she said to Melaenis, a madam.

MELAENIS: He practically shouted my name. Now I'm done for.

LAMPADIO: As soon as she announced the name, I
      questioned her.
   "Where does she live? I said. "Lead me there and show me."
   "She's gone away," she said, "to live abroad."

MELAENIS: That splashes a little cold water on things.

LAMPADIO: "Wherever she went, we'll follow her. So don't try
    That kind of lie. By God, you've had it if you don't
    Tell me where she lives right now!" Be damned
    If I didn't hang right in there until the old dame   710
    Swore she'd show me.

PHANOSTRATA: But you shouldn't have let her go.

LAMPADIO: She's safe. But she said she wanted to see some
     woman
    First, one of her friends who has a common interest
    In this business. And I know she'll come.

MELAENIS: She'll finger me,
    And hook her own woes to mine, the bitch, and allow
    Selenium to discover how I've deceived her.

PHANOSTRATA: What
    Do you want me to do now?

LAMPADIO: Go inside and keep
    Your chin up. If your husband comes, tell him to wait
    At home, where I can find him if I need him. I'll run
    Back to the old woman again.

PHANOSTRATA: Lampadio, I beg you,   720
    Take care.

LAMPADIO: I shall handle this business to perfection.

PHANOSTRATA: I put my trust in you and in the gods.

LAMPADIO: I'll put mine
    In the same place—as soon as you go home.

(PHANOSTRATA *exits*)

MELAENIS: Young man, stop and listen!

LAMPADIO: Are you speaking to me, woman?

MELAENIS: To you.

LAMPADIO: What do you want? I am more than busy.

MELAENIS: Who lives there?

LAMPADIO: My master, Demipho.

MELAENIS: Isn't he the one who has arranged such a rich match
   For his daughter with Alcesimarchus?

LAMPADIO: He's the one.

MELAENIS: Hold it you! Who, then, is this other daughter   730
   You all are looking for now?

LAMPADIO: I'll tell you:
   Not his daughter by his wife, but his wife's daughter.

MELAENIS: What's that supposed to mean?

LAMPADIO: She's my master's
   Daughter by a previous woman, so to speak.

MELAENIS: Didn't
   You just now say that you were looking for the daughter
   Of the woman who was talking to you here?

LAMPADIO: I did indeed.

MELAENIS: Then, God help me, how is she a "previous woman"
   If she's now his wife?

LAMPADIO: You're wearing me out with words,
  Woman, whoever you are. The middle woman he was
      married to,
  She's the mother of the daughter who's engaged to
      Alcesimarchus.   740
  That wife died. Now do you get it?

MELAENIS: That much I get.
  What I fundamentally don't get is how the previous one
  Is the posterior, and the posterior, the previous?

LAMPADIO: He raped
  This woman before he took her home as his wife; so before
      that,
  She was pregnant and gave birth to a daughter; and after the
      birth
  She ordered the baby to be thrown away. I myself
      abandoned her,
  And I watched another woman pick her up. Afterwards, my
      master
  Married her. And now we're looking for that girl, her daughter.
  But why are you twisting your neck looking up at the sky?

MELAENIS: Go on about your busy business. Don't let me
      keep you.   750
  I understand now.

LAMPADIO: Thank God—for if you hadn't figured it out,
  I don't believe you'd have ever let me go.

(*He exits*)

MELAENIS: Now I've got
  No choice but to be good, whether I want to or not.
  Everything is known. So I'll see to it that I get
  All the thanks and keep her from telling on me.
  I'll go home and bring Selenium back to her folks.

ACT III

(*Enter* MELAENIS, SELENIUM, *and* HALISCA)

MELAENIS: I've told you everything; walk this way, Selenium,
    So that you'll belong to those you ought to
    Rather than to me. Parting with you is such sweet sorrow,
    But I'm resolved to do it for the good it will do you.   760
    (*She reveals a little box*)
    In here are the toys you had with you when that woman
    First brought you to me; she gave them to me so that
    Your parents might recognize you more easily. Halisca,
    Take this little box. Then knock at that door.
    Say that I want someone to come out here right now.

ALCESIMARCHUS: (*Entering from his house with sword in hand*)
    Receive me, Death, your friend and well-wisher!

SELENIUM: Mama!
    How awful!

ALCESIMARCHUS: Shall I stick it on this side or on the left?

MELAENIS: (To SELENIUM) What's your problem?

SELENIUM: Don't you see
    Alcesimarchus?
    He's got a sword!   770

ALCESIMARCHUS: What are you doing: Killing time and not
    yourself?
    Go on and leave the light of day!

SELENIUM: Run! Help him!
    Please! He'll kill himself!

(*She and the others run to him,* HALISCA *dropping the little box*)

ALCESIMARCHUS: (*To* SELENIUM)   O Salvation who saves
  Me, my savior! Only you can make the darkness bright!
  Only you can make this change in me, my destiny; I live
  Whether I want to live or not!

MELAENIS: Were you really
  Going to do something so violent?

ALCESIMARCHUS: I've nothing to say
  To you—to you, I'm dead! But she is mine,
  And I'll never let her go, for, by God, she's mine,
  Crazy-glued to me from this moment on! Slaves,   780
  Where are you? Shut the doors and bar and bolt them
  As soon as I've carried her over the threshold!

(*He exits, carrying* SELENIUM)

MELAENIS: He's gone! He's carried off the woman! I'll go,
  I'll go after him right now and tell him all I know
  And see if I can't change his rage into tranquility.

(MELAENIS *and* HALISCA *follow him into the house*)

ACT IV

Scene 1

LAMPADIO: I don't believe I've ever seen a more excruciating
  Old broad than this one. Now she denies what she
  Just admitted to me. But look, there's my mistress!
  But what is this? Why is this little box
  Filled with toys lying here, and with no one else   790
  Visible in the street? I'll do a child's duty;
  I'll squat on the box.

PHANOSTRATA: What are you doing, Lampadio?

LAMPADIO: This little box—does it come from our house? It was
   Lying here by the door when I picked it up.

PHANOSTRATA: What news
   Do you have about the old woman?

LAMPADIO: That there's no one worse
   In the whole world. She denies everything that she just
   Confessed. For me, by God, to let that old bag
   Get the laugh on me is worse than any kind of death
   You'd pick.

PHANOSTRATA: (*Looking into the little box*)
          God, be merciful!

LAMPADIO: Why are you calling to God?

PHANOSTRATA: Save us!

LAMPADIO: What's the matter?

PHANOSTRATA: These are the toys   800
   My baby girl had with her when you left her to die.

LAMPADIO: Have you lost your senses?

PHANOSTRATA: They truly are.

LAMPADIO: Go on!

PHANOSTRATA: They are!

LAMPADIO: If any other woman talked to me that way,
   I'd say she was drunk.

PHANOSTRATA: No, by heaven, I do remember.

LAMPADIO: So, for heaven's sake, from where in the world
     Did it come? Did some express god deliver it
     Directly to our door, for some reason, right on time?

PHANOSTRATA: Heavenly Hope, help me!

Scene 2

HALISCA: (*Entering from* ALCESIMARCHUS's *house*)
     If the gods don't help me now, I'm done for, with no one   810
     To whom to lift up my eyes for help. My own carelessness
     Has made me so miserable! And how I fear for my own back
     If my mistress finds out just how careless I've been!
     I know I had that little box in my hands right here
     In front of the house. I don't know where it can be unless
     I dropped it somewhere around here. You good folks,
     My spectators, please tell me if you saw it, saw anyone
     Pick it up or carry it away. Did he go this way
     Or that way? I'm none the wiser for asking these fools,
     Or bothering them; they always like to see a woman
          in a fix.   820
     Now I'll look to see if there are any footprints.
     For if no one came by here after I went indoors,
     The little box would still be here. Why look here?
     I'm done for. I know it. It's over for poor unlucky me.
     It's nowhere, and I'm there, too! It's lost and me with it!
     But as I've started, I'll continue; I'll keep looking.
     I'm shaking on the inside, and terrified on the outside,
     Fear on both sides tossing me up and down.
     What wretched wretches human beings are!
     I'll bet he's happy, whoever he is, that has it—   830
     Of no use to him, but plenty to me. But I'm not helping
     Myself by not getting to it. Halisca, pay attention
     To what you're doing; look at the ground and all around.
     Focus like a laser beam; see like a seer.

LAMPADIO: Mistress!

PHANOSTRATA: Oh, what is it?

LAMPADIO: That's her.

PHANOSTRATA: That's who?

LAMPADIO: Who dropped the little box.

PHANOSTRATA: She surely is.
   She's looking for the place she dropped it. That's certain.

HALISCA: But he went this way; I see the print of his big shoe
   In the dust; I'll follow him this way. Here he stopped   840
   With someone else. And here I see a only a confusion.
   No, he didn't go forward this way, but he stopped here.
   And from here, he went over there. And talked to someone.
   So, there are two people involved; that's for sure.
   Oh! Now I can see the footprints of only one person.
   But he went this way. Let me see. He went from here
   To over there, and from over there to . . . nowhere.
   And I'm getting nowhere fast. What's lost is lost:
   The skin on my back along with the little box.
   I'd better go back inside.

PHANOSTRATA: You, woman, wait!   850
   Some people would like to meet you.

HALISCA: Who's calling me back?

LAMPADIO: A good woman and a bad man want you.

HALISCA: A good man
   May be hard to find, but this bad man does seem
   To know more about what he wants than this woman
   He's calling does. Back I go.

LAMPADIO: What were
   You looking for?

HALISCA: Greetings to you, sir and madam.

PHANOSTRATA: And to you. But what are you looking for?

HALISCA: I'm tracing footprints, trying to find where something
   Disappeared.

LAMPADIO: What is it? Whatever is it?

HALISCA: Something to bring bad luck to others and worse luck
   To my family.

LAMPADIO: She's bad goods, madam, and sly, too.   860

PHANOSTRATA: Heaven knows, she seems so.

LAMPADIO: She is imitating a bad
   And destructive animal.

PHANOSTRATA: For goodness sake, which one?

LAMPADIO: A caterpillar, which twists itself up in young vine
      leaves.
   That's the same way she's trying to twist this story up.
   Now, what are you looking for?

HALISCA: A little box, young man,
   Flew away from me here.

LAMPADIO: You ought to have put it in a cage.

HALISCA: My stars, it was no great prize!

LAMPADIO: It wouldn't surprise me
   If there were a troop of runaway slaves in that little box.

PHANOSTRATA: Do let her speak.

LAMPADIO: If she only would.

PHANOSTRATA: Now tell us
  What was in it?

HALISCA: Only toys.

LAMPADIO: There's a certain man   870
  Who claims to know where it is.

HALISCA: Well, for goodness sake,
  There's a certain woman who would be very grateful if he
  Would show it to her.

LAMPADIO: Well, this certain man would like
  A reward given to him.

HALISCA: Well, by heaven, this certain woman
  Who lost the little box has nothing to give
  The certain man.

LAMPADIO: Well, it seems that this certain man
  Might well prefer another kind of reward better than money.

HALISCA: Well, heaven knows, this certain woman makes a point
  Of not supplying certain kinds of rewards for free.

LAMPADIO: How convenient for the certain woman! But you have
    advanced   880
  Your cause this time. We admit that we have the little box.

HALISCA: Good fortune keep you both! Where is it now?

PHANOSTRATA: See, it's safe! But I want to talk with you
  About a secret matter of grave importance to me.
  I'm picking you as my partner in my deliverance.

HALISCA: What secret matter? Who are you?

PHANOSTRATA: I am the mother
    Of the girl who had these things with her.

HALISCA: Then you live here?

PHANOSTRATA: You must be psychic. But, please,
    Woman, no more riddles. Just get to the point: quickly,
    Where did you get those toys?

HALISCA: My mistress's daughter   890
    Had them with her.

LAMPADIO: Liar! Mine had them, not yours.

PHANOSTRATA: Take a chill pill!

LAMPADIO: My lips are sealed.

PHANOSTRATA: Go on, woman.
    Where's the one who had them?

HALISCA: Here, next door.

PHANOSTRATA: My God! My husband's son-in-law lives there,
    doesn't he?
    (LAMPADIO *clears his throat*)
    I told you to chill out! Please tell me more.
    How old is she said to be?

HALISCA: Seventeen.

PHANOSTRATA: She is
    My own!

LAMPADIO: Given her age, she surely is.

HALISCA: In that case,
  Madam, I'm looking forward to my half of the reward.

LAMPADIO: But, by God, madam, aren't there three of us
    in this?   900
  I'm looking forward to my third!

PHANOSTRATA: I've already found
  What I was looking forward to—my daughter.

(HIATUS *and* LACUNA, *even more disheveled, enter and listen
quietly*)

HALISCA: It's only
  Right that what was once trusted to you in good faith
  Should be given back, so that a kindness should not turn out
  To be a source of badness. She is our foster child
  And surely your daughter. . . .

HIATUS: Don't call her Shirley.

LACUNA: Jerk! But it does look like things have worked out
  While we were otherwise occupied.

HIATUS: Good things do happen
  To those who open and toy with little boxes,
  It seems. Certainly that's been true in my case.

LACUNA: Jerk off!   910

HIATUS: No way. You've made my day, and I'm the first to say it.

LACUNA: Then, if that's the case, my love, come with me
  This way.

HIATUS: Of course, we could stay and watch the ending
  Of the play.

LACUNA: You've seen enough. Back inside we go.
  If the play's the thing, it's time to play again—my way.

(LACUNA *exits, pulling* HIATUS *after her*)

HALISCA: . . . And my mistress is about to give her back to you;
  She left home for that purpose. But, I beg you, please
  Ask her about all the rest. I'm only a servant.

PHANOSTRATA: That's only fair.

HALISCA: I'd rather she gets the credit.
  But I beg you to give the little box back to me.   920

PHANOSTRATA: What should I do, Lampadio?

LAMPADIO: What is yours, keep as yours.

PHANOSTRATA: But I feel sorry for her.

LAMPADIO: Here's what I think you
    ought
  To do: give her the little box, but go inside
  With her.

PHANOSTRATA: I'll follow your advice. Here, you take
  The little box yourself. Let's go in. But what
  Is your mistress's name?

HALISCA: Melaenis.

PHANOSTRATA: After you, my dear.
  I'll follow right after.

ACT V

DEMIPHO: What is this business that everyone's talking about
   All over town—that my daughter has been found? They also
   Say that Lampadio has been looking for me in the forum.   930

LAMPADIO: (*Enters*) Master, where have you come from?

DEMIPHO: From a senate meeting.

LAMPADIO: I am happy to report that, thanks to me, your family
   Has grown larger.

DEMIPHO: Well, that doesn't please me!
   I do not care for the efforts of others increasing
   My family! But what's all this about?

LAMPADIO: Hurry up.
   Go into your new in-laws' house, and you'll soon meet
   Your daughter inside. Your wife's in there as well.
   Go quickly.

DEMIPHO: This certainly comes before everything else!

SPEAKING FOR THE CAST

LACUNA: I suppose it's only fitting since I had the first word
   That I should take the last.

HIATUS: And true to your nature.   940

LACUNA: I wouldn't be too eager to bring up other folks' natures
   When you seem to be having so much trouble bringing things
   Up on your own.

HIATUS: Don't be so touchy. I'm done.

LACUNA: You sure are, poor thing. I think it's time for bed
   For you.

HIATUS: But haven't we just come from there?

LACUNA: We may have come, but now it's time to go.
   But before we do go to a well-earned rest,
   I guess it's only fair to Plautus that we
   Close the play the way he wanted with a group farewell.

HIATUS: Since, as you said, you did begin, why don't
    you end?   950

LACUNA: As you said I said, we've only come to say
   We really must be going, but before we go:
   Spectators, don't bother to wait for the rest of the cast
   To come out here to you; not a one of them will.
   They'll all do their business backstage, and when
   That's done, they'll take off their clothes . . . costumes.
   And then the actor who blew his lines will get
   A beating, and the one who didn't, a drink or two.
   Now as to what's left—that, spectators, is for you
   To do, the way it's always been done, please lend   960
   Our comedy a big hand at this its very end.

PSEUDOLUS

Translated by Richard Beacham

PSEUDOLUS

Translated by Richard Beacham

INTRODUCTION

The *Pseudolus*, which was first performed in 191 B.C., has frequently been called Plautus's masterpiece. Cicero suggested that it was the playwright's own favorite work, and certainly, it has long been popular with audiences; it still held the stage at Rome a century and a half after its composition and has frequently been revived in the modern era. Its popularity is not difficult to explain. In no other extant work are the particular skills of the Father of Farce more exuberantly obvious. Indeed his evident desire to please a restive Roman audience (to whom the very concept of scripted comedy was relatively new) resulted in a virtuoso display of what we now consider the most characteristic qualities of Plautine farce. A brief description of some of these may also therefore serve as an introduction to the play.

The comic characters found in his Greek models are in Plautus's hands more vigorously drawn and more cynically motivated. In place of subtle characterization, Plautus tends to prefer caricatures, whose language is cruder, more ribald, and playful, but also much richer in complex and sometimes fantastical imagery. The dramatic personae of the *Pseudolus* reads like a who's who of such stock characters, from the simple-minded young lover, Calidorus, through the villainous pimp Ballio and stern father Simo, to the clever, calculating slave of the title role. Plautus's employment of such devices as soliloquies and overheard conversations is also amply displayed, as is his love of disguises and crude deception, slapstick, a certain preference for fooling over the development of emotional interest, and a fondness for a festive conclusion.

It has been noted by critics that one of the recurrent conceits of Plautus's plays is that the characters make up the comedy as they go along: they contrive the very plot in which they take a part. Probably this directly reflects the legacy of a more tentative dramatic fare: improvised, nonliterary entertainments long favored by his audience, which the actors are thought to have assembled on the basis of stock characters and situations, some well-worn but ever-popular bits of comic business, and the barest outline of a scenario. We trace the influence of such performances in Plautus's deliberate choice to make believe that his own plays are unscripted, taking shape in the presence of an audience that in turn assists in their formation. The *Pseudolus* has many such instances, as well as a refusal to attempt to maintain dramatic illusion in the usual sense of the conventions of realism; characters frequently acknowledge the audience, their own function as actors, and the play itself.

This sense of theatrical self-awareness permeates the play. To cite a single example, at one point, the old man Simo openly disdains to play his conventional role: "Now I think I'll prepare a little reception for Pseudolus. Not that nonsense with clubs and whips you normally see in most comedies. No, I'm going right inside and fetch the twenty *minae* I promised Pseudolus if he brought this off." The chief agent of such self-consciousness is usually the clever slave—of which Pseudolus is the prime example—who fashions the play around him to become simultaneously its author and hero. He fills this role by virtue of his wit and intelligence—even explicitly warning his master of how he plans to trick him—triumphing over adversity and the social facts of life in a way that no actual Roman slave could ever be seen to do. Like other slaves in Plautine comedy, Pseudolus can get away with it since all the plots and characters are notionally set safely in Greece, and ultimately in the even more remote world of topsy-turvydom where anything goes. Since there is no real offense, there is no real punishment. The clever slave enjoys impunity. In the surviving plays nothing dire ever actually happens to him despite circumstances of ever-present danger and threats of imminent torture.

I referred earlier to Plautus as the Father of Farce, whose characters, situations, and types of humor have been a staple of Western tradition and practice. But there is a still closer modern theatrical form analogous to the works of Plautus, and that is musical comedy. All of his works contain extensive sung passages, and in the course of his career, the percentage of musical content steadily increased. The use of lyric meters and song are not characteristic of the earlier Greek plays that Plautus took as his models, and which he so substantially adapted. The innovations are his and earn for him an additional claim to fame: the Father of Musical Comedy. Unfortunately, although the text can indicate to us where songs occurred, and their words and metrical pattern, the actual music itself is totally lost. But clearly, in seeking to revive Plautine comedy on the modern stage, the decisive role of music in structuring and modulating the performance of the work and its perception by an audience should be taken into account.

When I prepared the *Pseudolus* for staging, I attempted to turn it back into musical comedy. Of course, this genre has evolved a great deal since Plautus, and borrowing from its conventions inevitably involved compromise—both of those conventions and of the Plautine text itself. The *Pseudolus* contains five extensive *cantica* or sung passages. In my version each of these was rendered into one or more numbers. In addition, I inserted songs at those points in the plot where the conventions of musical comedy today would suggest one—a love duet between the protagonists, for example; a song deftly and efficiently revealing the emotional state of a character or highlighting a particularly significant juncture in the plot.

The music itself, prepared in collaboration with a composer-colleague, was original and modern, although we employed a great variety of styles and idioms to echo the metrical variety, linguistic styles, and parodies of other forms of theater employed by Plautus. In some cases (e.g., the pimp Ballio's entrance number, "Worthy of a Whopping Whipping"), we were able to compose songs by giving musical settings to lyrics that were a close translation of Plautus's text. In others, we used a single line or two from the text as the point of departure or opening phrase of a song whose ideas were then expanded and developed using extraneous material. In a few cases, we simply interrupted the Plautine text and introduced a song entirely of our own devising, with only the precedent that this was exactly the type of interpolation Plautus frequently allows his characters—to stop the action for jokes, irrelevant commentary, or banter, while in actual presentation such impromptu additions were probably an important element of the performance style.

"Musicalizing" the *Pseudolus* did allow me to iron out a few dramaturgical wrinkles in the text. For example, although the plot centers on the efforts of Pseudolus to assist his somewhat half-witted master, Calidorus, in tricking the evil pimp into releasing Calidorus's sweetheart, Phoenicium, the young lovers never have a scene alone together or exchange a single word. Indeed, Phoenicium remains mute throughout. So I gave them a love duet, and later had Phoenicium sing a torch song where the music carried the main burden of emotional expression. I also used an opening, end of act, and closing chorus to frame the play and make it self-conscious in a manner entirely true to Plautus's own approach. These additions to the script, which I mention to indicate the type of liberties that might be appropriate to a particular production, have not been included in the translation here, which adheres closely to the original Latin text.

My purpose in preparing this and other plays by Plautus for production was to enhance its appeal in contemporary production while respecting the meaning, method, and mood of the original text. My wish, which I commend to readers of this and the other translations in this volume, was to evaluate the texts not simply as literature to read but as scripts to be performed. Plautus's works, properly understood, are scenarios for actions in time and space whose meaning can only truly be understood or read when these scripts are allowed to take on shape, movement, and sound within an appropriate space in the conspiring presence of an audience, at the moment of performance. The meaning of a theater text is not simply in what the words say, but in the context they create, in the actions that inform the words, in the flow of rhythm and emotion, and tension and energy that they regulate, and even at times in the very sounds they make. Even on the page the texts demonstrate that Plautus was a virtuoso composer of such acts of theater; reconstituted on stage, they have the potential, nowhere better embodied than in Pseudolus himself, to take on life, strut, conjure, make us laugh, trick and delight us.

Richard Beacham

get another copy!
/ no music

PSEUDOLUS

CHARACTERS

PSEUDOLUS, a slave
CALIDORUS, his master
BALLIO, a pimp
SIMO, father of Calidorus
CALLIPHO, his neighbor
HARPAX, a military messenger
CHARINUS, a friend of Calidorus
SLAVE BOY of Ballio
COOK
SIMIA, slave of Charinus

SCENE: *A street in Athens with* SIMO's *house and* BALLIO's *brothel.*

PROLOGUE: You'd better stand and have a stretch: here comes a play
by Plautus—a long one!

(*Enter* CALIDORUS, *sighing and weepy-eyed, with* PSEUDOLUS *at his
heels, trying to get his attention and doing small gags, etc., to cheer
him up. He starts to speak, but is shushed by* CALIDORUS.)

CALIDORUS: Shhhh!

PSEUDOLUS: (*Echoing him*) Shhh! Shhh! SHHHHHHHHH! If such
solemn silence could share with me what secret serious sorrow
is making you so sad, your servant Pseudolus could certainly save
us both some effort—me in asking, and sir in answering! . . .

237

schweetheart! (*Pauses, then repeats the previous tongue-twisting passage at double time. Pauses again, then continues in a normal voice.*) But since it can't, well then, I'll ask! (*Loudly*) Why are you moping around so many days so moribund, moaning and moistening this message with tears, and never sharing your suffering with a single soul? Speak! *Speak!* Show Pseudolus your little secret sorrow.   14

CALIDORUS: (*Crying and collapsing on him*) Oh, Pseudolus, Pseudolus, I'm so, so sad!

PSEUDOLUS: (*In mocking horror*) Jupiter forfend!

CALIDORUS: Jupiter's not in charge here. It isn't Jupiter's judgment that afflicts me; it's Venus's envy!

PSEUDOLUS: (*Double-take, then*) Won't you let me in on it then? You've always used me as your closest confidential counselor.

CALIDORUS: And shall do now!   22

PSEUDOLUS: Then let me know what's up! (*Bit of bawdy business*) I mean, good deeds, good words, . . . or a good deal more! Pseudolus is at your service!

CALIDORUS: Take these tablets then, and let them tell you what titanic torment tortures me.

PSEUDOLUS: You bet! (*Aghast*) But what is this, I ask?!

CALIDORUS: What is what?

PSEUDOLUS: This.   30

CALIDORUS: What is this?

PSEUDOLUS: That's what *I'm* asking. The characters are scrambling all over each other—why, they're practically conjugating!

CALIDORUS: You and your jolly jests!

PSEUDOLUS: By Pollux, sir! Some sibyl could decipher this. No one else could make sense of a single syllable!

CALIDORUS: Why issue such ill insults on these little letters, etched on this tiny tablet by a teeny hand?

PSEUDOLUS: "Teeny"? *Weenie!* Lord preserve us! And, give this hen a hand! Some chicken scratched this out. 40

CALIDORUS: Don't make me sour, Pseudolus! Either read the tablets or give them back.

PSEUDOLUS: Alright, I'm reading, already! Give me your sole attention.

CALIDORUS: My soul's departed.

PSEUDOLUS: Well, fetch it up.

CALIDORUS: No, I am silent. Summon it yourself! There, from the wax! For there my soul is now, no more in this my breast!

PSEUDOLUS: (*Taking this in*) I see . . . (*Gazing at the tablets*) I say, I see! I see your sweetheart, I do, I do, I do! 50

CALIDORUS: Where, for goodness sake?

PSEUDOLUS: (*Aside*) Goodness has nothing to do with it. (*To him*) Why, look *here!* Stretched out on the tablets. Wallowing in the wax!

CALIDORUS: Why, you! May all the gods and goddesses . . .

PSEUDOLUS: . . . look after me!

CALIDORUS: (*Tragically*) I have flourished briefly like the grass of
summer; quickly I rose up, and ah, so quickly fell.

PSEUDOLUS: (*Nods and winks obscenely at the audience*) Shut up
while I plow . . . uhh, *read* through the letter.   60

CALIDORUS: Read already!

PSEUDOLUS: "Phoenicium extends greetings to her lover, Calidorus,
conveyed through this wood, wax, and writing, and, weeping,
craves help from you, her mind, and heart and soul all a-tremble."

CALIDORUS: Ah, Pseudolus, alas, alack! I lack the wherewithal to
help her.

PSEUDOLUS: What wherewithal?

CALIDORUS: Hard cash. Silver.

PSEUDOLUS: You want to send here wherewithal of silver when she
sent you a wooden wherewithal? What is this: *How to Succeed in
Business Without Really Trying?*   71

CALIDORUS: Just read on—you'll soon see how urgently I need to
get my hands on ready cash.

PSEUDOLUS: "My darling the pimp"— (*Aside*) You're wasting your
money—(*Aloud*) Ah! I mean, "My darling, the pimp has sold me
for twenty *minae* to a foreigner, a Macedonian soldier. And before
the soldier departed, he made a downpayment of fifteen *minae*.
Now only five *minae* remain to be paid. Because of this the soldier
left a token with the pimp—his own image sealed in wax. When
his agent arrives with an identical token, I'm to be sent off with
him. And the deadline set for this is the day before the next
Dionysia!" Ummmm. Dionysia, Dionysia—Ah! That's tomorrow!

CALIDORUS: My end is nigh. Unless you're able to help me.   83

PSEUDOLUS: May I go on with my reading?

CALIDORUS: Oh yes! Please! It's almost as if I'm conversing with her.
   Read on—though the potion you mix be both sweet and bitter
   to me!

PSEUDOLUS: (*Poetically*) "Now the familiar days
   and ways of love, the close loving cuddles of our bodies,
   our sweet lips' soft nibbles,   90
   our squeezing and teasing of nipples,
   our transports of delight:
   all these sweet blisses,
   of you and your missus,
   are lost—
   tossed—
   into eternity.
   Unless I suck—
   (CALIDORUS *looks alarmed, and* PSEUDOLUS *corrects himself*)
   succor you and you me.
   I've told you all I know.   100
   Now I shall learn,
   if you burn,
   with love, like I—
   or lie. Goodbye."

CALIDORUS: Is it not a sad little letter, Pseudolus?

PSEUDOLUS: Miserable.

CALIDORUS: Don't you just want to weep?

PSEUDOLUS: My eyes are like pumice. I can't squeeze out even one
   little tear.

CALIDORUS: Whyever not?   110

PSEUDOLUS: Our type has always had dry eyes.

CALIDORUS: Aren't you going to help me?

PSEUDOLUS: How can *I* help *you*?

CALIDORUS: Alas!

PSEUDOLUS: "Alas"? By golly, don't skimp on the alases. I've got plenty.

CALIDORUS: I'm so unhappy. I don't know where to borrow the money.

PSEUDOLUS: Alas!

CALIDORUS: And soon that man will take away my girl.   120

PSEUDOLUS: The lass!

CALIDORUS: Is that all the help you can offer?

PSEUDOLUS: I give what I've got. I've got an endless supply of alases hidden away at home.

CALIDORUS: This is the end of me! Can't you lend me just a single drachma—to be paid back tomorrow?

PSEUDOLUS: By golly, I couldn't, not even if I pawned my body. Besides, what do you want a drachma for?

CALIDORUS: I want to buy a rope.

PSEUDOLUS: What for?   130

CALIDORUS: To hang myself with. Ere evening's shadows fall, I shall be a shadow myself!

PSEUDOLUS: Who's going to give me back my drachma then? I see! You intend to go off and hang yourself, to cheat me out of that drachma you owe me!

CALIDORUS: I simply can't go on living if she's lost to me and taken far away!

PSEUDOLUS: Why are you weeping, you cuckoo? You'll survive.

CALIDORUS: Why shouldn't I weep—without a nickel to my name, or any hope in the world of raising a penny?   140

PSEUDOLUS: Well, as I gather from the letter, unless you're weeping pennies from heaven, displaying these tears is about as useful as collecting rain in a sieve. But fear not! I won't abandon you in your love. Somewhere today, by fair means—or by my own—I hope to find you some financial assistance. Just where it's coming from I can't say. I only know it's on its way! Look, my eyebrow is twitching!

CALIDORUS: If only your deeds were as good as your words!

PSEUDOLUS: By Hercules! You know what an ocean of commotion I stir up! Once I set things going with my magic wand!   150

CALIDORUS: My hope and dreams are in your schemes!

PSEUDOLUS: How about this? Either I get you the girl today—to have and to . . . *hold*—or else I give you the twenty *minae*?

CALIDORUS: That'll do nicely. If you can manage it.

PSEUDOLUS: Go ahead and ask me for twenty *minae*. So you're absolutely clear on what I'm promising. *Ask*, by Hercules! I'm longing to give you my word.

CALIDORUS: Will you give me twenty *minae* today?

PSEUDOLUS: You bet! Now leave me alone. Oh, and just so you'll
know—and don't say I didn't tell you—if no other sucker turns
up, I'll have to touch your father for it. 161

CALIDORUS: May the gods preserve you—for my sake! But, however, duty demands . . . that you try Mother, too, if you like!

PSEUDOLUS: Ah, as for that you can set your mouth at rest.

CALIDORUS: My "mouth"? Don't you mean my "mind"?

PSEUDOLUS: If you prefer, but that's such a cliché. Now, let everyone take notice, and let no one claim he wasn't told.
All of you here—the crowd assembled,
all of you here, my friends today,
all of you here, I give fair warning, 170
not to be deceived; don't even believe,
a single word I say!

CALIDORUS: Shhh! Shut up for goodness sake!

PSEUDOLUS: What's up?

CALIDORUS: I just heard the pimp's door rattle.

PSEUDOLUS: I'd like to make his shins rattle.

CALIDORUS: And here he comes himself, that old sink of sin! Ballio!

(*They withdraw.* BALLIO *storms out of his brothel, brandishing a
whip, and accompanied by several slaves.*)

BALLIO: Idle, worthless, all of you, scoundrels and rascals!
Come on, get out—look at 'em, stupid and worthless!
—Not worth buying, 180

—Not worth supplying, with food.
Good, just for nothing, and *this!*

(*He cracks his whip*)

(Ballio's Song): Worthy of a Whopping Whipping

Slaves more like asses than men!
Knaves, beaten senseless, and then,
Some more,
What a bore!
Hurting me more than them,
wasting this leather to keep them in trim!

Oh, they're so worthy,
Of a whopping whipping!   190
They're so deserving,
I can't desist.

Ye gods preserve me,
It's so very gripping!
It's so unnerving,
I can't resist!

Only one thought as they work,
never get caught, as they shirk,
and steal,
a good deal.   200
Scrounging both near and wide,
robbing and pinching, and learning to hide!

Never a thought for their lives,
You'd be better advised,
to let wolves manage sheep
than ever to keep
such men in your home.
You'll be beat poly-chrome!
If you don't take your orders from me.

So don't stand at ease! 210
Shake the sleep from your eyes
or I'll lash at your thighs
til they hang like a Napoli curtain—
brightly colored, and certain
to please!

If it's patterns you lack,
a rug from the East,
all embroidered with beasts,
can be etched on your back—
with a WHACK! 220

Orders, I give, but you're thick.
What's now required is my stick
to remind,
what's assigned.
Why, that's the least he'll do
for such impressionable scoundrels as you!

Look at them all, at a loss!
Don't give a toss for their boss!
It's true,
black and blue! 230
My whip deserves this bunch,
it will, by Pollux, have bollocks for lunch!

(*Striking one of the slaves*)

How's this for a start?
Does it smart?
You'll learn if you must, the hard way.
When a slave scorns his master,
he's in for disaster.
Now line up and do what I say!

(*Addressing each slave in turn*)

You first. With the bucket. Get water and fill cook's pot. Then you,
with the ax. I appoint you chief cutter-upper!   240

SLAVE: It isn't very sharp, sir.

BALLIO: So what? Neither are you! All dull with beatings! That
doesn't make me any less keen to use you for all you're worth! You
next. This house—make it shine. Get on with it—inside! As for
you . . . you'll be chief bed maker-upper. And you there can rub
the silver til it glows, and lay the tables. When I return from the
forum I'd better find everything
neat and tidy, swept and clean,
and given a sheen—know what I mean?   249

Today's my birthday, and you can help me celebrate in proper
style. Pig, fatback, tenderloin, cow's udder! (*They each react,
thinking he refers to them*) No! not you, for the stew! Didn't you
hear? I'm going to entertain some classy gents in the style they'll
think I'm accustomed to. Go on, get on with it! Time's a-wasting,
and the cooks awaiting. I'm off now to the market to see if I can
outshark the fishmonger. (*Takes one of the boy slaves*) As for you,
small fry—you can spy, and keep an eye out for pick-pockets. (*A
bit of obscene business between the boy and* BALLIO's *pocket*)

Hold it right there! (*More business with "holding it," etc.*) I
almost forgot the most important part: The *tarts!* Hey, there,
whores—out-of-doors!   261

(*Calls inside, and they troupe out.* BALLIO *continues his song.*)

Today, if you please, take a break in the ease
you enjoy, and the wiles you employ
As you make yourselves pretty for the gents in the city.

Today I shall learn which of you yearns to earn
her freedom and the means for her keep.
Or, contrarywise, puts weight on her thighs,
As she lazily lounges in sleep.

Today I shall see which of you should go free,
And which—what the hell!—is fit only to sell.   270
For today, let's be clear, I want gifts for a year
from your lovers who flock and adore.

It's my birthday today, and those who can't pay their way
will be banished my sweets, and put back on the streets
out-of-doors! Common whores!

So where, need I ask? Are the lads it's your task
to ensnare?
As with kisses and blisses you rapture and capture
their hearts (such good tarts)
in my lair?   280

So where are they then? I want masses of men
at the doors proffering presents for me.
Why do you suppose I fork out for these clothes,
and deck you girls out in such finery?

To fill your tummies with yummies,
guzzling the sauce,
and not giving a toss
while I make a loss?!!
I'd be better off running a winery!   289

Now let's have you one at a time. (*Shrieks from the girls*) So none
can say she wasn't told. So pay attention—all of you! You first,
Hedytium, you darling of the grain dealers. All your clients have
got enormous stocks (*more shrieks*)—stocks, I said, *stocks!* of
grain. See that enough of it is brought here to last all year. So
much grain for me and my household that they change my name
in town from Ballio, "the wimp of a pimp," to "old king corn."

CALIDORUS: Just hear how that gallows bird carries on. Hasn't he got
a magnificent air?

PSEUDOLUS: He sure has. All of it hot! But shhhh! Let's pay attention. 300

BALLIO: Aeschrodora. The favorite of the meat market! Your friends the butchers are as bad as us pimps. Always trying to flog off a scrap of stewing steak for best bit of bottom round. Unless I take delivery by tomorrow of three nice sides of beef, nicely hung, (*more shrieks*) I'll see that you're well-cured! What do you say to that—hooker on a hook?

CALIDORUS: Why that's just offal!

PSEUDOLUS: Why do the young men of Athens let such a creep flourish? Where are they, why are they laying low, those lusting lads who turn to the pimp for their low-life-lays? Why don't they gang up on him, and rid the town of this pest? But of course, that's just wishful thinking. Their passions enslave them to this knave of tarts. They'll never take a stand against him. 313

CALIDORUS: Do be quiet!

PSEUDOLUS: What's the matter?

CALIDORUS: You are. Your chattering keeps me from hearing him!

PSEUDOLUS: Well, I guess I'll be quiet then.

CALIDORUS: I'd rather you *be* so, than *say* so!

BALLIO: Now you, Xystilis, pay attention! Your lovers are into oil, lots and lots of olive oil, stored away. I want this place to be awash with it today, or tomorrow your salad days will begin in earnest— in the flophouse, where you'll have a bed, but not much sleep. You'll be well-oiled, my dear, "*Ultra-vergine*, cold-pressed," if you catch my drift! Yes, indeed, my little super serpent! All of your clients are slippery with oil, but not so much as a drop to smooth things for your fellow slaves or to season my supper! Of course, you're not into oil—it's wine that wins you! Well, by golly all of

you are going to settle accounts with me in one lucky "strike" if you
don't follow my orders—to the letter!—today.   329

So that leaves you, Phoenicium, you little morsel for the con-
noisseurs! You're always on the verge of buying your freedom off
me; always quick to make a deal, but slow to deliver the goods!
Well now, honey, hear this: if your friends' fortune fails to fill my
larder with food—by today!—well then, tomorrow, you'll have a
fabulous shade of phoenician purple on your fanny, Phoenicium,
followed by a frolic in the flophouse!

CALIDORUS: (*Aghast*) Pseudolus! Do you hear what he says!?

PSEUDOLUS: Indeed, I do. I'm concentrating with all my might.

CALIDORUS: What do you think I should do to keep him from de-
bauching my sweetheart?   340

PSEUDOLUS: Don't fret! Just keep calm. I'll do the fretting for both of
us. Fret, fret, fret, fret, fret! Ballio and I have been on close terms
for ages—we're old friends. I'll send him a nice gift for his birthday: a mound of monstrous mischief!

CALIDORUS: But what's the use?

PSEUDOLUS: Don't let it get you down.

CALIDORUS: But . . .

PSEUDOLUS: Tut, tut . . .

CALIDORUS: This is agony!

PSEUDOLUS: Stiff upper lip!   350

CALIDORUS: But it isn't!

PSEUDOLUS: Well, make it stiff!

CALIDORUS: How can I?

PSEUDOLUS: Get hold of yourself! Don't let your spirits droop when things are hard. Keep your pecker up.

CALIDORUS: But that's just absurd! What's the fun of being a lover, if you can't play the fool. (*Poses melodramatically*)

PSEUDOLUS: Oh, do can it! (*Grabs him*)

CALIDORUS: Pseudolus, dear, let me indulge myself! (*Weeps extravagantly on him*)

PSEUDOLUS: (*Lets him fall*) Okay. Go ahead. I'm off.   360

CALIDORUS: Oh, no! Please! Stay! I'll do whatever you say.

PSEUDOLUS: That's more like it!

BALLIO: (*Impatiently, at the door*) Time's awasting! Let's be off, boy.

CALIDORUS: Hey! He's leaving. Aren't you going to call him back?

PSEUDOLUS: There's lots of time. Keep calm!

CALIDORUS: But he's going to get away!

BALLIO: Come on, boy, get your arse in gear!

PSEUDOLUS: Hey there, birthday boy! Birthday boy, I'm speaking to you! Come on back, birthday boy, and show a little respect. I know business calls, but so do we! Come on, we want to have a word with you.   371

BALLIO: Hey! What gives? Why this delay when I'm on my way?

PSEUDOLUS: Someone who's done you good deeds.

BALLIO: Done deeds are dead deeds. What can you do today?

PSEUDOLUS: Why so haughty?

BALLIO: Why so naughty?

CALIDORUS: Stop him! Don't let him go!

BALLIO: Come along, boy.

PSEUDOLUS: Let's cut off his (BALLIO *reacts in horror*) . . . escape!

BALLIO: Whoever you are, you can go to hell!   380

PSEUDOLUS: I'd like you . . .

BALLIO: And I'd like you both—out of my way! Come, boy.

PSEUDOLUS: Just one little word?

BALLIO: Don't be absurd!

PSEUDOLUS: A word to the wise?

BALLIO: Damn your eyes! Will you or won't you get out of my way?

PSEUDOLUS: Stay, stay, just a little delay.

BALLIO: Away, away!

CALIDORUS: Ballio, I say . . .

BALLIO: What you say doesn't pay!   390

CALIDORUS: I've always paid in the past.

BALLIO: I'm not asking for past payment.

CALIDORUS: I'll pay you just as soon as I've got it.

BALLIO: Fine. When I've got it, you'll get it.

CALIDORUS: Alas, alack! When I think of all the money and gifts I've wasted on you!

BALLIO: You're wasting your breath, now. Idiot. Your words are worthless.

PSEUDOLUS: Now see here! Don't you know who this is?

BALLIO: I know who he was. What he is now's for him to say. Let's make tracks.   401

PSEUDOLUS: Oh, now Ballio—can't you give us just a tiny tid-bit of your time if there's *profit* in it?

BALLIO: (*Stopping in his tracks*) Profit? Did you say *profit?* Why even if I was busy at the altar sacrificing to Jove above, I'd put the innards on the back burner if someone mentioned profit. Say what you will, it's impious to poo-poo profit.

PSEUDOLUS: He dares disdain the very gods we all hold dear.

BALLIO: (*Aside*) I'll have a word with him. Greetings! You sneaky, Greeky slave.   410

PSEUDOLUS: May the gods love you as much as we do. In other words, love you and leave you.

BALLIO: Well, what's up, Calidorus?

CALIDORUS: I'm up. To my ears in misery, debt, and love!

BALLIO: What a pity! If only I could pay my bills with sympathy!

PSEUDOLUS: Very funny. Don't bother; we know all about your fine feelings. But do you know what we really want?

BALLIO: More or less: to see me ruined.

PSEUDOLUS: Well, sure. But also, the thing we called you back for, if you'll pay attention.   420

BALLIO: I'm paying and delaying. So make it snappy!

PSEUDOLUS: He's so *unhappy!* About not having paid you the twenty *minae* for the girl, as promised, by her "sell by" date.

BALLIO: No doubt. It's a good deal easier to feel sad than mad. He's sad not to have paid it; I'm mad not to have received it.

PSEUDOLUS: Yes, but he will pay—he'll come up with it. Just hang on for a few days. He's afraid you'll sell the girl out of spite.

BALLIO: He could have paid me the money long ago if he'd had a mind to.

CALIDORUS: Oh yeah? Just how, if I hadn't got it?   430

BALLIO: If you were *really* in love you'd have managed somehow. Taken a friendly loan, approached a moneylender, added a soupçon of interest, or fleeced your father!

PSEUDOLUS: (*Taken aback*) Fleece his father?! Why, you wicked, wicked, man! Can't you offer any *good* advice?

BALLIO: It's not in a pimp's job description.

CALIDORUS: How could I ever, ever, fleece my father? The old geezer's too damn clever for that. And anyway, of course even if I could, my sense of propriety would never allow it.   439

BALLIO: Oh, I understand entirely! So every night just curl up against your precious propriety instead of Phoenicium. But since I see your love takes second place to propriety, what about the others? They're not all your father! Can't you touch up someone for a friendly loan, interest-free?

CALIDORUS: "A friendly loan"? There's no such thing these days.

PSEUDOLUS: Good grief, no. No one dares lend money. Not since those bankers stuffed themselves and then went bust. Made their own pile, but couldn't pay off their depositors.   448

CALIDORUS: It's no use at all. I can't raise a penny anyplace. What a dire destiny to die a double death of destitution and desire!

BALLIO: Well, why not buy oil on credit, then sell it for ready cash? By golly, you could make two hundred *minae* in no time!

CALIDORUS: But damn it! I'm underage. It's illegal. No one dares give me credit.

BALLIO: Ah, the law binds me, too. I wouldn't dare give you credit.

PSEUDOLUS: What do you mean, "credit"? After all you've made off him already?

BALLIO: Lovers are meant to be soaked—continuously. He shall give, give, and give some more. And when it's all given out—he can give up.   460

CALIDORUS: Have you no pity?

BALLIO: Nope. Can't afford it. Fine words don't ring the cash register. Even so I wish you were alive and well.

PSEUDOLUS: By golly, he's not dead yet!

BALLIO: He might as well be as far as I'm concerned, with this line of talk. When a lover starts coming to pimps for pity, it's all over. Come see me any time you like, so long as there's money in your mission. But when you come around moaning about lack of money, it's like asking for comfort from a stepmother.

PSEUDOLUS: Good Lord, were you ever married to his father?

BALLIO: Heaven forbid!   471

PSEUDOLUS: Come on, now Ballio, do us a favor, Trust me, if you're worried about him. In three days I'll have your money back to you, come hell or high water.

BALLIO: *I* trust *you?*

PSEUDOLUS: Sure, why not?

BALLIO: I'd as soon tie up a runaway dog with a string of sausages.

CALIDORUS: How can you treat me so badly after all I've done for you?

BALLIO: Well . . . what do you want me to do?   480

CALIDORUS: Just delay selling the girl for a few days, and save the life of one who loves her.

BALLIO: Oh, come now, cheer up. I'll even wait six months.

CALIDORUS: Oh, super! You wonderful, wonderful man!

BALLIO: You want to know something even better?

CALIDORUS: What's that?

BALLIO: Well, Phoenicium's not for sale anymore.

CALIDORUS: She's not?

BALLIO: Not a bit!

CALIDORUS: Run, Pseudolus! Bring sacrifices, gifts, priests, that I may worship this almighty Jupiter. Yes, yes, more Jupiter than Jupiter himself. 492

BALLIO: Ah, please, no sacrifices. A nice bit of lamb will do fine for me.

CALIDORUS: Go on. What are you waiting for? Fetch some lambs; didn't you hear Jupiter's orders?

PSEUDOLUS: While I'm at it, shall I fetch a few extra rods to warm up Jupiter with?

BALLIO: Go to hell!

PSEUDOLUS: That's where this prince of pimps is heading. 500

BALLIO: Oh, come now! You'd be sorry to see me dead. Admit it.

PSEUDOLUS: Why?

BALLIO: Well, because then *you'd* be the most despicable wretch in Athens!

CALIDORUS: For goodness sake, tell me the truth! Seriously! My sweetheart Phoenicium's not for sale?

BALLIO: Absolutely not. I've already sold her.

CALIDORUS: (*Aghast*) But, *how?*

BALLIO: Oh, the usual way. No clothes included, but with all the other bits intact. 510

CALIDORUS: (*Hysterically*) You've *sold* my sweetheart???

BALLIO: But of course. For twenty *minae*.

CALIDORUS: Twenty *minae?*

BALLIO: Yes, or four times five, if you prefer. To a Macedonian soldier from whom I have a downpayment of fifteen *minae*.

CALIDORUS: What am I hearing!?

BALLIO: That your girl's as good as gold!

CALIDORUS: How could you dare . . .

BALLIO: With ease. She was mine.

CALIDORUS: AHHHHHHH!!! Pseudolus, quick! Bring me a sword!

PSEUDOLUS: What do you want with a sword?   521

CALIDORUS: To end his life and mine.

PSEUDOLUS: Just attend to your own. His will end soon enough in starvation.

CALIDORUS: Answer me! You most wicked man that ever walked the earth! Didn't you solemnly swear you wouldn't sell her to anyone but me?

BALLIO: Exactly.

CALIDORUS: Indeed. And in legally binding terms.

BALLIO: That's right. Bound and gagged.   530

CALIDORUS: Well then, you've perjured yourself, you scoundrel!

BALLIO: But I've put money in my purse! And I, the scoundrel pimp, have got plenty in my pocket, while you, the pious paragon, for all your pedigree, haven't got a penny pot to pee in!

CALIDORUS: Pseudolus, go stand over there and bombard him with insults.

PSEUDOLUS: Delighted. Why, I wouldn't run faster for my freedom.

(*They stand on either side of* BALLIO *and proceed to hurl abuse*)

CALIDORUS: Crush him with curses!

PSEUDOLUS: I'll tear you to tatters with torment from my tongue! Wicked thing!

BALLIO: I like the ring!   540

CALIDORUS: Scoundrel!

BALLIO: It's true.

PSEUDOLUS: Hangdog!

BALLIO: Like you.

CALIDORUS: Tomb-robber!

BALLIO: I dare say.

PSEUDOLUS: Breaker of oaths.

CALIDORUS: Gallows bird!

BALLIO: The very word!

PSEUDOLUS: Scurvy slave!   550

BALLIO: Of course!

CALIDORUS: Unholy knave!

BALLIO: Endorsed!

PSEUDOLUS: Corrupter of youth!

BALLIO: Nicely expressed!

CALIDORUS: Perjurer!

BALLIO: I'm impressed!

PSEUDOLUS: Patricide!

BALLIO: I've nothing to hide.

CALIDORUS: Villain most vile!   560

BALLIO: I like your style!

PSEUDOLUS: Crock full of Ca Ca!

BALLIO: La de bloody da da!

CALIDORUS: Filthy pimp!

BALLIO: Rather limp!

PSEUDOLUS: Slime!

BALLIO: Sublime!

CALIDORUS: Keeper of whores!

BALLIO: What a sweet chorus!

PSEUDOLUS: Utterly worthless!   570

BALLIO: At your service!

CALIDORUS: You abused your own father and mother!

BALLIO: Oh, I murdered them as well! To keep from feeding them. Nothing wrong in that, surely?

PSEUDOLUS: We're wasting our words, like water in a sieve.

BALLIO: Is there anything you wish to add?

CALIDORUS: Can nothing shame you?

BALLIO: I'd be ashamed to be like you. A lover, flat broke like an empty nut. Nevertheless, despite all the abuse you've heaped on me, I can promise you this: unless the soldier comes up with the five *minae* that's due today on our "lay-away" plan, I shall unhesitatingly fulfill my duty.   582

CALIDORUS: Which is?

BALLIO: Bring me the money yourself, my boy, and I shall dishonor my agreement with him. That's my pimpish duty. Now I'd just love to chat some more with you, but "tempus fugit"! Now, no mistake: no money from you, no mercy from me. That's my position, so think it over, and act accordingly.

CALIDORUS: You're not rushing off?

BALLIO: I've got a lot to do. (*He exits*)

PSEUDOLUS: There's more to come! Now I've got him, if the gods and men are with me. I'll skin and skewer him like a cook with an eel. Now, Calidorus, I shall need your assistance.   592

CALIDORUS: At your service.

PSEUDOLUS: I shall surround this *bast*ion, and capture it today. To
do so, I shall require an assistant: clever, crafty, knowledgeable,
and quick—one who knows how to follow orders precisely, and
won't fall asleep on the job.

CALIDORUS: Tell me what your plans are.

PSEUDOLUS: In due course. I don't want to repeat myself. Plays are
quite long enough as it is.   600

CALIDORUS: A sound and sensible observation.

PSEUDOLUS: Hurry along then, and produce our man.

CALIDORUS: I've lots of friends, but hardly anyone I can count on.

PSEUDOLUS: I don't doubt it. So you've got a double-duty. Make a
long list of the lot; then choose one man we can rely on.

CALIDORUS: I'll have him here in a jiffy!

PSEUDOLUS: Well get on with it. Don't waste time talking.

(CALIDORUS *exits on the run*)

PSEUDOLUS: Well, with him gone, you're on your own, Pseudolus.
Having entertained our young master with fine talk, it's "what to
do" time. Here you are without a shred of a plan, cashless and
clueless. No idea where to start or finish weaving one's web. Well,
after all, that's how a poet works when he takes up his pen in hot
pursuit of something that doesn't exist—yet somehow finds it and
fashions fantasy into fact. I fancy I'll play the poet now; those
twenty *minae* are nowhere to be found, and yet, I'll find them!
After all, I already promised it once before and planned to bamboozle the old boy. But somehow he got wind of it first.   617

But now I'd better curb this talk. There's my master, Simo,
coming this way with his neighbor, Callipho. Now I've got to rob

this corpse of twenty *minae*, to give to Calidorus today. I'll just
withdraw back here for a bit of eavesdropping. (*Moves upstage*)

SIMO: Why, if you wanted a prime minister of all the spendthrifts
and libertines in Athens, no one could outqualify my son for the
job! Why, man, it's the only thing the town's talking about! How he
wants to buy freedom for his girlfriend, and can't come up with
the cash. I've heard all about it, although, of course, I suspected—
sensed and scented—it for some time, but kept it to myself.

PSEUDOLUS: So . . . he's got wind of sonny already! That's a mortal
blow to my plan; that scheme's scuttled! Just when I'm about to go
foraging for cash, I find he's headed me off at the pass! With his
cunning there's nothing for con artists to con.   631

CALLIPHO: If I had my way, all those who traffic in tattletales would
be suspended: the tellers by their tongues, and the listeners by
their ears! Now these rumors you hear—all about your son's phi-
landering and plans to fleece you—it's all most likely just a pack of
lies. Why, even if they're true, is that so surprising? Moral stan-
dards being what they are, these days? What's so new about a lusty
lad longing to liberate his lady love?

PSEUDOLUS: What a pleaser-geezer!

SIMO: Well, it's not a tradition I approve!   640

CALLIPHO: What difference does that make? Why, you did the same
thing yourself at his age! Only a decent daddy dare demand his
son disdain doing dastardly deeds—identical deeds he did! But
you, why you've sown enough wild oats to cover the whole city!
And you're surprised to discover "like father, like son"?

PSEUDOLUS: By Jove! A sensible man—how very few like you there
are! Gosh, that's just the sort of father a son ought to have!

SIMO: (*Hearing him*) Who speaks there? Ah, it's my slave, Pseudolus! It's he that's debauched my son—that sink of sin! He's my

boy's instructor, the one who strings him along, whom I'd love
string up!   651

CALLIPHO: Throwing an angry scene won't help now. Far more sensible to go up pleasantly and find out whether all these rumors are
true or false. A good humor can lessen bad fortune.

SIMO: I'll take your advice.

PSEUDOLUS: Ready or not, Pseudolus, here they come! Get ready to
address the old boy. Greetings! First to my master, as is proper,
then a share of what's left over for his neighbor.

SIMO: Good day to you. What are you up to?

PSEUDOLUS: Oh, just standing about, like this. (*Poses*)   660

SIMO: Get a load of that regal bearing, Callipho!

CALLIPHO: Definitely a man who knows how to stand up for himself!

PSEUDOLUS: It's right, I take it, that a guileless slave with a clear
conscience should stand proudly—particularly in the presence of
his master.

CALLIPHO: There are one or two things we've had wind of in a
nebulous sort of way, that we'd like your help in clearing up.

SIMO: He'll so cloud you with words, you'll think you're in a dialogue
with Socrates instead of Pseudolus!

PSEUDOLUS: Indeed. I know you've long held me in contempt.
Why, I even believe you doubt my loyalty! You wish to think of me
as good for nothing, but I must disappoint your expectation.

SIMO: Pray, throw open the portals of thine ears, O Pseudolus, that
my words may seek humble lodging within.   674

PSEUDOLUS: Oh, do speak frankly, even though you have incurred my displeasure!

SIMO: The slave is displeased with his master?

PSEUDOLUS: That surprises you, does it?   678

SIMO: Egad! From what you say, I guess I'd better avoid your wrath! Why you evidently intend to beat me in a different way than I'm accustomed to beating you! What's your opinion, Callipho?

CALLIPHO: Well, golly, I do think he's entitled to resent it if you doubt his loyalty.

SIMO: So all right! Let him have his resentment. I can look after myself. Now, how about it? What do you have to say about the matter at hand?

PSEUDOLUS: Ask away. Whatever I know, you'll have in Delphic utterance.

SIMO: Then pay attention, and mind your promise. Now tell me: do you know anything about my son's affair with a music-girl?   690

PSEUDOLUS: Yea, verily.

SIMO: Whom he wants to set free?

PSEUDOLUS: Yea, yea, verily.

SIMO: And you're about to try to get twenty *minae* off me by stealth and trickery?

PSEUDOLUS: *I*, get money from *you*?

SIMO: Just so. In order to give it to my son so he can free his girl-friend. Out with it! Speak up!

PSEUDOLUS: Yea, very verily.

CALLIPHO: He's confessed!   700

SIMO: What did I tell you, Callipho?

CALLIPHO: I remember.

SIMO: As soon as you heard of all this, why didn't you inform me? Why wasn't I told?

PSEUDOLUS: I'll speak. The reason is . . . I wasn't willing to engage in the base practice of a slave denouncing his master to his master.

SIMO: (*To* CALLIPHO) Wouldn't you have him dragged off to the mills at once?

CALLIPHO: Ah, but Simo, there's no real harm done.

SIMO: On the contrary—the most appalling!   710

PSEUDOLUS: Save your breath, Callipho. I know how to look after myself. The fault is mine. Now pay attention, please, and I'll tell you why I left you in the dark about your son's love affair. I knew if I told you, I'd be sent packing to the mill.

SIMO: And you didn't reckon that *I'd* send you to the mill if you kept quiet?

PSEUDOLUS: I knew it.

SIMO: Then why not tell me?

PSEUDOLUS: It was a choice of evils—the one at hand, the other still approaching. Present punishment or a few days' grace.   720

SIMO: What will you do now? 'Cause no one is going to get any money from me, believe me, now I'm on the alert. And no one else will let you have a penny, soon as I've passed the word.

PSEUDOLUS: By golly, I wouldn't think of trying to fleece anyone. Not while *you're* around! My goodness, no. It's you I'll have the money from: you're going to give it to me.

SIMO: You're going to get it from me!?

PSEUDOLUS: Absolutely.

SIMO: By Hercules, may the gods strike me blind if I give you a thing!   730

PSEUDOLUS: You'll give, alright. I'm letting you know so you'll be on the lookout.

CALLIPHO: By Jove, if you succeed, I'll never doubt you've done a mighty marvelous miracle!

PSEUDOLUS: I'll succeed.

SIMO: And suppose you fail?

PSEUDOLUS: Flog me. But what if I succeed?

SIMO: Then with Jove as my witness, you need never fear a flaying for the rest of your life.

(*They shake hands*)

PSEUDOLUS: Make sure you remember!   740

SIMO: Do you really doubt that forewarned is forearmed?

PSEUDOLUS: Well, I am warning you: watch out! I repeat, watch out, *watch out!* Before the day is over, you'll be handing over the money to me with these very hands.

CALLIPHO: By Pollux, if he's as good as his word, he's a marvelous masterpiece of a man!

PSEUDOLUS: Take me as your slave, if I fail.

SIMO: Oh, that's well said! Now it seems you don't already belong to me.

PSEUDOLUS: You two want to hear something even more wonderful?

CALLIPHO: Why sure. I'm longing to listen. I just love it!   751

SIMO: Absolutely right. I can't get enough of your talk.

PSEUDOLUS: Before this battle takes place, I shall wage another that will make me famous far and wide.

SIMO: What'll that be?

PSEUDOLUS: Well, your next-door neighbor, the pimp Ballio, brilliantly bamboozled by my artifice and wily ways,
(*going into a can-can rhythm*)
shall soon give o'er,
the girl next door,
the one your son is pining for!   760

SIMO: How's that?

PSEUDOLUS: I shall accomplish both these tasks by evening.

SIMO: Well, if you bring them off as promised, your prowess will surpass that of King Agathocles. But, should you fail, you won't mind me commissioning you to the mill?

PSEUDOLUS: Oh, not a bit! (*Sings*) "Not for just an hour, not for just a day, not for just a year, but always!" However, if I succeed, will you agree to give me the money to recompense the pimp?

CALLIPHO: Pseudolus is making a fair deal. Go ahead and agree.

SIMO: Yes, but you know what just occurred to me? Suppose, Callipho, that these two crooks are in cahoots, and have cooked up this cunning concoction to con me out of my cash?   772

PSEUDOLUS: Now would I dare to do a dastardly deed like that? Look, Simo, if we've conspired, cooked up, or concocted anything —well then, I'm an open book. You can inscribe my backside with your birch rods as if applying pen to paper.

SIMO: Well, alright. As you like. Let the entertainments begin!

PSEUDOLUS: Okay. Callipho, I want you to clear your diary and work for me today.

CALLIPHO: Well, I had planned to travel out to the country today.

PSEUDOLUS: Couldn't you turn your tactics to a different task?

CALLIPHO: Okay. On your account, I'll stay instead. Besides, I'm looking forward to your feats, Pseudolus. And if I find Father here failing to keep faith and follow through on the money, why, rather than see things fall flat, I'll finance it myself!   785

SIMO: I won't default.

PSEUDOLUS: By golly, that's for sure. If you don't pay up, I'll punish you with potent and prolonged protest—in public! Now let's have the two of you tucked away inside, to give my tricks a turn.

CALLIPHO: Whatever you say!

PSEUDOLUS: But I want you, ready and waiting at home.

CALLIPHO: At your service!

SIMO: Well, I'm off to the forum. I won't be long.

(*The two old men exit in opposite directions*)

PSEUDOLUS: Don't delay! (*Dropping the grand manner*)

I begin to detect
that you folks now suspect
all the deeds that I've promised today,
shall go unrealized,
and were only devised
to amuse you during our play!   800

Well, such doubts are absurd.
I'm as good as my word,
so be certain of that and don't scoff.
As for what I *shall* do . . .
well, I haven't a clue!
Still, I know I'll somehow bring it off!

When an actor's on stage
it's his job to engage
in some intrigues both novel and droll.
If he fails in that task   810
let him turn in his mask
to another more fit for the role!

Now then, if you'll allow
I'll withdraw to plot how
best to muster my powers of invention.
Oh, and while I'm away,
the musicians will play.
So please give them your closest attention!

(*He exits*)

ACT II

(*Enter* PSEUDOLUS)

PSEUDOLUS: Praise be to Jove! How lovely and how fine
our plot's progressing with these plans of mine!   820

What need for doubt, away with every fear!
For Pseudolus has a scheme stored, right up here!

How vain and foolish, to trust the faint of heart!
Each makes his own fate, so write and play your part!

Now I've prepared my forces, summoning all hands,
lined up in treble ranks, my stratagems and plans.

I'll meet the enemy, let come what may,
defeat him easily, and rout him in the fray.

Just like my slavish forebears, whose noble spirit and wiles
inspired my own skullduggery, my artifice and guiles.   830

Today I'll fight for you and me, against our common foe.
So if you please, with grace and ease, we'll batter Ballio!

Just watch me. For today, I shall besiege and take this citadel.
(*Indicating* BALLIO's *house*) I'll lead my legions there. Once I've
captured it, and given aid to my allies, I'll next lead my troops
against this ancient stronghold. (*Points to* SIMO's *house*) In there
my friends and I will load ourselves with loot, letting my enemies
know that I was born to fill them with fear and force them to flight!
For I am sprung from a noble line; 'tis fitting that I perform such
daring deeds as shall be spoke of in ages yet to come!   840

(*Sees* HARPAX *approaching*) But what's this I see? Who's this
strange guy I spy? I'd like to know what's with him and that sword.
I'll just hide over here and see what he's about. (*He withdraws*)

(HARPAX *enters in full military regalia*)

HARPAX: This is the neighborhood and place I was told about, if my eyes can interpret what my military master told me. . . . It's supposed to be the seventh house after the city gate. The place the pimp Ballio lives to whom I'm supposed to give this token and money. If only someone would tell me which home is where the tart lives! (*Chuckles to himself*)   849

PSEUDOLUS: (*Concealed*) SHHHH! Quiet please! This is my man, unless all the gods and men deceive me. I need a new plan now that this option's opened up! Let's try this for a start and set the other ploys aside. By Pollux, now's the time to nail this military messenger who's just arrived!

HARPAX: I'll just knock on this door and summon someone out.

PSEUDOLUS: (*Approaching*) Whoever you are, will you kindly knock off the knocking? I've come out as advocate and protector of the doors.

HARPAX: Are you Ballio?

PSEUDOLUS: Not quite. I'm Sub-Ballio.   860

HARPAX: What does that mean?

PSEUDOLUS: I'm his "in and out" man. (HARPAX *assumes an obscene interpretation*) His superintendent of stocks.

HARPAX: Oh, a sort of head butler.

PSEUDOLUS: Oh, no! I instruct the head butler.

HARPAX: Slave or free?

PSEUDOLUS: Well, at the moment I've got a position as a slave.

HARPAX: I see . . . if appearances are any guide, you don't deserve anything else.

PSEUDOLUS: Have a good look at yourself, before slighting others!

HARPAX: This man is bad news! 871

PSEUDOLUS: (*Aside*) The gods are on my side! This guy's a regular anvil on which I'll hammer out a heap of hoaxes today!

HARPAX: (*Aside*) Why's he talking to himself?

PSEUDOLUS: What's that, sonny?

HARPAX: Pardon?

PSEUDOLUS: You've been sent by that Macedonian military master, haven't you? You're the slave of that man who's brought one of our girls, gave my master, the pimp, fifteen *minae*, and still owes five?

HARPAX: That's me. But where in the world did you ever see or speak to me? I've never been to Athens before, or laid eyes on you until today. 882

PSEUDOLUS: You just looked the part. When the soldier left, today was set as the deadline for final payment, and we haven't received it yet.

HARPAX: It's just arrived.

PSEUDOLUS: You've got it?

HARPAX: You bet.

PSEUDOLUS: Then why not hand it over?

HARPAX: Give it to you?

PSEUDOLUS: But of course! I handle all Ballio's finances and accounts. I receive all payments on his behalf, and settle all expenses.   892

HARPAX: Well, by Hercules, I wouldn't entrust a penny to you, even
if you were treasurer to almighty Jove!

PSEUDOLUS: Why, before you could sneeze we could settle the matter at hand.

HARPAX: I'd rather keep the matter *in* hand, if you please.

PSEUDOLUS: Go to hell! You've come to castigate my character! As if
I don't manage mounds more money myself all the time!

HARPAX: Others may see fit to trust you; I don't!   900

PSEUDOLUS: Why, you might as well suggest I'm out to rob you!

HARPAX: No, I'll let you say that; I'll only think it. What's your
name, anyway?

PSEUDOLUS: (*Aside*) The pimp has a slave named Surus. I'll say I'm
him. (*Aloud*) I'm Surus.

HARPAX: You're Surus?

PSEUDOLUS: Yes, I'm absolutely sure I'm Surus.

HARPAX: Well, we're wasting words. Whatever you call *yourself*,
why not call *him*—your master—if he's at home? So I can do the
business I was sent here for.   910

PSEUDOLUS: If he was inside, I'd call him out. But if you'd just like to
let me have the money, your business would be over in a jiffy—
faster than hanging around to give it to him.

HARPAX: Yes, but you don't get it, do you? My master sent me to *use*, not *lose* the money. And it's perfectly clear to me that you're getting in a sweat because you can't get your claws into it. I'm not giving a penny to anyone but Ballio, in person.

PSEUDOLUS: Ah, but he's engaged just now—with a case at court.

HARPAX: Good luck to him! When I think he's likely to be back, then I'll return. Take this letter and give it to him. It's got the token there, agreed upon by my master and yours, concerning the girl.

PSEUDOLUS: I know all about it. Master wanted the girl given to the person who brought the money, along with the seal bearing his image. He left me a copy of it.   924

HARPAX: You've got it all.

PSEUDOLUS: But, of course!

HARPAX: Okay, just give him this letter.

PSEUDOLUS: You bet! But what's your name?

HARPAX: Harpax. It's Greek for "Snatch."

PSEUDOLUS: Keep your distance, Harpax. We certainly don't need any "Snatch" around here. By Hercules, you certainly won't make it into our house.   932

HARPAX: I'm known for snatching my victims alive from the battle line—hence my name.

PSEUDOLUS: Much more likely, I should think, from snatching ornaments from people's houses.

HARPAX: Not at all. But you know what I'd like to ask you, Surus?

PSEUDOLUS: I will, just as soon as you tell me.

HARPAX: I'm staying at a tavern—third house outside the gate—the place kept by that old broad who's built like a barrel: Chrysis.

PSEUDOLUS: So what?   941

HARPAX: Do come and fetch me when your master returns.

PSEUDOLUS: Oh, by all means—Surus is at your service!

HARPAX: I'm a little fatigued from my journey, and want to freshen up.

PSEUDOLUS: Sound and sensible. I quite approve. Only kindly make sure you're around when I call.

HARPAX: As soon as I've luncheoned, I'll take a little nap.

PSEUDOLUS: Sane and sensible.

HARPAX: Anything else?

PSEUDOLUS: No, you just go and have a nice rest.   950

HARPAX: I'm off.

(*He exits*)

PSEUDOLUS: (*Calling after him*) Oh, and listen, Snatch, see that they give you plenty of bedclothes. A little sweat might do you good.

By the gods, now he's gone, we'll be happy today;
I had strayed from the path that was best.
Now I'm back on the track, and he's paying my way,
Opportunity's knocking, I guess!

For they say that good fortune doth favor the brave.
'Tis good fortune that fortune's on time.   960

For this fortunate letter has favored this slave,
And a rich cornucopia's mine!

It holds tricks, it holds schemes, it's got money for dreams
to bring Master the girl he desired.
We're in luck; I can crow, I can boast though it seems
that the plans I contrived weren't required!

I had carefully plotted each step of the way
to deliver our girl from the pimp.
But when faced by the goddess of luck, I must say,
most men's cockiest concoctions go limp!   970

For 'tis true, he who uses his luck, we call "wise."
We respect him and honor his name.
While the fellow whose projects are flops, we despise.
But for fortune—both men are the same!

We are fools not to know what great folly we show.
All our scurrying and worrying's absurd.
Sometimes joy grows from woe, or the high are brought low;
And, as always, Death has the last word!   978

But that's quite enough philosophising! I'm chattering away far too
long. By the gods! That little lie I conjured up just now was worth
its weight in gold! Saying I was Ballio's boy. Now with this one
letter, I can ensnare three people: Master, the pimp, and the chap
I got it from. (*Sees* CALIDORUS *approaching*) And, hey! Here
comes something else just as good! Look—Calidorus is coming
this way, and he's got someone in tow.

CALIDORUS: (*Entering with his friend,* CHARINUS) Now, I've shared
all the facts with you, sweet and sour.
the girl I desire,
my troubles so dire,
and the help I require.   990

CHARINUS: I've got it all down pat. All I need to know is how you
intend to use me.

CALIDORUS: Pseudolus ordered me to fetch him someone energetic
and sympathetic.

CHARINUS: You've followed orders admirably! You've got someone
here who's a friend in deed and in need. But his Pseudolus is new
to me.

CALIDORUS: There's no finer fellow alive. He's my savant servant! A
real ideas man who's promised to promote the scheme I told you
about.   1000

PSEUDOLUS: (*Aside*) I shall address him in my dandiest diction!

CALIDORUS: Hark! Heard I a voice?

PSEUDOLUS: (*Grandly*) I, 'tis I that doth require thee, thee, O Sire,
who doth command Pseudolus!

I bring thee something very nice:
A treble triumph, three times thrice.
Three pleasures, so neatly won,
Three treasures, discreetly wrung,
from three distinct and different men,
by guile, deceit, and stratagem!   1010
And all these things are given thee
In this sealed letter, brought by me!

CALIDORUS: The very man!

CHARINUS: The scoundrel carries on like some tragic hero.

PSEUDOLUS: Approach and meet me man to man—
And greet good fortune from my hand!

CALIDORUS: Well, Pseudolus, am I to greet you as good fortune in hand, or fortune yet to come?

PSEUDOLUS: Verily, both!

CHARINUS: Well, greetings, both! But what happened?   1020

PSEUDOLUS: Fear not!

CALIDORUS: Here's the man I caught.

PSEUDOLUS: What's that—"caught"?

CALIDORUS: I meant, "brought."

PSEUDOLUS: What's he called?

CALIDORUS: Charinus.

PSEUDOLUS: Bravo! Carry on, Charinus!

CHARINUS: Your wish is my command, just let me know.

PSEUDOLUS: Well, don't call us, Charinus, we'll call you. But, we probably won't bother.   1030

CHARINUS: Oh, it's no bother at all!

PSEUDOLUS: Okay then, wait a second. (*Turns to* CALIDORUS *to reveal what he's holding*)

CALIDORUS: What's that?

PSEUDOLUS: The letter and token that I intercepted just now.

CALIDORUS: "Token"? What token?

PSEUDOLUS: The one brought from the soldier. His slave carried it here, along with the five *minae* cold cash to carry off your sweet-heart. Boy, did I bamboozle him!

CALIDORUS: But how? 1039

PSEUDOLUS: Now look. This play's being performed to entertain our audience. They were here, and know all about it already. I'll fill you in later.

CALIDORUS: What do we do now?

PSEUDOLUS: This very day you shall have your girl free, and in your arms.

CALIDORUS: Who, me?

PSEUDOLUS: The very same. I promise. Provided I keep my head above water and you two manage to find me a man super soon.

CHARINUS: What sort? 1049

PSEUDOLUS: Wily and smart, who can play his part right through, and improvise on his own, once he's grasped the general plot. And one who's not too well-known around here.

CHARINUS: Does it matter if he's a slave?

PSEUDOLUS: Actually I'd *prefer* a slave.

CHARINUS: I think I can provide you with just the right chap. Clever and sly—my father brought him over from abroad. He's not yet stepped foot outside our house. And until yesterday, never even been in Athens! 1058

PSEUDOLUS: That's just great! Now I also need five *minae*—on loan—which I'll repay today. His father owes it to me. (*Points at* CALIDORUS)

CHARINUS: Look no further. I'll supply it!   1061

PSEUDOLUS: What a swell fellow! I also need a military cloak, a sword, and a wide-brimmed hat.

CHARINUS: You got it!

PSEUDOLUS: By the immortal gods, this Charinus is ingenious! But this slave of yours—has he got any sense?

CHARINUS: Smells just like a goat.

PSEUDOLUS: He'd better wear a long-sleeved tunic. And is he sharp?

CHARINUS: Like acid.

PSEUDOLUS: And if he gets called on for some sweet-talking, can he manage that?   1071

CHARINUS: Need you ask? Syrup, liquor, cordial, honey: all sorts of delicacies. Why he's a walking sweets shop!

PSEUDOLUS: I like it! You're just great, Charinus! Matching me in my own line of wit. But I'd just like to know the name of this slave.

CHARINUS: Simia.

PSEUDOLUS: Can he twist himself out of a tight corner?

CHARINUS: Faster than a top!

PSEUDOLUS: He's got a way with words, huh?

CHARINUS: Yes, gotten away with plenty of other things, a lot worse!

PSEUDOLUS: Suppose he's caught in the act?   1081

CHARINUS: He'll slip away like an eel.

PSEUDOLUS: This man sounds smart.

CHARINUS: Smarter than the law allows!

PSEUDOLUS: Outstanding fellow, from all you say.

CHARINUS: Wow, if you only knew him! As soon as he sees you, he'll
tell *you* everything you want him to do! But what *do* you want him
to do?

PSEUDOLUS: Listen, When I've got him all decked out, I want him to
pretend to be the soldier's slave. He must take this token to the
pimp, along with the five *minae,* and relieve the pimp of the girl.
There you have the whole scenario. As far as handling the details
—I'll coach him myself.   1093

CALIDORUS: (*Who has been growing impatient*) Well, then, what are
we waiting for?

PSEUDOLUS: I want this man—dolled up and decked out—brought
to me. We'll meet at the bank. Now hurry!

CALIDORUS: We'll be there before you!

(CALIDORUS *and* CHARINUS *exit*)

PSEUDOLUS: Then get going!

Any doubts that I had now have vanished away,   1100
for my mind is at rest, and I'm happy to say,
that the bird is in hand, and our omens are fine.
Yes, my legions stand ready, and ranked in a line.

Soon I'll lead them in battle, and conquer our foe.
Now I'm off to the forum, where Simia, I know
will receive my instructions, then use all his skill
to ensure without slip we go in for the kill!

We'll encircle their citadel, led by this slave,
and then capture the town of the tarts and their knave!   1109

(He exits quickly. Enter an unkempt boy from BALLIO's *brothel.)*

BOY: There's one thing you gotta hand to the gods; they sure know
how to kick a fellow when he's down. When they were up there on
Olympus passing out glamor and fortune they seem to have
scraped the bottom of the urn on my turn. I mean, what can be
worse than keeping house for a pimp, I ask you? On second
thought, don't tell me—I *know!* The things I have to put up with,
big and small, oh my, oh my, oh *why*, don't they leave me alone?
They say it's the oldest profession. Some career structure! You
work your way to the bottom, and stay there. And the overtime!
The customers never seem to have a day "off." Just when you think
it's quiet, there they are again, knock, knock, knock! Importunity
knocking. Let me tell you, compared to the things that go on in
this place, I'd rather be self-employed. At least it's with someone
you love! Nobody here loves me. Not really. Do I look like anyone
brings me fancy finery or food? Forget it.   1124

And to make matters worse, today's the pimp's birthday. You
never heard such a carry-on! Such threats! Presents today, or
perish tomorrow's his motto. The whole house is in such a state!
Girls screaming and scheming how to save their skins. As for the
boys—why they're all on their knees . . . praying! Absolutely
scared stiff, they are! What's a poor chap like me supposed to do?
Grin and bear it? Just open wide and try not to show any teeth?
I'm a nice boy, I am, no chance of me making a bit on the side to
give to the pimp. I'm terrified, I tell you; don't know which way to
turn.   1134

Still, I'd better get a grip on things—even though they seem
too big to handle—if I know what's good for me. Here comes the
pimp now. And he's got a cook with him. I'm history.

(He exits. BALLIO, *a boy slave, and a* COOK *and his assistants enter.)*

BALLIO: They call the place you find cooks for hire "cooks' square," but that's a joke—they should call it "crooks' square"! Even if I tried I couldn't have found a worse one than this cook here—*very-boastful*, stupid, and useless. The only reason this cook-from-hell is still around is that someone has to fix food for funerals, and this one fits the job—the dead don't complain!

COOK: Well, if that's how you feel, why did you hire me?   1144

BALLIO: No choice—you were the only one there. But why were you the only "left over" in the square?

COOK: I shall explain. It's not my fault, but a fundamental flaw in human nature that limits my desirability.

BALLIO: How do you figure that?

COOK: I shall tell you. It's like this. No one looking for a cook wants one that's good, and expensive—oh no!—they always go for the dregs. That's why I alone was still available today. Those other jerks are a dime a dozen—I won't go for less than twice the going rate! You see, I prepare my dishes differently than other cooks who serve up whole fields of vegetables for their bovine bosses to graze upon. Then they proceed to season that stuff with even more greenery! They pile on sorrel, cabbage, beets, spinach, and flavor it with coriander, fennel, garlic, parsley, then pour on a pint of "flavor enhancer" and grate on a load of that dreadful mustard that's enough to make you weep even as you grate it! Why, when it comes to seasoning it's not mustard but *buzzard* they use—to tear out the innards of your guests. Oh yes, 'tis this, *this* that shortens men's lives, stuffing their bellies with all that stuff that's too ghastly to mention, much less eat!   1164

BALLIO: And you? You who so condemn the condiments of others? I suppose your seasonings are just too, too divine—blessing one with a long life?

COOK: Oh absolutely. Why, with my food, you can *dine*, and not *die* for some two centuries. Oh yes! I just sprinkle a touch of *sparsely, page, toesmerry,* and *rhyme* into the pan and they practically do the cooking themselves. These be my seasonings for the fishy flock of Neptune; beasts of the field I prepare with *dasel, tallspice,* or *parragon.*   1173

BALLIO: Yeaaghhh! May Jove and his crowd wipe you out, together with all your spices and lies!

COOK: If perhaps I might continue.

BALLIO: Continue and be damned!

COOK: Well then, when all the pots are hot I uncover them and the scents ascend heavenward with arms upraised.

BALLIO: Scents ascend with upraised arms?   1180

COOK: Oh, I misspoke myself.

BALLIO: How's that?

COOK: I should have said "with feet upraised." And such scent Jupiter doth dine upon every day.

BALLIO: And suppose you're not cooking. How then doth Jupiter dine?

COOK: Oh, he goes to bed without his dinner.

BALLIO: Well, you can go to hell. And I'm supposed to give you money today for that?

COOK: Well, of course as cooks go, I don't come cheap. But when I work for you, you get real cost-effective value for money.

BALLIO: Yeah, in the form of pilfering.   1192

COOK: Now surely you don't suppose you'll find any cook without a sharp beak or claws?

BALLIO: And surely you don't suppose to go a-cooking without having your claws clamped while you're about it? (*To his boy*) Now, then, my little piece of property, I hereby order you to shift all our stuff to safety, and then keep your eyes glued to his; where he looks, you look; if he makes a move, you move too; if he lifts a hand, your hand is next to it; if he touches any of his own stuff let him do it, but if it belongs to us, don't let go. He takes a step, you step; stands still, so do you; and if he squats in a corner, corner him and squat alongside. And each of his minions shall have his own personal guard.   1204

COOK: Come now, just relax!

BALLIO: How am I supposed to relax when I'm about to let the likes of *you* into my house?

COOK: Ah, but think of what I'll brew for you today! Why just as Medea cooked up old Pelias with her drugs and potions, changing him from an aged slab of backside into a nice young piece of tenderloin, that's what I'll do for you!   1211

BALLIO: Cripes! Are you a poisoner as well?

COOK: Good Lord, no! Why I *serve* mankind.

BALLIO: (*Thinking this over*) I see. . . . And what's the charge for teaching me the best cooking trick of all?

COOK: Your meaning?

BALLIO: Having something "left-over" after your pilfering.

COOK: Well, if you'll just trust me, a mere trifle; if not, the sky's the limit! But tell me now, is this dinner of yours today for friends or foes?   1220

BALLIO: Why, for my friends of course!

COOK: Why not invite your foes instead of the friends? After all, the dinner I have in mind for your guests today will be so sensationally seasoned that once they've tasted one of my specially spiced dishes they'll be gnawing on their knuckles.

BALLIO: Well then, by Hercules, before you serve any of the guests, try some yourself, and give it to your other shifty chefs as well, so you can keep your nimble fingers for nibbling.

COOK: Is it possible you don't trust me?

BALLIO: Oh, don't be such a pain! That's quite enough chatter. Can't you can it? Now over there is my house. Go on inside and prepare dinner. Move it!   1232

COOK'S BOY: Sit yourself right down and call in your guests. Dinner is served!

(COOK *and his assistants leave*)

BALLIO: Get a load of that young squirt! The cook's lowest licker-upper is already a scoundrel. I really don't know which way to turn in being on guard. I've got thieves in my own house, and a robber in residence next door! My neighbor, Calidorus's father, expressly warned me a little while ago in the forum to be on alert against his slave Pseudolus, and not trust him an inch! He's on the prowl, determined if he can, to get the girl away—this very day! He even promised the old boy that one way or another he'd fiddle me out of Phoenicium! I'm going in right now to sound the alarm. I'll warn the whole establishment to be supersuspicious of Pseudolus.

(He exits inside. PSEUDOLUS *comes hurtling on.*)

PSEUDOLUS: If the gods up above ever had it in mind   1245
to support men below with assistance divine,

they must wish Calidorus and me to survive.
While leaving the pimp more dead than alive!   1248

Why, why else would they provide such a bold and brainy chap as
you to assist me? (*Looks offstage behind him*) But now where has
the fellow got to? Am I losing my marbles, talking to myself like
this? By Hercules, I think maybe he's pulled a fast one on me!
Things have come to a pretty pass when one scoundrel can't keep
track of another! By golly, I'm a goner, if this guy has got away! I
won't be able to pull off this job today! Ah! But here he comes! The
very image of a walking whipping! Just look how nobly he bears
himself. By Hercules, man, I was looking everywhere for you. I
was frantic with fear you'd turn fugitive.   1258

(*Enter* SIMIA, *disguised as* HARPAX. *Although there is no such suggestion in the text, having the role of* SIMIA *played by* CALIDORUS
*enhances the comic effect of the scene, both in terms of its suspense
and by providing the opportunity for a surprise meeting between*
PHOENICIUM *and her disguised lover.*)

SIMIA: A fitting function for me, I frankly confess.

PSEUDOLUS: Where were you?   1260

SIMIA: Some place I'd rather be.

PSEUDOLUS: Well, I was well enough aware of that.

SIMIA: Then why ask me?

PSEUDOLUS: I thought I'd give you a little advice.

SIMIA: Don't bother. You need all you've got.

PSEUDOLUS: You're being awfully naughty and haughty with me!

SIMIA: "Haughty"? Why not if I'm supposed to be a mighty military
master-mind?

PSEUDOLUS: Right! But I want to move quickly on our mutual ma-
neuvers.   1270

SIMIA: Do I look like I've got anything else in mind?

PSEUDOLUS: Double-time, then. Look lively!

SIMIA: I'd prefer to look leisured.

PSEUDOLUS: But now's our chance! While the real Snatch is asleep, I
want you to make your move.

SIMIA: What's your hurry? Take it easy, fear not! By Jupiter, I hope
that other one does turn up—that soldier's surrogate. By golly, I'll
be a better Snatch than him any day! So don't worry. I'm the right
one to do this job for you. In style! With all my deceits and double-
dealing, I'll give the soldier boy such a fright he'll deny his own
identity, and swear I'm really him!   1281

PSEUDOLUS: But how?

SIMIA: Your doubts will be the death of me!

PSEUDOLUS: What a fabulous fellow!

SIMIA: Why, when it comes to trickery and lies, you'll see how I'll
outdo you too, tutor.

PSEUDOLUS: May the gods preserve you, for my sake.

SIMIA: For my sake too. But take a look. Does my costume suit me?

PSEUDOLUS: It's just fabulous!

SIMIA: Great.   1290

PSEUDOLUS: I only hope the gods grant your desires, and not your deserts. You'd find the latter lacking! I've never known a better man for badness than you.

SIMIA: You're far too modest!

PSEUDOLUS: Mum's the word! By Jove, I'll give you gobs of goodies if you bring off this job!

SIMIA: Oh, do be quiet! Don't remind me to remember when my mind's made up for mischief. I've got it all here; wits and wiles are waiting.

PSEUDOLUS: What a fabulous felon!   1300

SIMIA: You and me both.

PSEUDOLUS: Don't you slip up!

SIMIA: Won't you *shut* up?

PSEUDOLUS: May the gods not love me if . . .

SIMIA: Don't worry, they won't! Wait for it, here comes a load of lies.

PSEUDOLUS: I just love you for being such a liar! I really respect and admire you.

SIMIA: Don't try and pass off that pap on me; I'm a master at putting out that line of patter myself.

PSEUDOLUS: Ah, what a dandy dainty you'll get today, if this job comes off!   1311

SIMIA: Ha!

PSEUDOLUS: Fine wining, dining, and reclining! Yes, and a lovely lady, to kiss and cuddle in the cutest, kindest way.

SIMIA: How nicely you entice me!

PSEUDOLUS: Oh, that's nothing to what you'll say—if you succeed.

SIMIA: If I don't, I'll hand myself over for the hangman to have. But
hurry up and point me toward the pimp's place.

PSEUDOLUS: Right over there!

SIMIA: Shhh! Hold it, its maw is gaping!   1320

PSEUDOLUS: I think the house must feel wretched.

SIMIA: Why's that?

PSEUDOLUS: Because, by golly, it's about to retch out the pimp.

(BALLIO *enters onto the porch in front of his house*)

SIMIA: Is that him?

PSEUDOLUS: Sure is.

SIMIA: Real damaged goods!

PSEUDOLUS: Just look! Even his walk is crooked, slipping sideways
like a crab.

PSEUDOLUS: (*To* SIMIA) Right! Now's the time for your task!

SIMIA: You said it!   1330

PSEUDOLUS: Make your move carefully; I'll lie in wait here.

SIMIA: (*Approaching* BALLIO) I'm sure I'm right about the number;
he said it was the sixth turning after the city gate: that's the street
I'm supposed to take. But now, how many houses along did he
say it was?

BALLIO: (*Aside*) I wonder who's the chap in the military getup? Where he's from, and who he's after? Nobody I recognize—looks like some sort of foreigner.

SIMIA: (*To* BALLIO) Ah, now there's someone who can help me out.

BALLIO: (*Aside*) He's heading this way. Wonder where in the world he's from?   1341

SIMIA: Hey there, you with the goatee like a goat—tell me something!

BALLIO: Well that's a fine "how do you do"!

SIMIA: Sorry, I'm fresh out of greetings.

BALLIO: Then you'll get the same from me.

PSEUDOLUS: (*Concealed, aside*) Things are off to a great start!

SIMIA: You know anyone living in this street? Hey, I'm asking you a question!

BALLIO: I know one: myself!   1350

SIMIA: Few can claim as much. Why in town there's hardly one man in ten who knows himself.

PSEUDOLUS: I like it! He's a philosopher!

SIMIA: The man I'm looking for is a real scoundrel: a criminal, deceitful, godless slimebag!

BALLIO: (*Aside*) Goodness! Sounds like he's after me. I answer to all of those. Wonder if he knows the name? (*To* SIMIA) Does the fellow have a proper name?

SIMIA: Ballio the pimp.

BALLIO: What did I tell you! Ah, 'tis I, I myself, young man, whom you're seeking. 1361

SIMIA: So you're Ballio?

BALLIO: The very same.

SIMIA: You're dressed like a burglar.

BALLIO: Well then perhaps you wouldn't bother to mug me in the dark!

SIMIA: My master's asked me to extend his best wishes. Here's a letter he's instructed me to give you.

BALLIO: What's his name?

PSEUDOLUS: (*Aside*) Damn! He's deep in do-do now! He doesn't know the name! We're caught! 1371

BALLIO: Well, who was it then that sent this?

SIMIA: Look at the seal. Then you tell me who it is, to prove you're really Ballio.

BALLIO: Let's have it then.

SIMIA: Take it. Now identify the seal.

BALLIO: Ah, it's Polymachaeroplagides all right, plain as day. I know him all right: it's Polymachaeroplagides.

SIMIA: (*Relieved*) That's right. Polymachaeroplagides. Good thing I gave you the letter. 1380

BALLIO: What's he up to?

SIMIA: Oh, whatever works are worthwhile for a worthy warrior. But what you've got to do now, is read the letter double-quick, and as soon as you've got the money give me the girl. If I don't get back to Sicyon today, I'll be a dead man tomorrow. My master is really strict!

BALLIO: How well I know!

SIMIA: Then hurry up and read the letter.

BALLIO: Just shut up, and I'll do it! "Polymachaeroplagides, Soldier, to Ballio, Pimp, sends this letter sealed with the hithertofore agreed upon token."   1391

SIMIA: That's the seal on the letter.

BALLIO: Yes, I've gathered that. But does he usually begin his letters so abruptly?

SIMIA: Oh, that's just soldier-speak, Ballio. A soldier's greetings to his friends is the protection of his sword. And his sword brings ill to his opponents. But read on.

BALLIO: Shut and listen! "I send my orderly, Harpax, to you . . . " So you're Harpax, are you?

SIMIA: My friends call me "Snatch."   1400

BALLIO: ". . . bearing this letter. Kindly take the money from him, and let him take away the girl. It is customary to close with respects to respectable people, hence the omission in your case."

SIMIA: So how about it?

BALLIO: Just give me the money, and take the girl!

SIMIA: Who's delaying?

BALLIO: Come on inside.

SIMIA: You bet!   1408

(*They enter* BALLIO's *house*)

PSEUDOLUS: Wow! That Simia's the craftiest con man I ever saw! Good golly, he's got me in a sweat! Now I'm worried with things working out so well, he'll turn his wiles on me, as well as Ballio! I hope he doesn't want to use his winsome ways to wage war on me! I would he won't, because I wish him well! By Pollux, my bollocks are in a triple twist! First, I'm afraid my confederate will do a flimflam and transfer his forces to the foe. Second, I'm fearful Master, fresh from the forum, will find us filching that filly from the fold. And finally I'm afraid my final fear is the real Snatch will turn up before the false one has fled the field with Phoenicium! Hell and damnation, they're taking their time! My heart's about to depart for foreign parts! (*He sees* SIMIA *and* PHOENICIUM *in the doorway*) Ah, victory is mine! Whew! The woman's wary wardens were outwitted!   1422

SIMIA: Now don't cry, Phoenicium. You don't yet know what's up, but you soon will, when we're comfy on a couch somewhere . . . having dinner. You're crying because you think I'm taking you to that man-eating Macedonian military man, aren't you? Well, soon you'll be where you're longing to be: in the arms of your own dear Calidorus!

PSEUDOLUS: What took you so long? My heart's been pounding me to pieces!   1430

SIMIA: How can you ask at a time like this, when we're still in enemy territory? Let's get out of here—feet on the street—double-quick!

PSEUDOLUS: You're right, by Castor, you disaster of a man! Forward march! Time for a drink to celebrate our triumph!

(*They leave. Enter* BALLIO *from his house.*)

BALLIO: Well, well, I'm certainly relieved now that fellow's taken
the girl off with him. Now let that sink of sin Pseudolus try to con
me out of her! If there's one thing I'm certain of, it's that I'd rather
swear and perjure myself a thousand times over, than ever let
Pseudolus make a fool of me! Now, by Hercules, the laugh's on
him. The next time we meet, I suppose he'll be slaving in the
mill—right where he belongs! Now if only Simo would turn up to
share the joy of this moment.   1443

(*Enter* SIMO, *from the forum*)

SIMO: Well, I wonder how my slave Ulysses has gotten on in his
schemes for plundering Ballio's Troy here!

BALLIO: Oh, you happy man! Let me shake your happy hand!

SIMO: What's this . . . ?

BALLIO: Well . . .

SIMO: Well, *what?*

BALLIO: There's nothing more to fear?   1450

SIMO: What's happened? Pseudolus hasn't paid you a visit, has he?

BALLIO: No.

SIMO: Then why so happy?

BALLIO: The twenty *minae* that Pseudolus swore he'd swindle out of
you today . . .

SIMO: Yes, yes?

BALLIO: It's safe and sound!

SIMO: Oh, by Hercules, if only that's true!

BALLIO: Why, if he succeeds in getting the girl, or hands her over to your son today, I'll give you twenty *minae* myself! Go ahead and ask me to promise; I'm longing to prove to you your money's absolutely safe. (*In a confident tone*) I'll even throw in a girl for free to sweeten my promise.   1463

SIMO: Well those are terms I can hardly refuse! Okay. So you promise to give me the twenty *minae* yourself?

BALLIO: I do.

SIMO: (*Aside*) Nothing bad about this bargain! But did you actually encounter Pseudolus?

BALLIO: Sure did. Him and Calidorus both.

SIMO: What did he say to you? What sort of line did he try to spin? Come on, I'm longing to know what he said.   1471

BALLIO: Oh, mere theatrical patter; the usual line of abuse a pimp gets in comedies; stuff schoolboys know. He said I was nasty, and wicked, and a liar.

SIMO: Gee, he didn't exaggerate!

BALLIO: Indeed. Consequently I took no offense. What good is it to insult a man like me, who's beneath reproach and not bothered by abuse?

SIMO: Okay for you. But why don't *I* need to worry about him anymore? Tell me; I can't wait to hear!   1480

BALLIO: Because now there's no way whatever he can cheat me out of the chick. Remember I told you she was on layaway to that Macedonian soldier?

SIMO: Yes, yes!

BALLIO: Well his chargé d'affaires has just given me the money and the letter with the soldier's seal . . .

SIMO: How's that?

BALLIO: . . . as per our agreement! He took her away just a few moments ago.

SIMO: Word of honor?   1490

BALLIO: Where would I get any of that?

SIMO: You're certain he's not been up to some razzle-dazzle deception?

BALLIO: The letter and the seal were absolutely genuine. In fact, the man's already out of the city on his way to Sicyon.

SIMO: Well then, congratulations! Now then, shall we sign Pseudolus up for a little holiday at Milltown? (*Sees the real* HARPAX *approaching*) But who's this chap in the military getup?

BALLIO: Damned if I know. Let's see where he's heading and what business he's about.   1500

HARPAX: It's a slob of a slave that doesn't mind his master's business, or can't be bothered to do his duty unless reminded. The sort who—the moment they're out of Master's sight—live it up like freemen. Wasting away in the fleshpots. Why they'll never better themselves that way! Once a slave, always a slave! Nothing going for them at all, except more of the same brazen badness! Me, I try to avoid all contact or conversation with such types—I keep my distance. I believe in doing just as I'm told, even when Master's absent. After all, if I show respect when he's away, I'll have nothing to fear when he's around.   1510

Now for the business at hand. All this time I've been waiting at the tavern, just as that Surus told me to when I gave him the letter. He said he'd come and fetch me the moment the pimp returned home. Well, since he didn't summon or send for me, I've come unsummoned to find out what's going on, and to make sure he's not up to any mischief. (*Approaching* BALLIO's *house*) The best thing I guess, is just to knock on that door, and summon someone. I want to give this money to the pimp so I can take the girl with me.

BALLIO: (*Hearing* HARPAX's *last line*) Well, now!   1520

SIMO: What?

BALLIO: This man is for me.

SIMO: What do you mean, "for you"?

BALLIO: He's ripe for plucking. He's got money and he wants a honey! My mouth is watering!

SIMO: So you want to gobble him up?

BALLIO: You bet, Best swallow him whole; fresh, hot, and stuffed with cash! Good men are no good to me; it's those of ill-repute who put food on my table.

SIMO: And the gods give you your just deserts!   1530

HARPAX: Well, there's no use hanging around. I'll knock and see if Ballio's about.

BALLIO: (*Gleefully*) Venus is smiling on me, keeping me supplied with all these spendthrift losers and lovers, out for a good time of eating, drinking and making merry with the misses. (*To* SIMO) Not your type at all, who don't know how to enjoy yourself, but begrudge those who do!

HARPAX: (*Knocking*) Hello! Anybody home?

BALLIO: There now, he's walking right into my hands. I'm just sure I'll soon make a pile off this one: the omens are auspicious!

HARPAX: Hello! Will someone open the door?   1541

BALLIO: Hey there, soldier boy! Who are you looking for?

HARPAX: The owner of this establishment. The pimp, Ballio.

BALLIO: Well, young fellow, look no more!

HARPAX: Why not?

BALLIO: Because he's standing here right in front of you.

HARPAX: (*Thinking he means* SIMO) Oh, are you Ballio?

SIMO: You better be careful, soldier, unless you're bent on a beating. Point at him; he's the pimp.

BALLIO: And he's the respectable gentleman. Your solid citizen who, incidentally, often can't produce a penny for his creditors in the forum, without a little timely assistance from his friendly pimp!   1553

HARPAX: Can we talk?

BALLIO: Let's talk. What can I do for you?

HARPAX: Take this money.

BALLIO: Why didn't you ask sooner?

HARPAX: Here it is. Five *minae*, cold cash. I have orders from my master, Polymachaeroplagides to give you this, the sum owed on your layaway plan for Phoenicium, who's to come with me now.

BALLIO: Your master . . .   1561

HARPAX: That's correct.

BALLIO: . . . A soldier . . .

HARPAX: Right again.

BALLIO: A Macedonian, possibly?

HARPAX: No doubt about it!

BALLIO: You were sent to me by Polymachaeroplagides?

HARPAX: You got it.

BALLIO: To give me this money?

HARPAX: Yes indeed. Provided you're Ballio the pimp.   1570

BALLIO: And you're to get a girl from me?

HARPAX: Exactly.

BALLIO: Name of Phoenicium?

HARPAX: Your memory's perfect!

BALLIO: Would you excuse me for just a moment? I'll be right back.
     (*Goes over to* SIMO *to confer*)

HARPAX: Okay, but make it snappy. I'm running late.

BALLIO: Yes, I can see that. I just want to consult with my adviser
     here. Just wait a second; I'll be back in a jiffy. (*To* SIMO) Well, now
     Simo, how about this! I've caught this soldier with the money, red-
     handed.   1580

SIMO: I don't get it.

BALLIO: Don't you see what's going on?

SIMO: It's over my head, I'm afraid.

BALLIO: Your slave Pseudolus has sent *him* to pretend to be the Macedonian's military attaché.

SIMO: And did you get the money off him?

BALLIO: (*Shows him the money*) What does this look like?

SIMO: Well, don't forget to give me half the haul; share and share alike!

BALLIO: What the hell! It's probably all yours, anyway!   1590

HARPAX: How long do I have to wait?

BALLIO: (*To him*) Oh, only a minute now! (*To* SIMO) What's your advice, Simo?

SIMO: Let's have a bit of fun with this surrogate of Pseudolus, and see how long he takes to realize we're on to him.

BALLIO: Follow me. (*To* HARPAX) Well, now, so you're the soldier's slave, are you?

HARPAX: Obviously.

BALLIO: How much did you cost him?

HARPAX: He had to win me through valor on the field of battle. I was leading the opposing forces.   1601

SIMO: He was raiding a prison, was he?

HARPAX: If you're going to insult me, you'll get as good as you give.

BALLIO: How long did it take to get here from Sicyon?

HARPAX: A day and a half.

BALLIO: A real speed demon!

SIMO: Oh, he's fast all right! Just look at those legs—just right for wearing chains.

BALLIO: Aren't they just! Tell me, when you were a little boy, did you used to lie in a cradle?   1610

HARPAX: Of course.

BALLIO: And did you used to make—you know what?

SIMO: Of course he did!

HARPAX: (*Bewildered*) Are you two nuts?

BALLIO: And tell me now, at night when you and soldier boy were out on patrol together, did you ever offer him a nice place to sheathe his sword?

HARPAX: Go to hell!

BALLIO: That's just what's in store for you, this very day.

HARPAX: Now see here. Either give me the girl, or return the money.   1621

BALLIO: Wait a moment.

HARPAX: Why should I?

BALLIO: (*Pulling at his cloak*) How much did it cost you to hire this cloak?

HARPAX: What?

SIMO: And this sword. What did they charge you for that?

HARPAX: These two are missing some marbles!

BALLIO: (*Grabbing his hat*) Whooopee!

HARPAX: Hey, let go!   1630

BALLIO: What did the owner of this hat charge to lend it?

HARPAX: What owner? Are you two out of your heads? I paid for all these things out of my own pocket.

BALLIO: The one between your legs, no doubt!

HARPAX: (*Erupting*) You two old fools are well-oiled. What you want is a good old-fashioned massage.

BALLIO: Now hold on, by Hercules. Seriously, just answer one little question for me. *The price?* What's Pseudolus paying you for this?

HARPAX: Who's Pseudolus?

BALLIO: Why, the author of this mischief of course! The one who's coached you to con me out of the concubine.   1641

HARPAX: What mischief? I don't know this Pseudolus of yours; I haven't a clue who he is!

BALLIO: Oh, come off it! There's nothing for felons to fiddle here today. So just tell Pseudolus that someone beat him to the prize: Snatch got here first.

HARPAX: But damn it all man, *I'm* Snatch!!

BALLIO: You are? You're *not!* (*To* SIMO) Why, he's an impostor, sure as shooting!

HARPAX: Look, I gave you the money, right here a few moments ago, right? And earlier, when I first arrived, I gave your slave a letter with my master's seal, Right?   1652

BALLIO: Right! I mean, wrong! You gave a letter to my slave? Which slave?

HARPAX: Why Surus, of course.

BALLIO: You're sure it was Surus? (*Aside to* SIMO) That rogue Pseudolus has thought of everything. He gave this impostor the exact sum owed by the soldier, and decked him out to abduct the girl. But he's overplayed his part. (*To* HARPAX) Now see here, Snatch himself brought the letter to me.   1660

HARPAX: But I tell you, I'm Snatch! The servant of a Macedonian soldier. I'm not trying to fiddle anyone out of anything! And I never met, and never heard of anyone named Pseudolus!

SIMO: Sounds to me, pimp, that short of a miracle, Phoenicium has finally flown the flock.

BALLIO: Oh, mercy me, the more I hear, the worse I fear! Good Lord, yes, when he mentioned Surus, my heart did a frozen flip flop. Assures us he gave the letter to Surus, does he? It'll be a miracle if it wasn't Pseudolus himself! (*To* HARPAX) Wait! Listen! What did this fellow you gave the letter to look like?   1676

HARPAX: Let's see now . . . red hair . . . pot belly . . . thick calves . . . swarthy complexion . . . large head . . . sharp eyes . . . ruddy face . . . and, oh yes! tremendous feet!

BALLIO: (*Falling faint*) Oh, Lord! You've flattened and finished me with those feet! It *was* Pseudolus! I'm dead and done for, Simo: a limp pimp!

HARPAX: You speak too soon. Hang on, by Hercules, until you hand over my twenty *minae!*

(*Draws his sword*)

SIMO: And I want my twenty *minae* too!

(*Raises his stick*)

BALLIO: (*To* SIMO) Oh, now surely you're not going to hold me to a wager I made in jest!?   1681

SIMO: Why it's a civic duty, unburdening bullies of their bets and their booty.

BALLIO: Well then at least let me get my hands on Pseudolus!

SIMO: Give Pseudolus to you? Why blame him when I warned you a hundred times to beware of him?

BALLIO: But he's wiped me out!

SIMO: Yes, and lightened me by twenty *minae!*

BALLIO: Oh, whatever shall I do?

HARPAX: As soon as you've given me my money, you can go flog yourself.   1691

BALLIO: And you can go to blazes! Alright, follow me to the forum, and I'll pay up.

HARPAX: I'm following.

SIMO: What about me?

BALLIO: I pay off my foreign trade deficit today; the domestic account can wait till tomorrow. Oh, I've been overdrawn and quartered by Pseudolus today, when he put up that impostor to gull me out of the girl! (*To* HARPAX) Come on then. (*To audience*) Don't expect me to show my face on this street again. I'll slink back home through the back alley.   1701

HARPAX: We'd be in the forum already, if you walked as fast as you talked.

BALLIO: And this is supposed to be my birthday. Better call it my "deathday."

(BALLIO *exits with* HARPAX *toward the forum*)

SIMO: (*To audience*) Well, I scored one on him alright, and my slave bashed Ballio beyond belief. Now I think I'll prepare a little reception for Pseudolus. Not that nonsense with clubs and whips you normally see in most comedies. No, I'm going right inside and fetch the twenty *minae* I promised Pseudolus if he brought this off. He won't even have to ask; I'll just give it to him! By golly, he's the cleverest thing on feet! No one's ploys are so nifty or shifty! Why, Ulysses and that business with the Trojan Horse were child's play compared to Pseudolus. I'll go in and get the cash, and then prepare a little surprise for Pseudolus.   1715

(*Exits into his house. Enter* PSEUDOLUS, *inebriated. The text for this song is fragmentary.*)

PSEUDOLUS: Feet, you're not doing your thing! Time to make a stand; no falling down on the job. That's the problem with drink; it always goes for you feet first. Now mind, do you hear? (*To audience*) I've been soaking it up in the best society. And mercy me, I had the most marvelous things to munch on! A proper party, fit for the gods. It's what life's all about, isn't it? Having a good time, being on top of . . . the world . . . enjoying yourself . . . and others!   1722

When a lover is hugging his lover,
lips and tongues exploring each other,
soon their limbs are entwined,
and their—well, never mind.
What comes next must take place under cover!

I've been living it up with young Master
and toasting our opponents' disaster.
We've been wining and wenching,   1730
and dining and drenching,
while the world turns faster and faster!

I was spinning about in a trance.
Even led everyone in a dance!
I fell flat on the floor,
while the crowd yelled "Encore!"
and my dignity wasn't enhanced!

So here I am, out for a draft of fresh air. Now's the time to turn my
attention from one master to another, and remind the senior—
Simo—of our bargain. (*Goes up and knocks on* SIMO's *door*) Hey
in there, open up! Open open, up up! Someone say to Simo, his
servant Pseudolus is summoning him!   1742

SIMO: (*Appearing in the doorway*) Well, if it isn't the voice of the
vilest villain alive that calls me out! My goodness, what's this
I see?

PSEUDOLUS: A man wearing a garland . . . your own sweet Pseudolus, soused!

SIMO: Enjoying a bit of freedom by the look of it! Just look at him—
not precisely a picture of piety in my presence!

PSEUDOLUS: Pseudolus the rogue greets Simo the gentleman!

SIMO: Gods bless you, Pseudolus. (*Embraces, then pushes him away*)
Pheww! Keep the hell away!   1752

PSEUDOLUS: Why all this to-ing and fro-ing?

SIMO: Why these belches in my face, you brazen beer bag?

PSEUDOLUS: Look, handle with care, please, "this side up." Can't
you see I'm already slightly smashed?

SIMO: Now Pseudolus, what are you thinking of, going around like
this and dolled up and drunk in broad daylight?

PSEUDOLUS: It's very nice?

SIMO: Nice? My nose knows it not nice!   1760

PSEUDOLUS: Oh, don't let that bother you, it's just a sweet little
(*Burps*) . . . belch!

SIMO: Why, you old souse! I shouldn't doubt you could soak up
several seasons' wine harvest in under an hour.

PSEUDOLUS: What a worthy way to while away a winter hour!

SIMO: You've got a point. But tell, where have you been sailing in
this bloated barge of a body?

PSEUDOLUS: Your son and I have been taking a drink together.
(*Starts to giggle*) Oh, but *Simo*, didn't we just bamboozle Ballio
brilliantly? Just like I promised?   1770

SIMO: What a rascal you are!

PSEUDOLUS: It's all the girl's . . . doing! Now she's free, very free
indeed, with your son . . . on a couch!

SIMO: I know all about what you've been up to.

PSEUDOLUS: Well then, why the delay in giving me my reward?

SIMO: It's your due, I admit it. Here.

PSEUDOLUS: And you said I'd never get it out of you! Well, let's have it, and then follow me this way.

(*Points offstage, intending to parade* SIMO *through the town*)

SIMO: (*Aside*) What am I going to do with him? He intends to take my money and publicly humiliate me as part of the bargain.

PSEUDOLUS: Woe to the vanquished!   1781

(*Indicating that* SIMO *should fall on his knees*)

SIMO: I never thought I'd be brought so low, on my knees before you! Oh dear, oh dear, oh dear!

PSEUDOLUS: Now cut that out!

SIMO: Just think how I suffer!

PSEUDOLUS: I'm thinking how *I'd* be suffering if you weren't.

SIMO: You really intend to take this from your own dear master?

PSEUDOLUS: With the greatest possible pleasure.

SIMO: Oh, now dear Pseudolus, do please let me keep some of it for myself.   1790

PSEUDOLUS: No way! Call me a greedy cheeky Greeky slave, but you'll never get a penny. How much mercy would you have shown my hide and backside, if I'd failed today?

SIMO: All right, then, take it.

(PSEUDOLUS *does so and strides away, leaving* SIMO *on his knees*)

PSEUDOLUS: Now come over here!

SIMO: Come over there? Why?

PSEUDOLUS: Just come over. There's no catch.

SIMO: Here I am.

(*They stand face to face.* PSEUDOLUS *points to the slave collar and cuffs he wears, which* SIMO *removes one by one, as* PSEUDOLUS *counts out the money to him.* SIMO *hesitates, then gives the money back. They embrace.*)

PSEUDOLUS: I want to invite you to go drinking with me.

SIMO: You do?   1800

PSEUDOLUS: That's right. I'm giving the orders now. Obey, and I'll share some, maybe all of this with you!

SIMO: Who can resist an invitation like that?

PSEUDOLUS: What about it, Simo? Are you still angry with your son or me on account of all this?

SIMO: No, not a bit.

PSEUDOLUS: Let's go.

SIMO: After you. Shall we invite the audience as well?

PSEUDOLUS: Good Lord, no! Not that lot! When did they ever invite me for a drink? Well, tell you what. If you'd like to show your appreciation of our company and play, I'll invite you after all . . . to tomorrow's performance!   1812

(*They leave, arm in arm*)

STICHUS

Translated by Carol Poster

INTRODUCTION

I don't know whether it is desirable for a translator to approach a literary work without any preconceptions at all, but in most cases it is probably not possible. Even when I translate minor French symbolists with whom I have little previous acquaintance (e.g., Herold, Leberghe, and Samain), I still have some general notions of how to approach a late-nineteenth-century French lyrical poem. In the case of an author as familiar as Plautus, the problem is complicated by having seen his works in performance, read them in translation, and studied them in Latin classes.

Before I started translating the *Stichus*, I hadn't looked at Plautus for several years. I vaguely remembered a few common generalizations about his work—that it was low comedy, boisterous, vulgar, filled with sight gags, mistaken identities, and broadly sketched stock characters. I also remembered that Roman comedy, although not quite as obscene and scatological as the Greek, used language much cruder than the Ciceronian standard followed in most Latin texts, made frequent use of demonstratives, and employed elaborate and exotic meters.

When I began to work with the *Stichus*, I found some of my preconceptions quite accurate—demonstratives abounded, there was a tremendous variety of meters, and colloquial usages predominated —but I also discovered that the play violates many of what I had considered the characteristic rules of Plautine drama.

The play opens with a dialogue between Panegyris and her sister, two young married women who are both intelligent, witty, decent, and loyal to their husbands. They are not autocratic matrons, silly girls, or grasping prostitutes; instead, they are as charming a pair of heroines as might be found in any author. While their father, Antipho, the parasite, Gelasimus, and the running slave,

Pinacium, are stock characters, the humor of the discussions between Pinacium and Panegyris is far greater than might be expected, and the husbands, when they finally do arrive, prove to be a
pair of very nice young men. Even during the celebration at the end
of the play, the two slaves, Stichus and Sangarinus, share their girlfriend Stephanium in perfect drunken amiability.

After having read the Latin text and both available translations
of the play, I began to consider how I might best approach the task of
translation. The central stylistic problem was how to use language
that would express the charm of the two young women, the extravagant enthusiasm of Pinacium, the pomposity of Antipho, the extravagant humor of Gelasimus, and the vulgar ribaldry of the slaves.
Originally, I had planned to use meter to construct these distinc-
tions, making the two young couples speak in iambs and having the
remaining characters speak in anapests. I attempted a complete first
draft of a strictly metrical translation—and it was incredibly bad.
The language was awkward, stilted, and unactable.

My previous translation experience had been confined to short
poems, in which every line demanded lyric intensity. In Plautus, as
in Homer or Shakespeare or any extended epic or drama, there are
many lines that are quite prosaic, and serve only to further the plot,
such as lines 582–583 of the *Stichus:*

> sed videone ego Pamphilippum cum fratre Epignomo? atque is
> est. adgrediar hominem . . .

> [but do I see Pamphilipus with his brother Epignomus? Yes it is.
> I will go to him . . .]

Rendering such lines into elegant verse would be a task almost
impossible for any translator except Alexander Pope.

Despite a strong preference for strictly metrical translations of
verse, I finally decided to let my ear control the rhythm of the lines
rather than trying to conform to some predetermined metrical
scheme. The rhythmical idiom I eventually found to work best was
an accentual line with frequent, though irregular, use of full or
partial rhymes at caesuras and ends of lines.

Once I had found a comfortable rhythmical idiom for the play, I
was forced to address one remaining difficult issue: the structural

dilemma of the play. The first act of the play provides an obvious dramatic conflict. The two husbands have been absent for three years. Antipho wants to take his daughters back and marry them to rich men. The two women want to remain faithful to their husbands. This conflict is resolved with the return of the husbands at the end of the second act. The main plot is resolved and the play is less than half over. Two minor subplots—whether the parasite Gelasimus will get his dinner (acts 3 and 4) and which slave will get the girl (act 5)— don't seem sufficiently substantial to sustain the action of the play.

A minor, and not fully articulated, subplot seems to run just below the surface of the play. The two young families are impoverished. The women appear concerned that the husbands will blame them for bad household management. Just at the end of act 4, however, it becomes apparent that Epignomus blames Gelasimus for their earlier poverty, and martial harmony is restored. I did consider interpolating a few passages (in square brackets) to fully articulate this subplot in order to extend the central action of the play through the end of act 4, but eventually I decided to stay as close to the original text as possible.

The only other feature of this translation that some readers might find somewhat idiosyncratic are the frequent overt references to oratory. Although the reason I might tend to notice or emphasize these references more than many translators no doubt has something to do with my scholarly involvement in classical rhetoric, I do think that my reading of these allusions is justified because rhetoric was not only an extremely important part of Roman education but was also almost as ubiquitous in antiquity as television is today.

I hope that the end result of my various decisions is a translation that is, on the one hand, faithful to the original text, and, on the other hand, actable on the contemporary stage.

Carol Poster

STICHUS

CHARACTERS

PANEGYRIS, wife of Epignomus

SISTER of Panegyris, wife of Pamphilippus

ANTIPHO, elderly father of Panegyris

GELASIMUS, a parasite

CROCOTIUM, maid and slave of Panegyris

PINACIUM, young boy, slave of Panegyris

EPIGNOMUS, husband of Panegyris and brother of Pamphilippus

PAMPHILIPPUS, husband of Sister of Panegyris and brother of Epignomus

STICHUS, slave of Epignomus

SANGARINUS, slave of Pamphilippus

STEPHANIUM, maid and slave of Sister

SCENE: *Main stage represents street in front of three houses, which
belong to* ANTIPHO, PANEGYRIS, *and her* SISTER. *Wide doors enable
audience to watch scene inside* PANEGYRIS's *house. Orchestra
(in classical theater) or thrust (in proscenium theater) represents
streets in other areas of city. As the play starts,* PANEGYRIS *and her*
SISTER *enter together.*

ARGUMENT

Panegyris and her sister have married two rich brothers, Epignomus and Pamphilippus. The brothers lose their money, and leave on a long journey to recover their fortunes. When the play opens, the father, Antipho, tries to force the sisters to leave their husbands. The sisters remain faithful. The husbands return, their fortunes restored. The slaves celebrate.

ACT I

Scene 1

PANEGYRIS: Sister, I weave in my soul
  Like Penelope wove on her loom.
  I've been feeling like her—lonely
  Since our husbands have been gone.
  We need to practice strategems,
  Quite as complex as hers,
  To take care of business
  And household budgets
  In our husbands' absence.

SISTER: It's only right   10
  We do our jobs,
  Obeying commands
  Of honor and gods.
  But come here, Sister, and sit down.
  I really need to talk with you now
  About our husbands.

PANEGYRIS: Is something wrong?

SISTER: I hope and pray they're well. That's not the problem.
    Until this time our father's
    Been a model citizen,
    Praised by everyone who knows him.   20
    But now he's changed.
    He threatens to recall us
    From the husbands to whom he gave us,
    An unmerited injustice,
    He plans to do in their absence.
    That's why I'm so depressed,
    So bored with life, and restless.

PANEGYRIS: Don't cry, my sister, or you'll
    Do to yourself the damage
    Our father tries to do to you.   30
    It's better by far to hope.
    I know our father, the way
    He likes to play these games
    With us. If he were offered
    A mountain made of gold,
    He'd never do what you fear.
    But even if he did,
    We'd have no right
    To fight him.
    It's been three years since our husbands left.   40
    They deserve it.

SISTER: I know.

PANEGYRIS: Where they are, how they're behaving,
    What they're doing, when they'll be back,
    If they're well, or even alive,
    For three years, we haven't heard
    Anything, haven't received
    A single word.

SISTER: Sister, are you sad because
   They're not doing their duties as husbands,
   While we're being dutiful wives?

PANEGYRIS: Absolutely.   50

SISTER: Be quiet, Sister. I never want to hear
   These ideas from you again.

PANEGYRIS: Why not?

SISTER: Because, in my soul, I know it's right.
   That's why in this (and only this)
   I can teach my older sister—and advise
   You to remember your duty.
   And if our husbands act badly,
   We must remember
   To behave even better,
   Become models of propriety.   60

PANEGYRIS: All right. I'll be quiet.

SISTER: And you'll remember what I said.

Scene 2

(*Enter* ANTIPHO *with slaves*)

ANTIPHO: How many times do I have to remind
   You slaves to do your duty?
   People who won't do their jobs
   Without frequent reminders
   Have no sense of common decency.
   Why are your minds so deficient
   When it comes to household chores?
   When it's time to collect your wages,   70

You're models of efficiency.
I'll want this house immaculate
When I get back from my visit,
And if you forget this task,
I'll whip your memories into shape.
I live with pigs, not people!
The furniture should shine,
The walls should gleam,
Not a speck of dust on the floor,
Or you'll be in trouble   80
When I get home.
I'm going to my older daughter's house.
If you need me, you'll find me there.
I'll be back soon.

SISTER: What shall we do, Sister, if he persists
    In holding out against us?

PANEGYRIS: If he commands us,
    We'll have to obey his parental authority.
    If we act rebellious, he'll oppose us.
    My best guess is that love and obedience
    Will have the greatest success with him.   90
    We can't disobey him and still act virtuously,
    But if we plead with him to arouse his pity,
    And stir his generosity with extravagant flattery,
    We can succeed. I know our father;
    He's easy enough to persuade.

ANTIPHO: (*To himself*) How shall I approach my girls?
    Shall I enchant them with my eloquence,
    Or tangle them in terrible tales,
    Condescend to them graciously
    Or rant at them ferociously?   100
    I know they'll want to keep their husbands,
    And I don't want to start any arguments,
    So, first, I'll baffle them with blandishments,
    And when they're overcome with my oratory,

And thoroughly perplexed by my perspicuity,
Then I'll advocate the divorces openly.
I've got a way with words.
                              There's the door.
    It's open.

SISTER: I'm sure I heard our father.

PANEGYRIS: You did.
    Let's overwhelm him with loving kisses.   110

SISTER: Hello, darling Father.

(*Both sisters embrace him*)

ANTIPHO: Hello. Stop that! Sit down!

SISTER: Just one more hug!

ANTIPHO: I've had enough of your hugs and kisses.

PANEGYRIS: Father, don't you love us?

ANTIPHO: Your tears have made my breath too salty.

SISTER: Sit here, Father.

ANTIPHO: You sit there. I'll take the bench.

PANEGYRIS: The bench is too hard; here's a cushion.

ANTIPHO: You take care of me well. I'm sufficiently padded. Now
    stop.

SISTER: Not quite enough.

ANTIPHO: What are you doing?

PANEGYRIS: Bringing another.

ANTIPHO: Whatever you want. That's fine. 120

SISTER: A daughter can never do too much
For the comfort of her parents.
And after her father she should care most
For the husband to whom he gave her.

ANTIPHO: Your loyalty is impressive.
You treat your husbands equally well
Whether they're absent or they're present.

SISTER: Since they have chosen to marry us,
It's our duty to act virtuous.

ANTIPHO: Are we alone? Can anyone overhear us? 130

PANEGYRIS: We're alone here.

ANTIPHO: Concentrate hard on what I say,
For I'm ignorant of women's ways,
And question you like a stranger
Asking a local about a foreign place.
What sort of women do both of you think
Make the best wives?

SISTER: Why are you asking?

ANTIPHO: I'm hoping to find another wife.
It's been several years since your mother died.

SISTER: There are many women far worse than her, 140
And I've never known any better.

ANTIPHO: And yet I've posed this question to you,
And also to your sister.

SISTER: I suppose that what's best is what's most proper.

ANTIPHO: I want to know what things you value most.

SISTER: A woman should do nothing that exposes her
   To mischievous rumors and gossip.

ANTIPHO: What do you think?

PANEGYRIS: What do you want to hear?

ANTIPHO: How can I tell by watching closely,
   What sort of woman will suit me best?

PANEGYRIS: Choose a woman who, when tempted to neglect her
      duty   150
   And given chances to behave badly,
   Consistently continues to act honorably.

ANTIPHO: How can a woman behave
      faultlessly?

SISTER: Never to do today an act she'll regret tomorrow.

ANTIPHO: What sort of woman do you think wisest?

PANEGYRIS: One who controls herself in prosperity,
   And remains steadfast in adversity.

ANTIPHO: You've defended your virtues cleverly,
   But the reason I came to see you really
   Was my associates argued persuasively
   That I should carry you back home with me.   160

SISTER: We're the people that choice would affect most.
   If you didn't approve of our husbands,
   You shouldn't have chosen them for us at all,

And to take us back from them while they're gone,
Is completely unjust.

ANTIPHO: But wouldn't it be more unfair,
   To leave you married to beggars?

SISTER: I'm perfectly happy with my beggar,
   And will love him as much in our current poverty
   As I did in our earlier prosperity.
   It was to the man, not his money, you married me.   170

ANTIPHO: They've abandoned you for the past three years.
   Why stay married to men who treat you so badly,
   When I could find you husbands
   Who'd care for you superbly?

PANEGYRIS: Father, you wouldn't expect dogs to hunt well
   If they went out unwillingly.
   An involuntary bride is a man's worst enemy.

ANTIPHO: Do you both refuse to obey me?

PANEGYRIS: We're obeying you by staying
   With the men to whom you gave us.   180

ANTIPHO: Goodbye. I'll repeat to my friends
   What you've just said.

PANEGYRIS: If you retell it skillfully,
   They'll agree with me.

ANTIPHO: Take care of your household now,
   To the best of your ability.

PANEGYRIS: That's good advice.
   See how well we obey you—when you're right.
   Now, Sister, let's go inside.

SISTER: No. I need to go
  And do some work on my own home.
  If you hear news of our husbands,   190
  Let me know.

PANEGYRIS: Of course. And you'll share with me
  Any word that comes your way.

(SISTER *exits*)

PANEGYRIS: Crocotium, come here!

(CROCOTIUM *enters*)

PANEGYRIS: Find the parasite Gelasimus, and bring him here
      with you.
  I want to send him to the harbor to see if there's any news,
  Of a ship from Asia having arrived today, or rumors
  That one's to be arriving soon. Although I send a slave
  To stay at the harbor from dawn to dusk each day,
  I want to be sure. Do this quickly, then return.

(PANEGYRIS *exits*)

                                    Scene 3

(*Enter* GELASIMUS, *downstage of* CROCOTIUM, *so he doesn't see her*)

GELASIMUS: I think that my mother was Hunger herself,   200
  For she's been with me since the day of my birth,
  My belly's been empty since I first walked on earth.
  I've more than repaid her for carrying me.
  For ten months she carried me in her belly,
  But for more than ten years she's been with me.
  And when she carried me I was extremely tiny.
  It mustn't have been much work for her,

But look at the size of the hunger I carry.
Bearing her is a Herculean labor,
For she's enormous, and very heavy.   210
My belly pains me almost daily,
But I can't give birth to my own mother;
Nothing will rid me of my hunger.
I've heard that elephants endure a ten-year pregnancy;
I wonder if an elephant planted this seed of hunger in me,
For that's how long it's been growing in my belly.
If anyone's in the market for a comedian,
I'm for sale, with all my routines.
I'd do anything for a meal.
When I was small, my father named me Gelasimus—   220
After his mule—because I always made a fool of myself.
I was born a fool,
And as poor as a mule,
But it was starvation that made a comedian of me.
Father always complained about the price of food,
I, too, have learned to scheme, because I've never had money.
But even though I'm poor, I still behave generously:
I never turn down anyone who offers to feed me.
Although I continue to live quite traditionally,
All around me I've observed a decline in oratory.   230
The best kind of speech I've ever heard,
Has almost completely vanished from earth—
The dinner invitation.
I'd always heard this kind of declamation:
"Come dine with me, if you please;
I'd like to invite you over for a meal—
If it's not inconvenient."
A new rhetoric has invaded our country,
Filled with vile and pernicious sophistries.
I hear it all around me: 240
"I'd like to invite you to dine at my house,
But I'm eating out tonight myself."
I want to take those words and rip their flesh from their bones,
Or worse, I'd like to make them eat at home.
These foreign words have forced me

To take barbaric measures.
Acting as my own auctioneer,
I'll sell myself to the highest bidder.

(CROCOTIUM *moves upstage of* GELASIMUS)

CROCOTIUM: The parasite I was sent to fetch is over there.
    I'll stay inconspicuous, and see what I can overhear.   250

GELASIMUS: There are many inquisitive people in this town,
    Who would turn strangers' business into their own;
    They'll pry into whatever they see,
    With no better excuse than curiosity.
    At the sight of an auction, they wonder what it can be:
    An estate sale, a divorce, or a bankruptcy.
    For a meal I'd subject myself to any indignity!
    I'll satisfy the vicious gossips,
    My enemies, and all the nosy busybodies.
    This is why I'm holding a sale;   260
    All my possessions have passed away.
    All my morning snacks and midday meals,
    Elaborate dinners and glasses of beer,
    Have completely disappeared
    Since my best friends left me alone here,
    Trading abroad for the past three years.
    I miss their lively company
    Almost as much as their dinner parties.

CROCOTIUM: He's so funny when he's hungry.

GELASIMUS: Now, I'll hold my auction. I plan to sell   270
    Every single one of my possessions.
    Come here! Step right up! You can't fail to profit.
    The first lot consists of funny stories.
    What do you bid? Do I hear a dinner?
    Or even a lunch: What do you offer for this lot?
    You there—did you nod? No?
    Nothing for this lot.

What about perfumed oils or rubbing alcohols?
Massage equipment or hangover cures?
Ancient aphorisms or parasitical perorations?   280
Creaky riddles or out-of-date jokes,
Famous one-liners or unpopular puns?
Or—to store the leftovers from your dinners
An empty parasite—hollow with hunger?
Help me out! Bid as much as you can.
I need the money to pay my taxes.

CROCOTIUM: I don't want to buy anything he's selling.
    His hunger seems to have increased the size of his belly.
    I'll interrupt.

GELASIMUS: Who's walking toward me? Oh, it's Epignomus's
    maid,   290
    Crocotium.

CROCOTIUM: Hello, Gelasimus.

GELASIMUS: That's not my name.

CROCOTIUM: That's what we used to call you.

GELASIMUS: Things have changed.
    You now should call me the Stand-up Scavenger.

CROCOTIUM: You've certainly entertained me today.

GELASIMUS: How? When?

CROCOTIUM: Just now, when you played the auctioneer.

GELASIMUS: I didn't know I
    was overheard.

CROCOTIUM: You got what you deserved.

GELASIMUS: Where were you going?

CROCOTIUM: To meet you here.

GELASIMUS: Why?

CROCOTIUM: Panegyris ordered me to bring you to her,
  As soon as possible.

GELASIMUS: I'll move as fast as I can.
  Has she made a sacrifice? Is she grilling a lamb?   300

CROCOTIUM: Nothing's cooking.

GELASIMUS: Then what sort of food does she
    talk about?

CROCOTIUM: Ten bushels of wheat, I think.

GELASIMUS: She plans to give them to me?

CROCOTIUM: Actually, she wants to borrow them from you.

GELASIMUS: I no longer have anything to give or loan.
  All I have left is this threadbare cloak.
  I even auctioned off my generous tongue.

CROCOTIUM: How will your mouth manage without a tongue?

GELASIMUS: Attached to my belly I've got another one,
  Quite capable of appreciating anything good.

CROCOTIUM: With *your* belly, nothing could get that close
    to you.   310

GELASIMUS: I could say the same of you.

CROCOTIUM: Well? Are you coming?

GELASIMUS: Of course, I'm going to Panegyris's house.
   Tell her I'm on my way.

(CROCOTIUM *exits*)

GELASIMUS: I wonder what this is all about.
   Since her husband left, I've never been asked to their house.
   I might as well go. It can't hurt to find out.
   Wait. There's Pinacium, Panegyris's young slave.
   Look at that. He's posturing like a bad actor
   On an empty stage. I remember him. He was always sneaking
   Small glasses of hard liquor from the best bottles
   When he thought no one was looking.   320

ACT II

Scene 1

(*Enter* PINACIUM, *carrying basket and fishing rod*)

PINACIUM: Mercury, the son of Jove,
   Never brought his father better news
   Than I carry to my mistress now.
   My heart is filled with a joyous message,
   I can't deliver until I have it perfect;
   I must select each word to sound as glorious
   As the sense it conveys.
                   Tears fill my eyes,
   As happiness overflows my heart.
   I love the world—and the world will respond
   By showering me with honor and glory.   330
   O feet! Hurry toward your home,
   So Pinacium can obtain his just reward.
   My mistress has been waiting anxiously

For the end to her husband Epignomus's journeys.
She loves her husband and longs for his return.
Now, Pinacium, don't relax,
Run like a sprinter with the wind at his back;
Run both nobles and peasants off the road,
If a king blocks your path, just knock him down.

GELASIMUS: What's Pinacium talking about?   340
    What makes him so energetic?
    Why is he carrying a creel and a fishing rod?

PINACIUM: But wait! It's wrong for me just to run back home.
    My mistress should send orators with bags of gold,
    To plead with me to return, and a four-horse chariot
    To convey me to her door. Pedestrian transport
    Won't do at all. I'll retrace my steps back to the port.
    It would be much more appropriate if she approached me,
    And asked me to tell her what message I carried.
    This news I've discovered at the harbor   350
    Is better than anything she could beg the gods for.
    If I just conveyed it spontaneously,
    Panegyris wouldn't be prepared to receive it properly.
    That wouldn't be the manly way to do my duty.
    Rather than run to her, I'll wait for her to approach me,
    Wear my good fortune with dignified masculinity.
    Stop! Think again. How could she know
    What I've just found out, until
    I return to tell her about it?
    I need to return as fast as I can,   360
    To sweep away her griefs and sorrows,
    Outstrip the achievements of my ancestors,
    And become the most famous of all the heralds,
    Better known than Agamemnon's Talthybius
    And the rest of his clan.
    I'd run like a racer at the Olympic Games,
    But there's not enough space.
    Alas! I can't run really fast on this short a track.
    What? The door is shut?

Well, then I'll knock.   370
Open it now! Hurry up!
Don't delay! How long must I wait?
Are you asleep on your jobs?
Or lazy and awake?
I'll test which is stronger,
My feet and arms or this door.
I wish this door had run away,
So it could be punished like a vagrant slave.
I'm exhausted from beating the door;
I'll try it again just once more.   380

GELASIMUS: I'll try talking to him. Pinacium, hello.

PINACIUM: Hello.

GELASIMUS: When did you become a fisherman?

PINACIUM: Since the day you started your diet program.

GELASIMUS: What's your hurry? What news do you bring?
Where have you been?

PINACIUM: It's none of your business.

GELASIMUS: What's in there?

PINACIUM: Worms for your dinner.

GELASIMUS: What's your problem?

PINACIUM: If you had one shred of
decency,
You'd go away and not bother me.

GELASIMUS: Could I possibly get a straight answer from you? 390

PINACIUM: You won't get dinner here today. That's the truth.

Scene 2

(PANEGYRIS *opens door and sees* GELASIMUS)

PANEGYRIS: What's going on? Who's trying to break my door
   down?
   Why are you pounding like a group of soldiers
   Battering the closed gates of a besieged town?

GELASIMUS: Good morning, madam. I'm here because you
   summoned me.

PANEGYRIS: Is that why you're trying to wreck my door?

GELASIMUS: If you're worried about someone wrecking the door,
   You should talk to your slave; it's not my fault.
   I'm a victim too—I feel sorry for it.

PINACIUM: So you rushed to its rescue?

PANEGYRIS: Who said that?

PINACIUM: Pinacium.

PANEGYRIS: Where is he?   400

PINACIUM: Behold me, Panegyris. Don't waste your time
   On that impoverished parasite.

PANEGYRIS: Pinacium!

PINACIUM: So my ancestors named me.

PANEGYRIS: What's going on?

PINACIUM: You question what's going on?

PANEGYRIS: Shouldn't I question it?

PINACIUM: Is it any of your business?

PANEGYRIS: Impudent brat. What's got into you?
   Pinacium, explain yourself—now.

PINACIUM: Then order my enemies to let me go.

PANEGYRIS: Who's holding you?

PINACIUM: You need to ask?
   Fatigue has all my limbs in its grasp.

PANEGYRIS: It doesn't seem to have slowed your tongue.

PINACIUM: I ran so fast from the port to your gate,   410
   I exhausted myself for your sake.

PANEGYRIS: Do you have anything good to report?

PINACIUM: My news surpasses all your hopes.

PANEGYRIS: I'm saved!

PINACIUM: And I'm in peril. Exhaustion has emptied
   All the blood from my veins.

GELASIMUS: And what of me? My stomach's been empty
   For days and days.

PANEGYRIS: Did you meet anyone there?

PINACIUM: Entire crowds.

PANEGYRIS: Husbands?

PINACIUM: Plenty, I'm sure.
   But not a single person worse than you have here right now.

GELASIMUS: What now? I've put up with this rudeness for far too
      long.   420
   If you provoke me any further I'll—

PINACIUM: Hunger even longer.

GELASIMUS: I'm persuaded. You're probably right.

PINACIUM: I'll rush to clean the house. Get brooms—
   And poles to knock the spider webs down:
   I'll kill every single vermin I can find.

GELASIMUS: Poor things. Without their webs, they'll freeze.

PINACIUM: You think they're like you, too poor to own
   A warm set of winter clothes?
   Grab that broom!

GELASIMUS: All right.

PINACIUM: I'll sweep here. You sweep there.

GELASIMUS: No sooner said than done.

PINACIUM: Will someone fetch a
      bucket of water?   430

GELASIMUS: He thinks he's been selected
   Commissioner of public works,
   Without the formality of an election.

PINACIUM: Hurry up. Moisten the ground,
   Get rid of the dust
   In front of the house.

GELASIMUS: I'm starting now.

PINACIUM: You should have finished hours ago.
    I'll work on knocking these spiders down.

GELASIMUS: What a busy day.

PANEGYRIS: I'm not sure what's going on,   440
    Unless perhaps guests have just arrived in town.

PINACIUM: Set the table.

GELASIMUS: The dining table. That sounds good.

PINACIUM: Clean the fish that I brought back. Chop the wood.
    You! Fetch the ham and the rest of the food.

GELASIMUS: Words of wisdom fall from his mouth.

PANEGYRIS: In my opinion, you're not being very attentive
    To your mistress.

PINACIUM: Not attentive!
    I abandon everything to fulfill your wishes.

PANEGYRIS: In that case, tell me what I want to know.
    What happened when you were at the port?   450

PINACIUM: I'll tell you. I left for the port as the sun
    Rose over the sea and started to shine.
    I asked at customs how many ships had come in
    From Asia, and they said none.
    As I turned to depart, a Cyprian ship
    Sailed into the harbor on a following wind.
    Everyone wondered whose ship it was,
    What cargo it carried, from whence it came,
    When I spotted your husband Epignomus,
    Closely attended by his slave Stichus.   460

PANEGYRIS: Really? You said Epignomus?

PINACIUM: Your husband.

GELASIMUS: And my host.

PINACIUM: He's come back.

PANEGYRIS: You saw him yourself? With your
    own eyes?

PINACIUM: Joyously. His ship brimmed over with silver and gold.

GELASIMUS: That sounds
    very good.
  I'll joyously apply myself with this broom.

PINACIUM: His ship was filled with virgin wool and purple cloth.

GELASIMUS: Soon my empty
    belly will also be full.

PINACIUM: Tables inlaid with gold and ivory.

GELASIMUS: On which he'll set a
    huge dinner for me.

PINACIUM: He carries Babylonian weaving, and carpets, and
    tapestries,
  And many other fine things.

GELASIMUS: I like what I'm hearing.

PINACIUM: And moreover, he brought lute-girls and harp-girls
  And flute-girls, too—all stunningly beautiful.   470

GELASIMUS: Well done! After I drink, I'll flirt.
  That's when I'm the most fun.

PINACIUM: And many exotic scents and perfumes.

GELASIMUS: I'll cancel my sale.
    After this windfall, I don't need to sell a single tale.
    The malicious gossips who mocked my auction can go away.
    I congratulate Hercules on the lavish offerings
    I'll give in return for answering my prayers.

PINACIUM: He also brought
    some parasites.

GELASIMUS: I'm ruined.

PINACIUM: The funniest ones alive.

GELASIMUS: I'll take the dirt I swept up and scatter it back
    around.

PANEGYRIS: Did you catch sight of Pamphilippus, my sister's
    husband?   480

PINACIUM: No.

PANEGYRIS: He hasn't arrived?

PINACIUM: The customs officer said he had—
    But I didn't see him—I was in such a hurry to get back
    And bring you the delightful message.

GELASIMUS: The stories I just refused to sell
    Are on the market once again.
    My enemies will celebrate.
    Hercules, you're not particularly infallible.

PANEGYRIS: Go into the house, Pinacium. Order the servants
    To get things ready for a sacrifice.

(PINACIUM *exits*)

PANEGYRIS: Goodbye.

GELASIMUS: Do you want me to help you get
    organized?   490

PANEGYRIS: I have enough slaves inside.

(PANEGYRIS *exits*)

GELASIMUS: Well, Gelasimus, things look bad for you.
    One of the brothers is of no use at all
    And the other one still hasn't gotten home.
    I'll head back to my house and search my books
    For elegant phrases and funny jokes.
    If I can't displace these foreign parasites,
    No one will offer me a dinner tonight.

(GELASIMUS *exits*)

ACT III

Scene 1

(*Enter* EPIGNOMUS *and* STICHUS. *Music-girls can follow or be indi-cated offstage.*)

EPIGNOMUS: For a good journey and a safe return home
    I thank the weather goddesses, and Neptune,   500
    And also Mercury, who helped me in my mercantile
    Ventures, quadrupling my money.
    The household that was mourning my departure,
    Now can celebrate the end of my adventure.
    I've already met with Antiphon,
    With whom I'd once been out of favor,

And found myself restored to grace,
There are many things of which money is capable.
Because I returned rich from my voyage,
Antiphon welcomed my ship with great affection,   510
Without the need for legal intervention.
He met me at the dock, and he agreed
To dine tonight with me, and my brother.
Yesterday, my brother and I were at the same harbor,
But I set sail first, and arrived home earlier.
Come on, Stichus, lead those girls inside.

STICHUS: Master, whether I keep silent or whether I remind you,
    I know you know how many hardships I've endured with you,
    And for just this day, for the Freedom Day festival,
    I'd like to beg you for a free afternoon   520
    In which to celebrate our return home.

EPIGNOMUS: Your request is fair and just.
    Stichus, you can have your holiday.
    Go where you please and do what you like,
    And I'll even supply you with a good jug of wine.

STICHUS: I'll find myself a girlfriend for the day.

EPIGNOMUS: You can have ten, if you can afford to pay.

STICHUS: And something else?

EPIGNOMUS: What is it? Explain.

STICHUS: Can I dine out tonight?

EPIGNOMUS: If you're invited.

STICHUS: Invited or not, I don't care. I've got it planned.   530

EPIGNOMUS: What do you intend to do?

STICHUS: I've got it figured out.
   I have a girlfriend, Stephanium, who lives nearby—
   Your brother's maid. We're going to a party
   With her fellow servant Sangarinus, a Syrian.
   She's his sweetheart too; we're rivals,
   But we've each paid our share for dinner tonight.

EPIGNOMUS: Go lead the girls inside, then take your holiday.

(EPIGNOMUS *exits*)

STICHUS: If I don't go out and paint the town,
   I'll have no one but myself to blame.
   I'll go through the orchard to my girlfriend's place,   540
   And prepare myself to seize the night. I'll pay
   My part for our dinner, select the food,
   Have it cooked and brought to Sangarinus,
   Who will be here soon, with his master.
   I know that he'll show up on time.
   Any slave who'd be late for dinner
   Would deserve a serious beating,
   Which I'd administer myself—it would be fitting
   To drive him home with a beating.
   I must rush to make things ready. No more malingering.   550
   You, in the audience, don't be astonished
   That slaves can dine out and drink and have mistresses,
   These things were perfectly legal in Athens.
   In order not to make anyone jealous,
   I'll go around to the back entrance.
   I'll use that route to bring in the provisions.
   Come on! Follow me! I'll make an epic of the day.

(STICHUS *exits, followed by music-girls*)

Scene 2

(*Enter* GELASIMUS)

GELASIMUS: I've finished looking through my books.
  I'm sure I now can please my patron,
  I've memorized all the latest jokes.   560
  I'll head on down to the harbor,
  And if he's there, I'll win him over.

(*Enter* EPIGNOMUS)

EPIGNOMUS: Here's the parasite, Gelasimus, just arriving.

GELASIMUS: When I left my house this morning, I saw the best of
    omens.
  A weasel pounced on a mouse almost between my feet.
  This is the most propitious of omens for me.
  A weasel ate in the morning; tonight I'm sure to dine.
  I see Epignomus standing over there. I'll go meet him.
  Epignomus, I'm so glad to see you,
  Joyous tears keep springing forth   570
  From my eyes. How have you been?

EPIGNOMUS: I've been well—and busy.

GELASIMUS: I greet you happily, with hungry heart and open
    mouth.

EPIGNOMUS: You're very friendly. I hope the gods grant all your
    wishes.

GELASIMUS: I'd like to celebrate your safe return
  By dining with you here at your home.

EPIGNOMUS: Thanks, but I have a prior engagement.

GELASIMUS: Accept my invitation.

EPIGNOMUS: I'm committed.

GELASIMUS: Do this, please.

EPIGNOMUS: It's a firm commitment.

GELASIMUS: Do me a favor.

EPIGNOMUS: When the time is right,
    I promise.

GELASIMUS: This is the right time.

EPIGNOMUS: Impossible.

GELASIMUS: Why demur?   580
    I don't know why I dressed up for dinner.

EPIGNOMUS: That's enough. Find yourself another guest
    With whom to dine tonight.

GELASIMUS: Why don't you promise?

EPIGNOMUS: If I weren't committed, I wouldn't refuse.

GELASIMUS: There's one certain thing I'll promise you;
    If you invite me to dine, I'll accept you.

EPIGNOMUS: Goodbye.

GELASIMUS: You're sure?

EPIGNOMUS: I'm certain—I will dine at home.

GELASIMUS: Since I haven't gotten anywhere by hinting subtly
  I'll try a new strategy—speaking plainly.
  Do you wish me to come to your house for dinner?

EPIGNOMUS: Were it possible,
    I would,   590
  But I have nine strangers dining with me.

GELASIMUS: You don't need to provide a couch for me;
  I'll be comfortable anywhere you place me.

EPIGNOMUS: These guests are orators, eminent men,
  Part of the Ambracian delegation.

GELASIMUS: Arrange these orators at the head of the table,
  A place well suited to their station,
  And me at the foot, listening to their orations.

EPIGNOMUS: Your dining with these orators would be quite
  improper.

GELASIMUS: Even though I speak in vain,   600
  I'm an orator just the same.

EPIGNOMUS: You can come over tomorrow for leftovers.
  Goodbye.

(EPIGNOMUS *exits*)

GELASIMUS: I'm finished, by Hercules. No one needs me.
  The world will be short a parasite after today.
  I'll never put my trust in a weasel again;
  It's the ficklest of beasts you'll ever see,
  It changes homes ten times a day.
  I shouldn't have bet on its prophecies.

I'll call my counsels all together,   610
And learn the laws about dying from hunger.

(GELASIMUS *exits*)

ACT IV

Scene 1

(*Enter* ANTIPHO *and* PAMPHILIPPUS)

ANTIPHO: The gods must love both me and my family well,
   To have saved my daughters like this;
   Pamphilippus, I'm very glad that you and your brother
   Have made it back to your native land with your finances intact.

PAMPHILIPPUS: Antipho, I understand you far too well,
   For me not to see you're being friendly;
   Now that you're behaving like a friend to me,
   That's what I'll now believe you to be.

ANTIPHO: I'd wanted to show my gratitude   620
   By better means than empty words.
   I'd wanted to invite you to dinner tonight,
   But your brother told me he planned to have us both over,
   And rather than ruin his plans, I changed my mind.
   For tomorrow, I'd like to invite both you and your wives.

PAMPHILIPPUS: And the day after, both of you are invited to my
      place.
   Antipho, have we now truly made our peace?

ANTIPHO: Your financial fortunes have gone as I wished;
   Now I can properly enjoy your friendship.

If you want good advice, consider this: ⚹   630
Wealth is the most solid of all foundations
On which people build mutual admiration;
If you want friends, pay attention to business;
Feelings of good fellowship depend on finances.

(*Enter* EPIGNOMUS)

EPIGNOMUS: I'll be back soon.
                        The best thing that could happen
    when you've been gone
Would be to find nothing wrong when you return home.
But my wife was so extravagant in my absence,
I would have been bankrupted by her negligence
If my voyage hadn't restored our finances.
But here's my father-in-law and my brother, Pamphilippus. 640

PAMPHILIPPUS: How have you been, Epignomus?

EPIGNOMUS: How about you? How
    long has your ship been in port?

PAMPHILIPPUS: Not long ago.

EPIGNOMUS: Long enough for peaceful relations
    to be restored?

ANTIPHO: Far smoother sailing than you've had in your travels
    abroad.

EPIGNOMUS: Just like old times.
    Brother, should we unload our ships today?

PAMPHILIPPUS: Let's take a day of rest,
    And weigh ourselves down with pleasures instead.
    When will dinner be ready? I haven't had breakfast yet.

EPIGNOMUS: Come inside and wash.

PAMPHILIPPUS: First I'll go home and greet my wife and my
    household gods,
And then I'll continue on over to your house.

EPIGNOMUS: Look! Your wife and her sister are rushing toward us.

PAMPHILIPPUS: That will save some time. I'll be back soon, so we
    can dine.   650

ANTIPHO: Before you go, I'd like to tell you a story.

PAMPHILIPPUS: Go ahead.

ANTIPHO: Once upon a time, there was an old man, just like me.
    He had two daughters, married to two brothers, just like mine.

EPIGNOMUS: I wonder how this
    story will end.

ANTIPHO: The younger brother had a lute-girl and a flute-girl,
    He'd bought in his travel abroad,
    And the old man was a widower, like I am now.

EPIGNOMUS: Go on. I think I see the relevance of your story.

ANTIPHO: The old man was talking to the young one who had the
    flute-girl,
    Just like I'm talking to you now—

EPIGNOMUS: I'm listening.

ANTIPHO: "I gave you my daughter to warm your bed at
    night,   660
    For you to give me a girl for my bed now would only be right."

EPIGNOMUS: Who said that? The old man like you?

ANTIPHO: The old man who was
    speaking like I am now.
The young man answered, "If one is not enough I'll give
    you two,
And I'll give you a foursome if a pair won't do."

EPIGNOMUS: Who said that? The young man like me?

ANTIPHO: The young man like you. Then the old man responded:
    "A foursome would be an appropriate gift,
    But feeding so many would drive me bankrupt,
    So you should supply me with their food as well."

EPIGNOMUS: That old man was certainly a miser, I see.   670
    The young one must have regretted his generosity.

ANTIPHO: The old man gave the young one a dowry along with his
    daughter.
    Shouldn't the flute-girls be endowed in a similar manner?

EPIGNOMUS: The young man must have evaded the request quite
    cleverly—
    It was sensible not to give away flute-girls with a dowry.

ANTIPHO: Although the old man bargained about the food,
    He decided he could be satisfied with just the girls.
    "Good enough," the young man said. "How generous!"
    The old man replied. "Then everything is settled?"
    "It certainly is," the young man agreed.   680
    I'll go inside to congratulate your daughters,
    Then soak away my years in a bath of steaming hot water.
    I'll take it easy until dinner.

(ANTIPHO *exits*)

PAMPHILIPPUS: He tells a good story, doesn't he?

EPIGNOMUS: I should send a girl to sing him a lullaby.
    What other use could a man his age have for a concubine?

PAMPHILIPPUS: How's our parasite Gelasimus? Does he prosper?

EPIGNOMUS: I saw him not too long ago.

PAMPHILIPPUS: How is he?

EPIGNOMUS: Hungry.

PAMPHILIPPUS: Why didn't you invite him along for dinner?

EPIGNOMUS: I was afraid he'd
    bankrupt me.
    Speak of the devil and there he is—across the street.   690

PAMPHILIPPUS: Let's have some fun with him.

EPIGNOMUS: No sooner said than done.

(*Enter* GELASIMUS)

Scene 2

GELASIMUS: As I was saying, since I left,
    I've consulted with my friends and relatives,
    Sought the best authorities about my plight,
    And been told I'll die of unsatisfied appetite.
    Is that Pamphilippus with his brother, Epignomus?
    I'll talk to them and see if there's any hope.
    O Pamphilippus! Feast for my eyes!
    I'm so glad you're safe! My soul and my stomach rejoice!
    You're back from your travels abroad!

PAMPHILIPPUS: Greetings, Gelasimus.   700

GELASIMUS: Have you been well?

PAMPHILIPPUS: Never better.

GELASIMUS: That's excellent news.
  If I only were rich, do you know what I'd do?

EPIGNOMUS: What?

GELASIMUS: I'd invite him out to dinner. I didn't ask you.

EPIGNOMUS: That won't help persuade him.

GELASIMUS: In that case, I'd invite
    both of you—
  There should be no hard feelings between us—
  But I have absolutely nothing in my house.

EPIGNOMUS: If I'd known sooner, I would have asked you over,
  But there's not a single place left at tonight's dinner.

GELASIMUS: I'm easy to please. I could stand in a corner,
  And gorge myself contentedly on scraps from your larder.   710

EPIGNOMUS: That would be proper. But after the guests have
    gone,
  Come on over.

GELASIMUS: Damn you.

EPIGNOMUS: I'll need someone to clean the dishes.

GELASIMUS: To hell with you.
  Pamphilippus, what about you?

PAMPHILIPPUS: Tonight I'd promised someone we'd dine out.

GELASIMUS: What? Out?

PAMPHILIPPUS: Yes.

GELASIMUS: How can someone as tired as you
 Go out to dine?

PAMPHILIPPUS: What would you advise?

GELASIMUS: Order a dinner cooked
  at your home,
 And send your host regrets.

PAMPHILIPPUS: You suggest I eat at home alone?

GELASIMUS: No indeed. Invite me over instead.

EPIGNOMUS: I disapprove.
 Deceiving his host would be extraordinarily rude.

GELASIMUS: I didn't ask you.
 I can see why you're urging him to go.   720
 He'll come back late. The streets are unsafe.
 He'll be found dead in an alley and you'll inherit his estate.

PAMPHILIPPUS: I'll ask for an escort of several slaves.

EPIGNOMUS: You've almost persuaded him.

GELASIMUS: Quick! Order a dinner
 Cooked at home for you and me and your wife.
 I won't tell anyone where you dined.

PAMPHILIPPUS: If this is your only chance for dinner, don't get too
 excited.

GELASIMUS: You're really going out to dinner?

PAMPHILIPPUS: I'm dining at my
 brother's—just next door.

GELASIMUS: You're sure?

PAMPHILIPPUS: Absolutely.

GELASIMUS: You deserve to be attacked.

PAMPHILIPPUS: I'll stay off the streets; I'll use the garden
     path.   730

EPIGNOMUS: Listen, Gelasimus.

GELASIMUS: You'll be busy with your orators. Why should I listen
     to you?

EPIGNOMUS: Because this speech may benefit you.

GELASIMUS: My empty stomach is at
     your service.

EPIGNOMUS: I think for tonight I could find you some space.

PAMPHILIPPUS: It could just be done.

GELASIMUS: Hero of our country!

EPIGNOMUS: That is, if you could make yourself fit.

GELASIMUS: I'll suck in my gut and hold my breath,
     Until I occupy no more space than a delicate sylph.

EPIGNOMUS: I'll arrange it. Come along.

GELASIMUS: Aren't we going in here?

EPIGNOMUS: No. This house wouldn't suit you at all.
     We're going to jail.

PAMPHILIPPUS: I'll go inside to pray,   740
   Then continue on to your place.

(PAMPHILIPPUS *exits*)

GELASIMUS: Well?

EPIGNOMUS: We're headed toward jail.

GELASIMUS: Your wish is my command.

EPIGNOMUS: This man would do anything for a meal;
   Even take the top place at a hanging.

GELASIMUS: That's my nature.
   I'd brave anything to assuage my hunger.

EPIGNOMUS: When you were the parasite of me and my brother,
   You almost ate us into bankruptcy.

GELASIMUS: I can't disagree.

EPIGNOMUS: I know what kind of luck you brought into my life;
   I won't let that happen a second time.

(EPIGNOMUS *exits*)

GELASIMUS: They're gone. Gelasimus, look at where   750
   Advice has led you. What can you do?
   Charity and benevolence have perished;
   There are no more rewards for the ridiculous.
   The best of parasites are no better than beggars.
   I'm completely without friends, utterly abandoned.
   I'll refuse to live a single day longer.
   If I fill my stomach with deadly poison,
   No one will be able to claim I died of hunger.

(GELASIMUS *exits*)

ACT V

Scene 1

(*Enter* STICHUS)

STICHUS: When you're waiting for people it's customary
    To look out for them anxiously,   760
    As if that would make them arrive more quickly.
    Although I think this custom dumb,
    I'm standing here, waiting for Sangarinus to come,
    Though that won't speed him up at all.
    I'll just go home to fetch the wine bottle,
    And if he's not here, I'll seat myself and drink alone.
    Before the day melts away like snow.

Scene 2

(*Enter* SANGARINUS)

SANGARINUS: Greetings, Athens, teacher of Greece.
    I'm glad we've finally reached
    My master's native land.   770
    But what matters most is my sweetheart,
    My fellow slave Stephanium,
    Where she is and how she's doing.
    I have asked Stichus to greet her for me,
    And tell her precisely when I'd arrive,
    So she'd have dinner ready on time.
    But here is Stichus.

STICHUS: Master, you did a good deed,
    When you gave this jug of wine to me.
    I'll be as intoxicated as the immortal gods,

Filled with laughter and kisses and jokes,   780
Dances and seductions and bonhomie.

SANGARINUS: Stichus!

STICHUS: What!

SANGARINUS: How are you doing?

STICHUS: Very well, my
    best friend Sangarinus.
I'm having a party with Dionysus—
And now with you. Dinner is cooked.
Since your master and mistress dine
With Antipho at my master's place tonight,
We've been given freedom of this house.
Here is the wine my master gave me.

SANGARINUS: Who dreamed of gold?

STICHUS: Why does it matter to you?
    Go inside and wash up.

SANGARINUS: I'm already clean.   790

STICHUS: Excellent.
    We should be extremely clean today,
To ornament Athens, since we've been away
So long. Follow me.

(STICHUS *exits*)

SANGARINUS: I'm coming. My return home has started right.
    This augurs well for the rest of the night.

(SANGARINUS *exits*)

Scene 3

(*Enter* STEPHANIUM)

STEPHANIUM: Spectators, I don't want you to think it strange,
That while I live in that house, I'm entering from this place.
When we heard that the sisters' husbands had returned,
We were summoned over here in a hurry,
To clean the house, cover the couches, and get everything
      ready,   800
But I haven't forgotten my friends Sangarinus and Stichus
No matter how busy I've been. I've remembered
To cook their dinner. Stichus bought the food; I did the rest,
Just like he said. Now I'll leave here, and wait for my friends.

(STEPHANIUM *exits*)

Scene 4

(*Enter* SANGARINUS *and* STICHUS)

SANGARINUS: March outside in a parade formation.
I appoint Stichus commander of libations.
Today we'll indulge in all types of temptations.
The gods must be pleased with me,
I'm so well entertained in this place,
If anyone walks by, I'd like to call him over   810
To be our guest.

STICHUS: Anyone can join us—
But only if he brings his own wine.
Nobody else gets a sip of our booze;
Tonight we'll use this gift to get thoroughly polluted.

SANGARINUS: This meal is certainly worth every penny.
  We've got figs, beans, olives, fish, and pastries.

STICHUS: More than adequate. It's best for slaves
  To enjoy themselves within their means.
  Everyone should behave in a manner that's appropriate:
  Rich people drink out of delicate porcelain cups,   820
  And use elaborate chamberpots,
  While we drink from plain earthenware jugs:
  But we all still perform the same physical functions,
  In the manner best suited to our social stations.

SANGARINUS: Come on; tell where we should lie.

STICHUS: It's logical that
    you lie above me.
  And I'll go there, and make a pact with you,
  To properly divide the spoils. Now claim your territory.

SANGARINUS: What are these territories?

STICHUS: Do you want to sit
  By the food or the wine?

SANGARINUS: The wine, of course.
  But while our girlfriend is dining and dressing,   830
  Let's entertain ourselves. I appoint you general of this party.

STICHUS: I just thought of something pleasant.
  We're eating outside—it's like a picnic.

SANGARINUS: Yes, indeed—but much more comfortably.
  But meanwhile, general, why has our jug stopped pouring?
  See how many cups we still have to drink?

STICHUS: As many as there are
    fingers on a hand.

Remember the words of the famous Greek song:
"Three or five but never four."

SANGARINUS: Your health.
   I'll have a tenth drink from that jug of yours;
   If you're wise, you'll refill your mug.   840
   Good health to you and me and the audience;
   Also to our Stephanium.

STICHUS: What a wonderful party!
   Here's your mug. You have the wine.

SANGARINUS: I also want some tender meat.

STICHUS: If this isn't enough to eat,
   Nothing will satisfy your appetite.
   Have some water.

SANGARINUS: You're right. I don't need gourmet foods.
   Come on, musician, have a drink. Don't refuse.
   Why are you so hesitant? You won't need to pay a single cent;
   This wine is provided for free by the government.
   Take that flute out of your mouth and have some booze.   850

STICHUS: After he's had his drink, refill your cup.
   If you're drinking with me, you'll have to keep up.
   I don't want to get too far ahead of your drinking,
   Or later tonight we'll be good for nothing.
   This jug leans over as often as it stands up.

SANGARINUS: What then? Although you were sober, and hard to
        persuade,
   Once you had your first sip, the wine didn't hurt one bit.
   Now you've finished your drink, return your flute to your lips.
   Play your music quicker.
   Puff out your cheeks like an adder.   860
   Come on, Stichus, let's make a bet;
   The next drink's on the first one to miss a step.

STICHUS: Well said. I'm convinced—I'll do what you request.

SANGARINUS: Get ready. Watch. Top that. If you trip, I'm prepared
　To claim my winnings.

STICHUS: That's fair.
　Now for the first of several rounds.
　It's good for rivals to share a lover,
　Kiss the same lips, drink the same wine.
　I am you; you are me; we are soulmates to one another.
　We both love one girl. So when she's mine, she's also
　　yours,　　　　　　　　　　　　　　　　　　　　　　870
　And when she's yours, she's also mine.
　Neither of us needs to feel jealous.

SANGARINUS: That's enough. I don't want to overdo it.
　Let's play something else.

STICHUS: Should we ask our girlfriend out? She'll dance.

SANGARINUS: Let's.

STICHUS: Charming sweet darling Stephanium, come outside
　to us.
　You're more than beautiful enough.

SANGARINUS: The beautifulest.

STICHUS: Come outside to your merry men, and double our
　merriment.
　If you like our loving ways, come outside and take your place.

Scene 5

(*Enter* STEPHANIUM)

STEPHANIUM: I'll yield to you, my darlings. I would have come
    out earlier,   880
  For Venus's sake, but I had to dress up and make myself
    prettier.
  It's the nature of women, I guess, to strive for elegance.
  Besides, if we didn't wear jewelry and makeup and sexy
    dresses,
  No one would pay any attention to us.
  No matter how often we appear utterly gorgeous,
  We can lose everything by a moment's uncleanliness.

STICHUS: She uses the most delicious phrases.

SANGARINUS: Venus must have taught her these orations.

STICHUS: Sangarinus!

SANGARINUS: What is it?

STICHUS: I'm aching this much.

SANGARINUS: How much?

(STICHUS *points between his legs to indicate the magnitude of the
problem*)

SANGARINUS: That's bad.

STEPHANIUM: Where should I lie?

SANGARINUS: Which place do you want?

STEPHANIUM: I'd like to lie with both of you, since I love you
     both.   890

STICHUS: My savings are dissipating.

SANGARINUS: My freedom's escaping.

STEPHANIUM: Give me a place to recline, you two, if you
     want me.

STICHUS: If I want you?

STEPHANIUM: I long to be with both of you.

STICHUS: I'm helpless. What about you?

SANGARINUS: What?

STICHUS: Gods! I don't want the day to last a minute longer,
     Without my having danced with her.
     My sweet honey, come on and dance, and I'll dance with you.

SANGARINUS: Never, by God, will you conquer me that way,
     Whatever pleasures that you claim, I demand the same.

STEPHANIUM: If I'm to dance, pour the musician a drink.

STICHUS: And one for us.

SANGARINUS: You first, musician.   900
     And when your cup is drained, start to play
     A sweet arousing salacious riff,
     Stimulate us to our fingertips.
     Add some water to this.

Scene 6

SANGARINUS: You, take this. Drink. He liked that sip.
   He's not half as reluctant as he was before.
   And while he drinks, you can give me a kiss.

STICHUS: How dare you kiss her while she's standing near you;
   The only women who give kisses standing up
   Are the lowest class of prostitutes.   910
   If you steal kisses, you'll be treated like a thief.

SANGARINUS: Come on, musician, fill up your cheeks.
   As we introduce
   New wine in our mugs,
   Play a new tune.

Scene 7

SANGARINUS: What exotic dancer could have done that step?

STICHUS: If I lost this turn, I challenge you again.

SANGARINUS: If you have the skill.

STICHUS: I will.

SANGARINUS: Wonderful.

STICHUS: What the devil?

SANGARINUS: Oh hell.

STICHUS: Oh well.

SANGARINUS: Both together. No stripper or exotic dancer
   Could have managed that any better.   920

STICHUS: Now, let's go inside.
   We've danced enough for our wine.
   Spectators, it's time to applaud.
   Then everyone, return to your home,
   And throw a party of your own.

THE TRAVELING BAG

(*VIDULARIA*)

Translated by John Wright

INTRODUCTION

The Plautine canon of twenty-one plays was arranged alphabetically by its early editors, and so the *Vidularia* (*Tale of a Trunk*), bringing up the rear of this arrangement, was in a particularly vulnerable physical position. In fact, the archetype of the manuscript family known collectively as the Palatine Recension concluded, on its last surviving page, with the tantalizing phrase *incipit Vidularia* ("Here begins the *Vidularia*"), and the bare title of this play was just about all anyone knew of it until 1815, when Angelo Cardinal Mai published a newly discovered manuscript now called the Ambrosian Palimpsest.

This manuscript gave us more, though not a great deal more, of the *Vidularia*: only about a tenth of the play at the very most survives. But these fragmentary remains, besides displaying the romantic charm common to all ruins, can be made to yield some valuable information about the work of Plautus and about New Comedy in general.

Most important, the *Vidularia* makes it clear that Plautus's *Rudens*, with its lonely seaside setting, its Prospero-like presiding elder, and its tempest that throws a mixed bag of characters together, was not unique. The *Vidularia* contains all these elements, and is in fact so similar to the *Rudens* as to suggest the existence of an established subgenre of the usually urbanocentric New Comedy.

Second, the setting of the *Vidularia* is no Ardenesque Green World. "Country life isn't easy," says Dinia, the old farmer in the play, thus reminding us of the complete disinclination of New Comedy as a whole to romanticize rustic existence. In most of Plautus's plays, the country is either a vague threat to the urban heroes—the location of the dreaded mills to which a misbehaving slave might be condemned—or the (offstage) home base of various uncouth agelasts who disrupt the gaiety of city life. And in the rare cases where the country is actually the setting of a comedy, it is a place of exile, loneliness, and penitential labor.

And finally, in the *Vidularia* and *Rudens*, as well as in Menander's *Dyskolus*, the country is—clearly by convention—a proving ground for the urban heroes, for the slave lover Trachalio in the *Rudens*, for the jeune premier in the *Vidularia* and the *Dyskolus*. It is a place to prove one's worth, and love, by the performance of hard physical tasks. The parallel with Shakespeare's *Tempest* is suggestive, but probably only coincidental. Such a development is almost demanded by this sort of setting: the plot comes from the plot, so to speak.

The translation that follows, fragmentary as it is, would have been even more fragmentary were it not for the heroic labors of reconstruction performed in the nineteenth century by Wolfgang Studemund (who destroyed his eyesight transcribing the Ambrosian Palimpsest) and Friedrich Leo (who produced a learned "disputation" on the *Vidularia* in 1895).

John Wright

THE TRAVELING BAG

CHARACTERS

ASPASIUS, a slave
NICODEMUS, a young man
GORGINES, a fisherman
DINIA, an old man
CACISTUS, a fisherman
SOTERIS, a young girl

SCENE: *A lonely spot by the sea.*

PROLOGUE

*	*	*	this business with an old name	
*	*	*	*	*
*	*	*	*	*
praised	*	*	*	thanks
*	*	*	*	*

Schedia is the Greek name of this comedy;
our playwright has called it *Vidularia*.
First know   *   *   he's the one.
I imagine you would like to know the plot;
well, you'll understand what happens when it happens.

*	*	*	warned at the right time	
*	*	*	*	*

*   *   *   *   *

*   *   *   *   *

Listen to him; I'll be back soon in another role.

ASPASIUS: A man, whom slavery once got possession of

*   *   *   *   *

NICODEMUS: That god's bacchants made a Pentheus of our ship.

*   *   *   *   *

Want, grief, sorrow, poverty, cold, hunger.

*   *   *   *   *

GORGINES: This is a house of poverty.

*   *   *   *   *

That's Venus's myrtle grove.

*   *   *   *   *

NICODEMUS: Wait! There's something I want from you.

DINIA: Take it easy.

NICODEMUS: What do you say? Got a minute?

DINIA: Of course, if it's any use.
But what's the matter?

NICODEMUS: I heard you say just now
you want to hire a laborer for your farm.

DINIA: You heard right.

NICODEMUS: What sort of work do you want done?   10

DINIA: What do you care? Have you been made my guardian?

NICODEMUS: I think I can offer you a pretty good worker.

DINIA: You have some slave you want to hire out?

NICODEMUS: I've got no slaves; I'm hiring out myself.

DINIA: What? You're looking for a job? I can't believe it.
　　You don't look like any wage-earner to me.

NICODEMUS: And so I'm not, if you won't give the wages.
　　But if you've got the money, take me with you.

DINIA: Listen, boy, this country life isn't easy.

NICODEMUS: City poverty's no bed of roses either.   20

DINIA: Throwing dice—that's what your hands are used to.

NICODEMUS: I know; that's why they need a good, hard workout.

DINIA: Your body's pale from that soft, shady city life.

NICODEMUS: The sun's a good painter; it'll make it black.

DINIA: Now look: the food at my place is pretty rough.

NICODEMUS: Rough food for a man who's had rough luck: it fits.
　　I know what I'm asking for, and I hope you'll oblige me.
　　If what you need's a decent man, an honest man,
　　a man who'll be more loyal than your slaves,
　　a sparing eater, an unsparing worker, ·   30
　　a straight talker, here I am! Hire me.

DINIA: By heaven, I still don't believe that you're a working man.

NICODEMUS: You don't believe it?

DINIA:　　　　　　　　　　And you're no bargain either, I suspect,
　　except—well, you do seem honest. But let me tell you now,
　　so you don't claim later that you didn't know it:
　　any worker that I hire, wherever he comes from,
　　is going to work a lot, earn a little, and eat a little.

NICODEMUS: I'll work at least as hard as your hardest worker,
   and all you'll have to give me is a bit of lunch,
   besides my wages.

DINIA: No snacks?

NICODEMUS: Nossir,   40
   no dinner either.

DINIA: No dinner?

NICODEMUS: No, I'll go home for that.

DINIA: Home? Where's that?

NICODEMUS: Here, with Gorgines the fisherman.

DINIA: Hmm! Seems from what you say that you're my neighbor.
   *   *   *   *   *

GORGINES: Both of you pay attention, if you please. Leave the
      trunk here.
   I'll keep it safe, on deposit, like; and I won't give it back
   to either one of you until this case is settled.

ASPASIUS: That deposit idea sounds fine to me.

(*He exits*)

      *   *   *   *   *

CACISTUS: I'll go see if I can find a friend of mine
   or anyone I know, to plead my case. I know this place.
   Do you live here?

GORGINES: Right in this house; bring him here.   50
   I'll take the trunk inside and hide it carefully;

if you want to find yourself a patron, go ahead;
there'll be no trickery here while I'm in charge.

(*He exits*)

CACISTUS: Why the hell should I look for a patron for a lost cause?
Why, what a rogue and peasant slave am I,
not to have looked around me a hundred times,
the moment I set eyes upon that trunk.
That devil hid among the myrtles and ambushed me.
As sure as I'm standing here, I know it: I've lost my loot,
unless I find a plot that's worthy of my character.   60
I'll stay here and keep my eyes open, in case I see an ally.

DINIA: By heaven, you've recited a whole heap of miseries
to me today; that's the main reason I told you
to leave off: you were making me miserable.

CACISTUS: (*Aside*) Hey! That's the young man who the storm
*   *   *   *   *
and I just heard   *   *   *
How quick he was to find himself a job!
Hardly waited for his feet to touch the shore.

DINIA: Strange: I think I've heard your voice somewhere before
*   *   *   *   *

NICODEMUS: I understand. By heaven, I weep with you.   70

DINIA: My boy is lost, and may be in greater want than you.

NICODEMUS: A man in greater want than me? I don't believe
there is or was or will be such a man.

DINIA: Now, don't say that. And look, as for that money
that you asked me to lend to you at interest,
it's yours. And you needn't pay any interest.

NICODEMUS: I pray the gods keep your son safe and sound,
   for helping me like this in my hour of need.
   But I don't ask to be forgiven the interest.

DINIA: I won't ask interest from a needy man.   80
   And don't you even say a word about when
   you'll pay me back.

NICODEMUS: Until I pay this debt
  *   *   *   *   *

CACISTUS: While I was fishing, my spear struck a trunk
  *   *   *   *   *

some slave or other jumps out of the myrtle grove
  *   *   *   *   *

Why say more? We fought like cats and dogs
  *   *   *   *   *

And now we've put the trunk on deposit.
  *   *   *   *   *

[THE RECOGNITION SCENE]

GORGINES (?): There's a seashell on the other side.

NICODEMUS: But I'll tell you
  what the seal says.   *   *
  *   *   *   *   *

ASPASIUS (?): Why don't you have this guy sewn up in a sack
   and tossed into the sea? That way you'll give the fish   90
   a good supply of food.

CACISTUS (?):   No, I think
   you ought to tie this guy to a fishing boat,

so he can keep on fishing, even in the middle
of a hurricane.
*   *   *   *   *

GORGINES (?): The seals match; I've compared his ring.
*   *   *   *   *

[UNPLACED FRAGMENTS]

I'd rather have my family die than beg;
better good men's mourning than bad men's scorning.
*   *   *   *   *
Now the slave will wheedle the money from the father.
*   *   *   *   *

NICODEMUS: No, no: this is our homeland and he's my father,
but that man's Soteris's father.
*   *   *   *   *

For I heard that a woman once gave birth to a lion.
*   *   *   *   *

He would steal every little flea he set eyes on.